STRUCTURAL
EQUATION
MODELING

to the memory of Jeffrey S. Tanaka

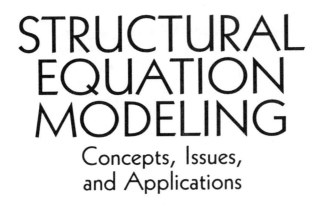

STRUCTURAL
EQUATION
MODELING
Concepts, Issues,
and Applications

Rick H. Hoyle
editor

SAGE Publications
International Educational and Professional Publisher
Thousand Oaks London New Delhi

For information address:

 SAGE Publications, Inc.
2455 Teller Road
Thousand Oaks, California 91320
E-mail: order@sagepub.com

SAGE Publications Ltd.
6 Bonhill Street
London EC2A 4PU
United Kingdom

SAGE Publications India Pvt. Ltd.
M-32 Market
Greater Kailash I
New Delhi 110 048 India

Printed in the United States of America

Library of Congress Cataloging-in-Publication Data

Structural equation modeling: concepts, issues, and applications / edited by
Rick H. Hoyle
    p. cm.
    Includes bibliographical references and index.
    ISBN 0-8039-5317-8 (acid-free). — ISBN 0-8039-5318-6 (pbk.: acid-free)
    1. Social sciences—Mathematical models. 2. Social sciences—Statistical methods. I. Hoyle, Rick H.
    H61.25.S767 1995
    300′.1′5118—dc20   94-47262

This book is printed on acid-free paper.

   97 98 99 00 01 10 9 8 7 6 5 4

Sage Project Editor: Susan McElroy

Brief Contents

Contents

Foreword

Structural equation models[1] have roots in the beginning of this century, but it is within the last three decades that the interest in them has surged. What are the "multiple indicators" of this interest? First, we have reached the point where the major social science statistical packages are sure to include procedures to estimate structural equation models or are seen to be incomplete. We have a number of stand-alone structural equation modeling programs as well. Second, SEMNET, an active list server devoted to structural equation modeling in the social and behavioral sciences, exists.[2] Third, major journals in a variety of social sciences regularly carry applications using, or methodological pieces on, structural equation modeling. *Structural Equation Modeling: A Multidisciplinary Journal* is a new publication from Lawrence Erlbaum Associates devoted to such models. Fourth, most major research universities and many other colleges and universities are offering courses on structural equation modeling or are incorporating material on structural equation modeling into their other courses. In sum, interest in structural equation modeling is strong.

Paralleling the growth in applications is the dynamic development of the structural equation modeling methodology. Methodologists have sought better understanding of fundamental aspects of modeling such as model fit, the robustness of estimators, testing distributional requirements, and building and rebuilding models. These self-critical examinations have led to new proposals and controversy. Much of the material originates in fairly technical presentations. This slows the diffusion of ideas from the specialized journals to the applied audience. *Structural Equation Modeling: Concepts, Issues, and Applications* helps to accelerate this diffusion. Rick Hoyle's edited collection provides readers a largely nontechnical review of some of the major issues facing researchers who wish to use structural equation modeling. It is a timely book, not only because of the high level of interest in structural equation modeling but also because it makes accessible, to a broad group of structural equation modeling users, current methodological developments. In addition to his overview chapter, Hoyle has assembled a useful set of chapters that present recent developments on specification (see chapter by MacCallum), estimation and testing (Chou and Bentler; West, Finch, and Curran; Hu and Bentler), philosophical underpinnings (Mulaik and James), statistical power (Kaplan), software comparisons (Byrne), writing up results from structural equation modeling analyses (Hoyle and Panter), analyzing multitrait-multimethod data (Marsh and Grayson), and examples of applications (Scott-Lennox and Lennox; Hull, Tedlie, and Lehn; Stoolmiller, Duncan, and Patterson).

The chapters from *Structural Equation Modeling: Concepts, Issues, and Applications* are practical and didactic. The methodological papers emphasize key points from recent technical works. Those wanting to consult the original sources can turn to the bibliography for a guide to the statistical literature behind the summaries in the book chapters. The practical emphasis of the book is reflected through all the chapters. For instance, Byrne's chapter compares LISREL and EQS, the two most popular structural equation modeling software packages. Hoyle and Panter's chapter provides advice on writing up structural equation modeling results. These are key topics for the researcher but rarely are discussed.

Readers new to the structural equation modeling approach will find the book a useful introduction to many aspects of structural equation modeling. Experienced structural equation modeling researchers will benefit from the summaries of recent methodological work and the bibliography. The volume provides researchers interested in structural equation modeling a valuable overview of contemporary issues in modeling.

KENNETH A. BOLLEN
Center for Advanced Study in the Behavioral Sciences
Stanford, California
March 11, 1994

Notes

1. Sometimes structural equation models are called LISREL models, analysis of covariance structures, or analysis of moment structures. Regardless of the name or notation, the terms refer to general models that include confirmatory factor analysis, classical simultaneous equation models, path analysis, multiple regression, ANOVA, and other common techniques as special cases.

2. SEMNET is a structural equation modeling special interest group organized to support the application of structural equation modeling across the social and behavioral sciences. The internet address is listserv@ualvm.ua.edu (bitnet is listserv@ua1vm). To subscribe, send the message SUBSCRIBE SEMNET first-name last-name.

Preface

The completion of this volume prompts vivid memories of two significant days in its development: the day it was conceived and the day it was born. The late Jeff Tanaka was a significant participant in both. The volume was conceived on a balmy Wednesday afternoon in late June of 1992 at Highland Beach, Florida. Oceanside, over drinks, we discussed the need for a book that we could recommend to students and researchers interested in learning the structural equation modeling approach to research design and data analysis. The discussion ended with a rough sketch of such a book scribbled in my legal pad and an agreement to complete a prospectus by early Fall. The book was born (i.e., the prospectus was accepted) on Monday, November 2, 1992, the day before Jeff died in a tragic automobile accident. The question of whether the project would proceed after his death was never considered. The editors at Sage and I agreed that the volume would stand as a tribute to Jeff and a reminder of his considerable influence on students and researchers.

Many of the contributors to this volume knew Jeff well and enthusiastically accepted my offer to contribute chapters to a volume to honor the memory of a valued colleague and friend. Those contributors who did not know Jeff personally know of his important contributions to the literature on structural equation modeling and reveal his influence in their individual contributions. Collectively, we dedicate this volume to the memory of Jeffrey S. Tanaka.

Jeff and I shared a vision of a volume on structural equation modeling that would bridge the gap between the technical literature that many students and researchers find intractable and the cursory treatment that structural equation modeling often receives in more general texts on linear models. Toward that end, this volume, from its inception, was intended for researchers, not methodologists and statisticians. Authors were challenged to write chapters that accurately summarize the technical literature on key topics and issues relevant to the structural equation modeling approach but to avoid technical jargon and notation and minimize the use of matrix equations. Also, authors were challenged to reach a "bottom line"—a practical recommendation or set of recommendations—without oversimplifying complex questions and controversies yet to be resolved in the technical literature on structural equation modeling. Although many of the authors are more accustomed to contributing to that technical literature, they willingly accepted these challenges and, as a result, produced a collection of informative, instructive, and surprisingly readable chapters directed toward researchers and students in the social and behavioral sciences.

The volume is organized around two themes: (a) concepts and issues and (b) applications. The first nine chapters define concepts and address issues associated with primary aspects of the structural equation modeling approach; the final four chapters either review or illustrate specific applications of the structural equation modeling approach. Chapter 1 provides an overview of the structural equation modeling approach with an emphasis on key concepts and issues. The material in that chapter sets the stage for Chapters 2 through 7, which cover the basic aspects of the structural equation modeling approach and are ordered according to the typical steps involved in planning and executing a structural equation modeling analysis. Chapters 8 and 9 cover practical matters that are not often addressed in treatments of statistical models. Chapter 8 describes and compares the most recent versions of the primary statistical software packages for estimating structural equation models; Chapter 9 addresses the task of writing manuscripts about research conceptualized and analyzed as structural equation models. Chapter 10 is a fitting bridge between the "concepts and issues" and "applications" sections of the book. It provides a review and recommendations regarding the use of structural equation modeling for construct validation, a particularly fruitful application of structural equation modeling. The final three chapters are primary research reports that illustrate the material presented in earlier chapters. Thus, as a package, the volume provides relatively complete coverage of fundamental aspects of the structural equation modeling approach with an emphasis on application.

Acknowledgments

A number of individuals contributed to the book by reviewing drafts of chapters: Peter M. Bentler, University of California, Los Angeles; David A. Cole, University of Notre Dame; William L. Cook, University of Texas; Anne M. Crawford, University of Kentucky; Robert Cudeck, University of Minnesota; Monica J. Harris, University of Kentucky; Deborah A. Kashy, Texas A & M University; Kimberly A. Kelso, University of Kentucky; Stanley Mulaik, Georgia Institute of Technology; Charles Reichardt, University of Denver; Joseph S. Rossi, University of Rhode Island; William R. Shadish, Jr., Memphis State University; Dean Keith Simonton, University of California, Davis; Gregory T. Smith, University of Kentucky; Irwin Waldman, Emory University; Thomas A. Widiger, University of Kentucky; and Alex Zautra, Arizona State University.

I am grateful to a number of individuals whose contributions either made this volume possible or helped make it better than it otherwise would have been. Kenneth A. Bollen introduced me to the structural equation modeling approach and continues to be a source of wisdom and encouragement concerning both methodological and professional matters. C. Deborah Laughton at Sage provided wisdom and encouragement at critical times during the process of editing the volume. Karyn S. McKenzie devoted many hours to the tedious tasks of formatting and copy-editing drafts of the chapters as well as compiling and editing the reference list. Finally, I thank the formidable group of contributors to the volume, who accepted the challenge of translating a burgeoning technical literature on structural equation modeling into practical and current chapters sure to appeal to researchers and students in the social and behavioral sciences.

RICK H. HOYLE
Lexington, Kentucky

1 The Structural Equation Modeling Approach

Basic Concepts and Fundamental Issues

RICK H. HOYLE

Structural equation modeling (SEM) is a comprehensive statistical approach to testing hypotheses about relations among observed and latent variables. Accounts of the statistical theory that underlies SEM as currently practiced appeared in the early 1970s (e.g., Jöreskog, 1973; Keesling, 1972; Wiley, 1973). Yet, several years passed before SEM began to receive widespread attention from social science researchers (e.g., Bentler, 1980; Bielby & Hauser, 1977; Jöreskog & Sörbom, 1979). With the increasing complexity and specificity of research questions in the social and behavioral sciences (e.g., Hoyle, 1994a; Reis & Stiller, 1992) and the appearance of flexible, user-friendly computer software (e.g., Bentler, 1992a; Jöreskog & Sörbom, 1993a; Muthén, 1988) has come increasing interest in SEM as a standard approach to testing research hypotheses. In addition to the appearance of at least three comprehensive texts on SEM (Bollen, 1989b; Hayduk, 1987; Loehlin, 1987), numerous didactic and illustrative chapters, journal articles, and special issues and sections of journals have appeared (e.g., Bagozzi, 1982; Connell & Tanaka, 1987; de Leeuw, Keller, & Wansbeek, 1983; Hoyle, 1994b; Judd, Jessor, & Donovan, 1986; Tanaka, Panter, Winborne, & Huba, 1990).

1

In this chapter I concisely outline the basic elements of the SEM approach; each element is covered in greater detail in one or more of the chapters that follow. The primary aim of this and all chapters in the book is to provide researchers and students trained in basic inferential statistics a nontechnical introduction to the SEM approach. Where possible, the presentation refers to concepts from standard statistical approaches in the social and behavioral sciences such as correlation, multiple regression, and analysis of variance.

Model Specification

SEM begins with the specification of a model to be estimated. Although the terms model and specification might be unfamiliar to some readers, the concepts probably are not. At the most basic level, a *model* is a statistical statement about the relations among variables. Models take on different forms in the context of different analytic approaches. For instance, a model in the correlation context typically specifies a nondirectional relation between two variables. Of course, more complex models are possible in the correlation context (e.g., partial and semipartial correlation, canonical correlation). The multiple regression and analysis of variance (ANOVA) approaches lend themselves to models that specify directional relations, although directionality cannot be tested statistically by those approaches.

Specification is the exercise of formally stating a model. Specification, too, varies in form across different analytic approaches. In the zero-order correlation context, the only model that can be specified includes a single nondirectional relation between two variables. Because variance typically is partitioned in a standardized fashion in ANOVA designs, researchers who use ANOVA rarely explicitly specify models. Research hypotheses that necessitate comparisons other than those provided by the standard main effect and interaction tests require explicit model specification (i.e., planned comparisons) on the part of the investigator. Exploratory factor analysis begins with no explicit model; however, decisions concerning such matters as how many factors to extract, how to extract them, and which rotation method to use involve implicit specification of a model.

The exercise of model specification is much more central in the SEM approach. Indeed, no analysis can take place until the researcher has specified a model of the relations among the variables to be analyzed.

In SEM, model specification involves formulating a statement about a set of parameters. In the SEM context, the *parameters* that require specification are constants that indicate the nature of the relation between two variables. Although specification can be quite specific regarding both the magnitude and sign of parameters, parameters typically are specified as either fixed or free. *Fixed parameters* are not estimated from the data and their value typically is fixed at zero. *Free parameters* are estimated from the data and are those the investigator believes to be nonzero. The various indexes of model adequacy, particularly the χ^2 goodness-of-fit test, indicate the degree to which the pattern of fixed and free parameters specified in a model is consistent with the pattern of variances and covariances from a set of observed data.

The pattern of fixed and free parameters in a structural equation model defines two components of the general structural equation model: the measurement model and the structural model. The *measurement model* is that component of the general model in which latent variables are prescribed. *Latent variables* are unobserved variables implied by the covariances among two or more indicators. Often referred to as factors, latent variables are free of random error and uniqueness associated with their indicators. Confirmatory factor analyses make use of only the measurement model component of the general structural equation model. The *structural model* is that component of the general model that prescribes relations between latent variables and observed variables that are not indicators of latent variables. The multiple regression model is a structural model without latent variables and limited to a single outcome. When the measurement and structural components are combined, the result is a comprehensive statistical model that can be used to evaluate relations among variables that are free of measurement error.

Relations between variables, observed or latent, in structural equation models are of three types. The *association* is a relation between two variables treated within the model as nondirectional; it is identical in nature to the relation typically evaluated by correlational analysis. The *direct effect*, which is the building block of structural equation models, is a directional relation between two variables; it is the type of relation typically evaluated by ANOVA or multiple regression. Within a model, each direct effect characterizes the relation between an independent and a dependent variable, although the dependent variable in one direct effect can be the independent variable in another. Moreover, as in multiple regression, a dependent variable can be related to multiple independent variables, and, as in multivariate analysis of variance, an independent variable can be related to multiple dependent variables. The capacity to treat a single variable as both a dependent and an independent variable lies at the heart of the indirect effect. The *indirect effect* is the effect of an independent variable on a dependent variable through one or more intervening, or mediating, variables (Baron & Kenny, 1986). In the case of a single mediating variable, the mediating variable is a dependent variable with reference to the independent variable but an independent variable with reference to the dependent variable. Thus the simplest indirect effect involves two direct effects. For instance, if x has a direct effect on y, and y has a direct effect on z, then x is said to have an indirect effect on z through y. The sum of direct and indirect effects of an independent variable on a dependent variable is termed the *total effect* of the independent variable.

A fundamental consideration when specifying models in SEM is identification. *Identification* concerns the correspondence between the information to be estimated—the free parameters—and the information from which it is to be estimated—the observed variances and covariances. More specifically, identification concerns whether a single, unique value for each and every free parameter can be obtained from the observed data. If for each free parameter a value can be obtained through one and only one manipulation of the observed data, then the model is *just identified* and has zero degrees of freedom. If a value for one or more free parameters can be obtained in multiple ways from the observed data, then the model is *overidentified* and has degrees of freedom equal to the number of observed variances and covariances minus the number of free parameters. If a single, unique value cannot be obtained from the observed data for one or more free parameters, then the model is *underidentified* and cannot be estimated. Thus a restriction on model specification is that for any model to be estimated it must be either just identified or overidentified. Determination of the identification status of a model can be difficult. Computer programs such as LISREL and EQS provide warnings when they encounter underidentified models; however, they do not always provide information about the location of the identification problem. Moreover, identification warnings can be misleading as they sometimes are triggered by characteristics of the data rather than characteristics of the model. MacCallum (Chapter 2) and Chou and Bentler (Chapter 3) provide additional detail about the general problem of identification, and Bollen (1989b) devotes extensive attention to evaluating identification.

The decision making associated with model specification in SEM is considerably more involved than specification of ANOVA and multiple regression models. Yet, the range of relations that can be specified in SEM far exceeds the range that can be specified in those and other more narrow statistical models. In Chapter 2, MacCallum covers the basic issues involved in model specification. Kaplan (Chapter 6) provides additional information about specification in the context of considerations about statistical power. These authors' treatments reveal the flexibility and comprehensiveness of the SEM approach (see also Hoyle & Smith, 1994). Indeed, it will be apparent that correlation, multiple regression, ANOVA, and factor analysis are themselves structural equation models (Tanaka et al., 1990). Thus SEM is a very general linear statistical model that can be used to evaluate statistically most research hypotheses of interest to social scientists.

Estimation

Once a model has been specified, the next task is to obtain estimates of the free parameters from a set of observed data. Although single-stage least squares methods such as those used in standard ANOVA or multiple regression designs can be used to derive parameter estimates, iterative methods such as maximum likelihood or generalized least squares are preferred. *Iterative methods* involve a series of attempts to obtain estimates of free parameters that imply a covariance matrix like the observed one. The *implied covariance matrix* is the covariance matrix that would result if values of fixed parameters and estimates of free parameters were substituted into the structural equations, which then were used to derive a covariance matrix. Iteration begins with a set of *start values*, tentative values of free parameters from which an implied covariance matrix can be computed and compared to the observed covariance matrix. Start values either are supplied by the researcher or, more commonly, are supplied by computer software, which either derives start values from the data (e.g., LISREL) or assumes a default value for all start values (e.g., EQS).

After each iteration, the resultant implied covariance matrix is compared to the observed matrix. The comparison between the implied and observed covariance matrices results in a residual matrix. The *residual matrix* contains elements whose values are the differences between corresponding values in the implied and observed matrices. Iteration continues until it is not possible to update the parameter estimates and produce an implied covariance matrix whose elements are any closer in magnitude and direction to the corresponding elements in the observed covariance matrix. Said differently, iteration continues until the values of the elements in the residual matrix cannot be minimized any further. At this point the estimation procedure is said to have *converged*. Convergence problems are not uncommon with models that have many free parameters, with models estimated from ill-conditioned data (see Chapter 4), and, particularly, with multitrait-multimethod models (see Chapter 10).

When the estimation procedure has converged on a solution, a single number is produced that summarizes the degree of correspondence between the implied and observed covariance matrices. That number, sometimes referred to as the *value of the fitting function*, approaches zero as the implied covariance matrix more closely resembles the observed covariance matrix. A perfect match between the two matrices produces a value of the fitting function equal to zero. The value of the fitting function is the starting point for constructing indexes of model fit.

Evaluation of Fit

A model is said to *fit* the observed data to the extent that the covariance matrix it implies is equivalent to the observed covariance matrix (i.e., elements of the residual matrix are near zero). The question of fit is, of course, a statistical one that must take into account features of the data, the model, and the estimation method. For instance, the observed covariance matrix is treated as a population covariance matrix, yet that matrix suffers from sampling error—increasingly so as sample size decreases. Also, the more free parameters in a model the more likely the model is to fit the data because parameter estimates are derived from the data. To complicate matters further, the different estimation methods vary in effectiveness as sample size and model complexity vary (see Chapter 3).

The most common index of fit is the χ^2 goodness-of-fit test, which is derived directly from the value of the fitting function. It is the product of the value of the fitting function and the sample size minus one, $F(N - 1)$. That product is distributed as χ^2 if the data are multivariate normal and the specified model is the correct one. At least one of those assumptions, particularly the latter one, probably is violated in most uses of SEM. As a result, considerable discussion has taken place about the validity of the χ^2 test as an index of fit. Chou and Bentler summarize that discussion in Chapter 3.

Growing dissatisfaction with the χ^2 goodness-of-fit test has led to the generation of a growing number of *adjunct fit indexes*, descriptive indexes of fit that often are intuitively interpreted. Bentler and Bonett (1980) are credited with pioneering the logic that underlies adjunct fit indexes in their *normed fit index* and their generalization of an extant index (Tucker & Lewis, 1973), which they termed the *nonnormed fit index*. Rather than comparing the implied and observed covariance matrices, these indexes and numerous others that follow similar logic (for reviews and comparisons, see Marsh, Balla, & McDonald, 1988; Mulaik, James, Van Alstine, Bennett, Lind, & Stillwell, 1989; Tanaka, 1993) derive from the comparison between the fit of a specified model and the fit of an independence, or null, model. The *independence model* is one in which no relations among variables are specified. In other words, all relational paths are fixed to zero and only variances are estimated. Thus most adjunct fit indexes reflect the improvement in fit of a specified model, which includes fixed and free structural parameters, over the independence model, in which all structural parameters are fixed at zero. Adjunct fit indexes are not statistics and, therefore, cannot be used to conduct formal statistical tests of model fit. Instead, they are treated as global indexes of model adequacy. For the most part, adjunct fit indexes vary between zero and 1.0, and .90 is widely accepted as a value such indexes must exceed before a model can be viewed as consistent with the observed data from which it was estimated. It is important to note that not all adjunct fit indexes follow the logic of the Bentler and Bonett (1980) indexes, although many vary between zero and 1.0 (e.g., the goodness-of-fit and adjusted goodness-of-fit indexes provided by LISREL). The use of multiple adjunct fit indexes sampled from different classes is recommended (Bollen, 1989b; Marsh et al., 1988; Mulaik et al., 1989; Tanaka, 1993).

An important distinction between the χ^2 goodness-of-fit test and adjunct fit indexes concerns the magnitude of the value that indicates acceptable fit of a model. The χ^2 is, in reality, a "badness-of-fit" index; therefore, smaller values indicate better fit. Indeed, a χ^2 value of zero, which would result from a value of the fitting function equal to zero (i.e., the residual matrix would contain all zeros), indicates a perfect fit. Recall, however, that the χ^2 variate is a statistic and, therefore, its values are evaluated relative to the number of degrees of freedom available for the test (see Chapters 2 and 5). Adjunct fit indexes, on the other hand, are *goodness*-of-fit indexes, which means that larger values are more desirable. Moreover, adjunct fit indexes are not statistics; therefore, there is no definitive critical value.

A final aspect of evaluating fit involves comparing two or more theory-based models of the same data. Such *model comparison* is statistical in nature, not unlike the comparison of models in hierarchical regression analysis. Model comparison requires the specification of two nested models. Two models are *nested* if they both contain the same parameters but the set of free parameters in one model is a subset of the free parameters in the other. A $\Delta\chi^2$ statistic, parallel to the F-change statistic consulted in hierarchical regression analysis, is used to determine which model better accounts for the observed data.

Model Modification

One of the more controversial aspects of SEM is modification, or respecification, of a model (MacCallum, Roznowski, & Necowitz, 1992; Chapter 2, this volume). *Model modification* involves adjusting a specified and estimated model by either freeing parameters that formerly were fixed or fixing parameters that formerly were free. The controversy surrounding model modification focuses more on the basis for modifying a model that the general notion of model modification. In that regard it parallels a similar point of discussion among ANOVA users regarding the usefulness of post-hoc comparisons of means: The act of comparing means is not at issue; rather the discussion centers around the basis for formulating mean comparisons. In the SEM approach, model comparison is analogous to planned comparisons, and model modification is analogous to post-hoc comparisons.

Model modification typically follows estimation of a model that resulted in unfavorable indicators of fit. In the absence of other theory-based models of the data, the basis for modification typically is an inspection of parameter estimates, an evaluation of some form of the residual matrix, or, in the spirit of stepwise regression, the use of statistical searches for adjustments that will result in more favorable indicators of fit. The most well-known of the statistical search strategies makes use of the modification index provided by the LISREL program. The *modification index* and the *Lagrange multiplier test* (provided by the EQS program) provide information about the amount of χ^2 change that would result if parameters that formerly were fixed were free in a specified model. The EQS program also provides information about the change in χ^2 that would result if formerly free parameters were fixed by means of the *Wald test*. The Wald and Lagrange multiplier tests can be used to evaluate χ^2 change as a result of respecifying one or many parameters; the modification index can be used to evaluate respecification of only one parameter at a time (see Byrne's comparison of these approaches in Chapter 8). Of course, such strategies sacrifice control over Type I error and, therefore, lead to a situation in which idiosyncracies of a particular data set might be interpreted as reliable findings (MacCallum et al., 1992).

Interpretation

If either the χ^2 goodness-of-fit test or adjunct fit indexes indicate acceptable overall fit of a specified model, then the focus moves to specific elements of fit. Individual estimates of free parameters are evaluated according to their difference from some specified null value, typically zero. The ratio of each estimate to its standard error is distributed as a z statistic and, therefore, must exceed 1.96 before the estimate can be considered reliably different from zero.

Tests and comparisons of parameter estimates involve unstandardized estimates, whereas presentation of results often involves standardized estimates. *Unstandardized parameter estimates* retain scaling information of the variables involved and can be interpreted only with reference to the scales of those variables. Unstandardized estimates indicate the number of units change in the dependent variable per unit change in the independent variable when all remaining independent variables are at their mean. *Standardized parameter estimates* are transformations of unstandardized estimates that remove scaling information and, therefore, invite informal comparisons of parameters throughout a model. Standardized estimates index the number of standard deviations change in the dependent variable per standard deviation change in the independent variable when all remaining independent variables are at zero (i.e., their mean in standard normal units). Standardized parameter estimates correspond to effect-size estimates, which are increasingly common adjuncts to standard statistical information from mean comparison procedures such as *t* test and ANOVA.

The most challenging and poorly understood aspect of interpreting SEM results concerns not the magnitude or direction of relations between variables but, rather, the nature of those relations. SEM often is described as a statistical means of testing causal hypotheses from correlational data. Perhaps stemming from that naive characterization of SEM, researchers often are too quick to infer causality from statistically significant relations in structural equation models (Cliff, 1983; Freedman, 1987). In reality, SEM does nothing more than test the relations among variables as they were assessed. In other words, SEM cannot overcome the limitations associated with nonexperimental data gathered in a single session.

So, what is the advantage of SEM over methods such as ANOVA or multiple regression for testing causal hypotheses? Consider briefly the necessary conditions for demonstrating a causal relation: association, isolation, and directionality (Bollen, 1989b). The most elementary condition is association; the cause and the effect must be related. In this regard, SEM enjoys no particular advantage over other statistical methods. Second, the putative cause must be isolated from other causes (i.e., extraneous and confounding variables), a condition established in experiments by random assignment to levels of the causal variable. Although partial correlation, ANOVA, and multiple regression analysis can be used to isolate putative causal variables from other variables, SEM is more flexible and comprehensive than any of those approaches, providing means of controlling not only for extraneous or confounding variables but for measurement error as well.

The condition with regard to which SEM is most frequently misunderstood is directionality. Directional arrows in path diagrams (described in the next section) are incorrectly interpreted by some as indicating that directionality has been tested using SEM or is implied by the investigator who has used SEM. In reality, SEM, like ANOVA or regression, cannot be used to test the hypothesis of directionality. Directionality is a form of association distinguished from nondirectional association either by logic (e.g., income cannot cause biological sex), theory (e.g., group cohesion affects group performance), or, most powerfully, by research design (e.g., a manipulated variable to which subjects are assigned randomly cannot be caused by a dependent variable). The use of theory to justify an inference of directionality is the most problematic because often there are competing theories that offer different accounts of the association among two or more variables (consider the plausible converse of the example cited in the previous sentence).

In the end, association in structural equation models is interpreted no differently from association in ANOVA or multiple regression. Directional arrows in path diagrams typically used to depict relations in structural equation models should not be taken to indicate hypotheses of causal direction unless explicitly designated as such (path diagrams of ANOVA or regression designs would include directional arrows as well). At the most generic level they distinguish between predictors and outcomes, a distinction that may have more to do with the focus of the research than concern over causal direction. Yet, if the study from which those variables arise is designed appropriately, then a causal interpretation of directional paths may be in order (see Martin, 1987; Chapter 7, this volume).

Communication

There is considerable inconsistency in the way results of SEM analyses are reported. Because of the large amount of statistical information that emerges from analyses of structural equation models and the variability in what portion of that information investigators include in their reports, some writers have called for increased attention to the communication of SEM results (e.g., Biddle & Marlin, 1987; Raykov, Tomer, & Nesselroade, 1991; Chapter 9, this volume). Informative and complete communication of SEM results is a challenging but essential aspect of the SEM approach.

A primary form of communicating SEM hypotheses and results is the path diagram. A *path diagram* is a pictorial representation of a structural equation model. The three primary components of a path diagram are rectangles, ellipses, and arrows. *Rectangles* are used to indicate observed variables, which may be either indicators of latent variables in the measurement model or independent or dependent variables in the structural model. *Ellipses* are used to indicate latent variables, independent and dependent variables as well as errors of prediction in the structural model and errors of measurement in the measurement model. *Arrows* are used to indicate association and are of two sorts. Straight arrows point in one direction and indicate direction of prediction, from predictor to outcome. Curved arrows point in two directions and indicate nondirectional association (i.e., correlation). In addition, MacCallum (Chapter 2) advocates sharply curved arrows that begin and end with the same observed or latent variable and indicate variance (i.e., a variable's covariance with itself). In the path diagram, the structural component of a model typically is arrayed so that directional arrows run from left to right. If the measurement component is included in the diagram, it sometimes is necessary to orient relations between indicators and their latent variables both vertically and horizontally in order to avoid cluttering the structural portion of the diagram.

The most informative path diagram includes an indication of all parameters in a model (Chapter 2, this volume). Such completeness is rarely the case in practice, however. Paths indicating error of measurement and error of prediction often are omitted from path diagrams and, on occasion, indicators of latent variables are omitted. Although such omissions are not, in principle, ill-advised, they may be misleading for two reasons. First, they do not clearly indicate the model specified and estimated. That problem is overcome by a caption that clearly specifies which aspects of the specified model were omitted from the diagram. Second, if, as is frequently the case, the path diagram is used to display parameter estimates, not all parameter estimates are presented in an incomplete path diagram. Thus, like an ANOVA display in which only a portion of the means is presented, the path diagram that includes only a portion of the parameter estimates raises questions about the status of the unreported estimates.

An additional issue associated with the use of path diagrams concerns precisely what the diagram should depict (Biddle & Marlin, 1987). A path diagram in a research report can depict one of the following: (a) the model originally specified and estimated by the investigator; (b) that portion of the original model for which parameter estimates were significant; or (c) a model that resulted from one or more modifications and reestimations of the original model. A virtue of the path diagram that depicts the full originally specified model is that it can be used as a basis both for presenting the conceptual hypotheses and for describing the model initially specified and estimated. The diagram that omits nonsignificant paths may be less cluttered than the full diagram but it contributes to incomplete reporting of results. A compromise between the full and partial diagrams is the diagram that depicts all parameters in the original model but uses dashed lines to indicate nonsignificant paths. The path diagram that depicts a model derived through modifications to an initial model should not be the only diagram provided as it belies the a priori specification and gives the appearance of a reliable model despite inattention to Type I error.

Of course, SEM results can be presented in other ways. For instance, tables provide a means of conveying a considerable amount of information in a limited space. Yet, unlike ANOVA tables, in which the design is conveyed through the format of the table, SEM tables do not provide information about the position of parameters in the model. On the other hand, path diagrams provide a clear sense of where particular parameters are located in a model, but they often become overly cluttered when parameter estimates are included in the diagram. Hoyle and Panter (Chapter 9) discuss further the virtues and drawbacks to various mechanisms for communicating SEM results. The authors of the final three chapters illustrate the use of tables and figures to communicate SEM results.

A final issue associated with communication concerns notation. Prior to the appearance of the EQS program, most SEM analyses were done using the LISREL program. Early versions of that program required the specification of as many as eight matrices, each identified by a Greek letter. Moreover, documentation associated with LISREL as well as computer output from it relied heavily on matrix representation of structural equation models; matrices and their elements were identified by Greek letters. As a consequence, early reports of SEM results are replete with Greek letters and matrix notation. As the SEM approach has entered the mainstream of statistical methods in the social and behavioral sciences, the use of those devices has been replaced by notation more consistent with notation used in other, more familiar, statistical models and, in many cases, verbal labels. Authors contributing to this volume were urged to avoid Greek letters and matrix notation in their presentations without compromising the completeness and accuracy of their coverage. A growing consensus among SEM users is that social and behavioral science researchers who use the SEM approach should do the same.

Summary and Recommendations

This brief survey of the basic concepts and issues associated with the SEM approach to research design and data analysis highlighted similarities and differences between SEM and standard approaches like correlation, multiple regression, and ANOVA. To summarize, SEM is similar to those approaches in four fundamental ways. First, both SEM and those approaches are based on linear statistical models. Indeed, standard linear models such as ANOVA, multiple regression, and factor analysis are special instances of the general structural equation model. Second, statistical tests associated with SEM and standard statistical approaches are valid only if certain assumptions about the observed data are met. For SEM, those assumptions are independence of observations (common to all approaches) and multivariate normality. A growing repertoire of estimation methods and mounting evidence that the maximum likelihood method is reasonably robust to modest violations of the normality assumption have helped curb earlier criticisms about the appropriateness of SEM for typical social and behavioral science data (cf., Hu, Bentler, & Kano, 1992; see Chapters 3 and 4, this volume). Third, neither SEM nor standard approaches offer statistical tests of causality. By virtue of their capacity to evaluate association, each approach can provide necessary but not sufficient evidence of causality. The SEM approach enjoys some advantage over the more restricted methods in evaluating causal hypotheses because of the ability to specify models in which the putative cause is isolated from extraneous influences and measurement error. None of the approaches can be used to test directionality, a condition established through logic, strong theory, or methodological strategies, not statistical design. Fourth, for SEM or any of the standard statistical models, adjustments to the initial statistical hypothesis after viewing the data dramatically increase the likelihood of sample-specific results. Post-hoc adjustments to statistical hypotheses tested by any statistical model necessitate cross-validation.

SEM differs from standard approaches in three important ways. First, the use of SEM requires formal specification of a model to be estimated and tested. Unlike ANOVA, which, as typically used, evaluates main effect and interaction hypotheses by default, and multiple regression analysis, which permits specification only of direct effects on a single outcome, SEM offers no default model specification and places relatively few limits on what types of relations can be specified. A frequently cited advantage of that characteristic of SEM is that it requires researchers to think carefully about their data and to venture hypotheses regarding each variable. Second, perhaps the most compelling characteristic of SEM is the capacity to estimate and test relations between latent variables. The isolation of concepts from uniqueness and unreliability of their indicators increases the probability of detecting association and obtaining estimates of free parameters close to their population values. Third, an unfortunate distinction between SEM and standard statistical approaches is the ambiguity associated with tests of structural equation models compared to the relatively straightforward tests that accompany standard models. At the heart of this ambiguity is the complex effect of data and model characteristics on the χ^2 variate on which most indicators of model fit are based. The development of new indexes of fit based on alternative distributions promises to curb that ambiguity in the near future. For now, the most defensible strategy for evaluating the fit of structural equation models is to consult fit indexes from multiple classes of indexes (Chapter 5) and evaluate the χ^2 goodness-of-fit test with reference to the statistical power of the test given the characteristics of the model and the data (Chapter 6).

The SEM approach is a more comprehensive and flexible approach to research design and data analysis than any other single statistical model in standard use by social and behavioral scientists. Although there are research hypotheses that can be efficiently and completely tested by standard methods, the SEM approach provides a means of testing more complex and specific hypotheses than can be tested by those methods. The chapters that follow dissect the structural equation model and, it is hoped, will demystify it for would-be users. Each chapter was written with the researcher in mind and is an invitation to consider thoughtfully the SEM approach to research design and data analysis. Read on. A worthwhile challenge awaits.

2 Model Specification

Procedures, Strategies, and Related Issues

ROBERT C. MACCALLUM

Any application of structural equation modeling (SEM) must involve the specification of one or more models to be evaluated. It is critical for researchers using SEM to have a sound working knowledge of procedures and strategies for model specification. This knowledge will allow researchers to specify models in a technically correct manner so that appropriate parameter estimates and measures of fit can be obtained and evaluated. Furthermore, such knowledge will provide the basis for employing strategies in model construction that will yield rigorous and clear resolution of research objectives.

In the present chapter I provide a detailed presentation of procedures for model specification as well as a discussion of related issues, such as the existence of equivalent models. In addition, I discuss and offer recommendations regarding strategies for model construction. I focus on the general case of conventional linear structural equation models. Although this presentation is almost entirely nonmathematical, readers should be aware that there exist several different but closely related mathematical frameworks for this general class of models (Bentler & Weeks, 1980; Jöreskog, 1974; McArdle & McDonald, 1984). Regardless of the framework employed, there also exists a variety of special cases of the general model, such as factor analysis, path analysis, and simultaneous equation models. I focus here on the general class of models, but readers should recognize that in any particular application they may define a model that fits into one of many special cases. In addition, there exists a variety of covariance structure models that do not fit into the class of linear models represented by these frameworks; e.g., the multiplicative model for multitrait-multimethod data (Browne, 1984b; Cudeck, 1988). Many of these models are quite important and useful, but they fall outside the scope of the present chapter.

Model Specification Procedures

A linear structural equation model is a hypothesized pattern of linear relationships among a set of variables. The purpose of such a model is to provide a meaningful and parsimonious explanation for observed relationships within a set of measured variables. That is, one observes correlational relationships within a set of measured variables, and one attempts to explain those relationships using a model that is substantively meaningful and also is parsimonious in the sense of being substantially less complex than the observed data themselves. A critical principle in model specification and evaluation is the fact that all of the models that we would be interested in specifying and evaluating are wrong to some degree. Models at their best can be expected to provide only a close approximation to observed data, rather than an exact fit. In the case of SEM, the real-world phenomena that give rise to our observed correlational data are far more complex than we can hope to represent using a linear structural equation model and associated assumptions. Thus we must define as an optimal outcome a finding that a particular model fits our observed data closely and yields a highly interpretable solution. Furthermore, one must understand that even when such an outcome is obtained, one can conclude only that the particular model is a plausible one. There will virtually always be other models that fit the data to exactly the same degree, or very nearly so, thereby representing models with different substantive interpretation but equivalent fit to the observed data. The number of such models may be extremely large, and they can be distinguished only in terms of their substantive meaning. In the absence of considering all possible such models, a finding that a particular model fits observed data well and yields an interpretable solution can be taken to mean only that that model provides one plausible representation of the structure that produced the observed data.

Let us now turn to some details of model specification. The set of variables within a given model includes both measured variables (MVs) and latent variables (LVs). An MV is simply a variable that is directly measured, whereas an LV is a construct that is not directly or exactly measured. LVs are routinely relevant and central in research in behavioral sciences (and in many other disciplines as well). Constructs such as intelligence, depression, and attitude are LVs. In the general class of models, MVs typically serve as approximate measures, or indicators, of LVs. For instance, the Beck Depression Inventory could serve as an indicator of the LV depression. In a structural equation model it is desirable for each such LV to be represented by several distinct indicators. The LV, then, is defined in effect as whatever its multiple indicators have in common with each other. LVs defined in this way are equivalent to common factors in factor analysis and can be viewed as being free of error of measurement. Without multiple indicators we rely on single error-perturbed MVs to represent constructs of interest. This approach is problematic in that constructs are not well defined and estimates of effects among constructs are biased by the influence of error of measurement.

Given a set of MVs and LVs, a model postulates a pattern of linear relationships among these variables. Within the model there exist two types of relationships: directional and nondirectional. Directional relationships represent hypothesized linear directional influences of one variable on another. For instance, the notion that stress causes depression implies a directional influence between two LVs. Nondirectional relationships represent hypothesized correlational associations between variables, with no attempt to postulate direction of influence. For example, the hypothesis that verbal ability and mathematical ability are correlated represents a hypothesized nondirectional association between two LVs. Essentially, the task of model specification requires that the researcher specify a pattern of directional and nondirectional relationships among the variables of interest. Of course, it is not necessary for there to be some type of relationship for each pair of variables. In fact, in typical models, many pairs of variables are hypothesized to be not directly associated by either type of relationship.

Each of these directional and nondirectional associations can be thought of as having a numerical value associated with it. Numerical values associated with directional effects are values of regression coefficients; that is, weights applied to variables in linear regression equations. Numerical values associated with nondirectional relationships are values of covariances between variables (or correlations, if variables are standardized). These weights and covariances can be thought of as parameters of the model. A major objective in applications of SEM is to estimate the values of these parameters.

Each variable in the system can be designated as either an endogenous or an exogenous variable. An endogenous variable is one that receives a directional influence from some other variable in the system. That is, an endogenous variable is hypothesized to be affected by another variable in the model. It may also emit a directional influence to some other variable, but not necessarily. An exogenous variable is one that does not receive a directional influence from any other variable in the system. Exogenous variables are typically associated with one another by nondirectional relationships, but such associations are not required, and exogenous variables typically exert directional influences on one or more endogenous variables.

An important feature of an endogenous variable involves the fact that we generally do not view such a variable as being perfectly and completely accounted for by those variables hypothesized to exert directional influences on the endogenous variable in question. Therefore, we generally define each endogenous variable as being influenced also by an error term, which represents that part of the endogenous variable that is not accounted for by the linear influences of the other variables in the system. These error terms can be viewed as consisting partly of random error and partly of systematic error that is not explained, but could theoretically be explained by variables or effects not included in the model. Note that the error terms themselves can be considered to be LVs in that they are not directly observed. Also, in most applications, the error terms will be exogenous variables, not receiving directional influences from other variables. This last feature is not a requirement, however, in that it is useful in some special situations to consider directional influences among error terms.

In the general case, a model will involve a hypothesis about a pattern of linear relationships among a set of LVs, with each LV measured by multiple indicators. Relationships of a latent variable to its indicators are usually defined as directional, from the LV to each indicator. For example, the LV depression would be hypothesized to exert a linear influence on each MV used as an indicator of that LV, such as the Beck Depression Inventory and the Hamilton Depression Rating Scale. Parameters associated with these linear effects are equivalent to factor loadings in factor analysis; that is, they are regression coefficients representing the linear influence of common factors on measured variables. The observed correlations among indicators of a given LV are thus hypothesized as arising from the joint dependence of those indicators on the LV. Note that each such indicator is an endogenous variable in that it receives a directional influence from the LV it is measuring. Therefore, we conventionally represent each indicator as being influenced also by an error term. These error variables are analogous to unique factors in factor analysis in that they represent that part of each indicator not accounted for by the common factor(s).

An alternative view of relationships between LVs and indicators is receiving attention in recent literature (Bollen & Lennox, 1991; Cohen, Cohen, Teresi, Marchi, & Velez, 1990; MacCallum & Browne, 1993). In this alternative view, some LVs could be defined as being influenced by their indicators, rather than vice versa. For example, clinical and social psychological researchers are often interested in the construct of social support, represented by measures such as frequency of positive social interactions in a given period of time. Rather than viewing social support as a construct influencing such measures, it might be more reasonable to view the MVs as giving rise to or influencing the construct. In such a construction the MVs are called causal indicators. Those indicators are then typically exogenous variables, thereby not containing a specified error term, and the construct automatically becomes an endogenous variable. In the process of model specification it is recommended that the researcher consider the nature of each LV of interest and decide whether it is most appropriate to define its indicators as effects of or causes of the LV and to specify the model accordingly. Cohen et al. (1990) provide some guidance for making such determinations. Bollen and Lennox (1991) discuss implications of this type of model specification, and MacCallum and Browne (1993) discuss and illustrate problematic issues that often will arise when causal indicators are embedded in larger models in practice.

With regard to the relationship between MVs and LVs, it is also important to note that MVs do not have to serve as indicators of LVs. An MV can stand alone in a model as either an exogenous or an endogenous variable. Some models, called path analysis and simultaneous equation models, contain only MVs and no LVs (other than error terms associated with endogenous MVs). A model could also contain a mixture of stand-alone MVs and LVs with multiple indicators. Researchers should be aware, though, that, without additional information such as reliability estimates, MVs standing alone in a model are considered and specified to be free of error of measurement. Therefore, the presence of such error in the measurements will contaminate estimates of model parameters. Thus it is generally advantageous to employ LVs with multiple indicators.

A model will also contain hypothesized relationships of LVs with one another. Following principles stated earlier, such relationships can be either directional or nondirectional, and each LV can be defined as either exogenous or endogenous. An endogenous LV will generally be specified as being influenced also by an error term representing that part of the LV not accounted for by the linear influences specified in the model. For example, if we hypothesize that stress causes depression, depression will contain an error term representing that part of the construct not accounted for by stress. Every error term in the model can be viewed as an LV that exerts a linear influence on the variable with which it is associated.

Let us now carefully consider the nature of all of the parameters in a structural equation model. First, every exogenous variable in the entire system (including every MV, LV, and error term that satisfies the definition of an exogenous variable) will have a variance that is defined as a model parameter. Endogenous variables also have variances, of course, but those variances are not parameters. Rather, variances of endogenous variables are implied by other variables and influences in the model. For instance, in the example mentioned earlier, the variance of depression is implied by the variances of stress and the error term, and their influences on depression. That is, because depression is modeled as a linear function of stress, plus an error term, the variance of depression could be expressed algebraically as a function of the variance of stress, the influence of stress on depression, the variance of the errors, and the covariance of stress and error, which is zero. More generally, the variance of any endogenous variable can be expressed algebraically as a function of the variances of exogenous variables, including error terms, and parameters associated with linear influences in the model. Thus the variances of endogenous variables are not themselves parameters but are functions of other parameters in the model.

Next, any covariances (i.e., nondirectional associations among exogenous variables of any kind) would be parameters of the model. Such parameters can involve exogenous variables only. It is not permissible to specify nondirectional associations involving any endogenous variable because all such associations are implied by other variables and influences in the model. Just as the variance of an endogenous variable can be expressed as a function of other model parameters, so also can covariances (or correlations) of endogenous variables with other variables. Thus such relationships are not specifiable as model parameters. For example, if we hypothesize that stress causes both depression and fatigue, we would not be permitted to specify a nondirectional association between depression and fatigue. The model already implies a relationship between these constructs in that both are influenced by a common cause, stress. Specifically, the covariance between depression and fatigue could be shown to be an algebraic function of the variance of stress and the linear influence of stress on depression and fatigue. Therefore, that covariance is determined by other parameters and can not be specified as a distinct parameter. The same phenomenon holds for all nondirectional relationships involving endogenous variables.

Finally, all directional effects specified in the model constitute a third category of parameters. These directional effects include effects of LVs on other LVs, LVs on their indicators, error terms on associated variables, and so on. To summarize, we can define three classes of parameters in a structural equation model: variances of exogenous variables, covariances among exogenous variables, and weights representing directional linear influences among variables.

Each of these parameters is designated as being either a free parameter, which means its value is unknown and to be estimated, or a fixed parameter, which means it is provided with a specified numerical value in the original model. For free parameters, it is also possible to define constraints involving estimates of individual parameters or combinations of parameters. For example, one can require that the estimate of a given parameter be greater than or equal to zero or that estimates of several parameters be equal. Such aspects of model specification must be carefully justified based on theory or research objectives. For example, equality constraints among parameters are especially useful in longitudinal models and in models fit simultaneously to multiple samples. In longitudinal models, equality constraints can be used to formulate hypotheses of invariance of linear influences among variables at different time points or across successive time intervals. In multisample analyses, equality constraints are often used to test equality of model parameters in separate groups of individuals.

Values of fixed parameters are generally defined based on requirements of model specification. A critical requirement is that we establish a scale for each LV in the model, including error terms. LVs are constructs not directly measured and thus have no scale of measurement. However, because we wish to estimate values of parameters representing associations among LVs and between LVs and MVs, it is essential that each LV have a defined scale. For example, a regression coefficient representing the predicted change in depression associated with a one-unit increase in stress cannot be estimated without defining a scale, or unit of measurement, for stress and depression. To resolve this dilemma, we provide each LV with a scale in the model specification process. This objective can be achieved in one of two ways. The first is to fix the variance of each LV at a specified numerical value, typically 1.0. Each such LV is thus defined as a standardized variable, which can greatly simplify interpretation of subsequent parameter estimates. Establishing a scale for each construct in this way allows us to interpret coefficients associated with directional effects among LVs as standardized regression weights, and those associated with nondirectional relationships as correlations. If MVs have also been standardized (i.e., if the model is fit to a correlation matrix) then coefficients associated with relationships of LVs to MVs, or MVs to one another, can also be interpreted as standardized. Thus this scaling procedure is recommended for each substantive construct in the model. A second procedure for establishing a scale for an LV is to fix the value of one parameter associated with a directional influence emitted by the given LV. This procedure is recommended for each error term in the model. In effect, this means that we simply assign a value of 1.0 for the influence of each error term on its associated endogenous variable. Recall that in typical models the error terms are exogenous variables and their variances are parameters to be estimated. Thus the estimate of each such error variance parameter will tell us how much variance in the associated endogenous variable is not accounted for by other influences in the model.

One loose end in the procedure just described involves how to establish a scale for an endogenous LV. The variance of an endogenous LV is not a parameter but rather is implied by other variables and influences in the model. For such a case we have two options. We could use the second procedure just described and fix at 1.0 one parameter representing an influence of that LV on another variable. This is typically done by fixing at 1.0 the parameter representing the influence of the LV on one of its indicators. An alternative is to fix the implied variance of the endogenous LV at 1.0. Because that implied variance is not a parameter, however, this procedure actually represents the introduction of a constraint on other parameter estimates. The second procedure is much more desirable because it allows us to define endogenous LVs as standardized, which simplifies interpretation of parameter estimates. However, this approach is not widely available in SEM software. It was introduced by Browne and Mels (1992) in their RAMONA program. Lacking such software, one is limited to using the first procedure just described for establishing a scale for an endogenous LV.

Path Diagrams

It is very common and useful in practice to represent models using path diagrams. Although there are some standard conventions in constructing such diagrams, there are also variations in how certain details of models are represented. For example, some researchers construct diagrams so as to explicitly display error terms as LVs whereas others do not do so. I find it useful to construct path diagrams so as to represent all information about the model. Such an approach requires the researcher to be completely explicit about model specification and also can be quite helpful in converting the model into instructions for SEM software. Therefore, I will describe a procedure for constructing complete path diagrams for SEM.

It is standard convention to use squares or rectangles to represent MVs and circles or ellipses to represent LVs, including error terms. Directional effects between variables are specified using single-headed arrows, and nondirectional relationships are represented using double-headed arrows. It is also useful to represent the variance of a variable, as necessary, using a double-headed arrow from a variable to itself. With one exception, each of these arrows, or paths, represents a parameter of the model and has either a free or fixed value. The exception involves cases in which we specify the variance of an endogenous LV as being fixed at 1.0. Such a variance is not a parameter but is rather implied by the model. Each path is then labeled using an appropriate symbol for free parameters to be estimated, or a numerical value for fixed parameters. In various mathematical frameworks for SEM (Bentler & Weeks, 1980; Jöreskog, 1974; McArdle & McDonald, 1984), these parameters are denoted using mathematical symbols, usually Greek letters. In the present introductory presentation, however, such notation is not really necessary. A simple alternative to be used here is to represent fixed parameters by their numerical values and free parameters by the symbol *.

Illustration

To illustrate procedures for specification of a model and construction of a corresponding path diagram, suppose we were to study relationships among depression, functioning of the immune system, and physical illness. These three constructs could be considered LVs, and we could obtain multiple measures of each. Depression could be measured by conventional scales such as the Beck Depression Inventory and the Hamilton Depression Rating Scale. Immune function could be assessed by a variety of blood chemistry measures. Illness could be measured by such measures as the frequency of physician-diagnosed infectious illnesses, number of days in bed, and so on. Assume that we select three appropriate indicators for each LV. For simplicity, the indicators for depression will be called Dep1, Dep2, and Dep3; the indicators for immune function and illness will be labeled in a corresponding fashion. Suppose finally that we hypothesize that depression influences immune function which in turn influences illness.

From this information, and following the procedures and rules defined earlier for model specification, we can construct a complete structural equation model and corresponding path diagram. The diagram is shown in Figure 2.1. The three LVs are shown as ellipses, with single-headed arrows representing the hypothesized associations among them. Those paths are labeled as * to represent the unknown values of the corresponding parameters. Depression is an exogenous LV because it receives no single-headed paths from other variables. Therefore, its variance is a parameter of the model and is fixed at a value of 1.0 to establish a scale. Immune function and illness are endogenous LVs. Their variances are not model parameters but can be defined as fixed at 1.0, thereby establishing a constraint on other parameters. On the path diagram those fixed variances are enclosed in parentheses to indicate that they are not parameters. Because immune function and illness are endogenous LVs, it is conventional to specify associated residual terms, which are shown in the diagram as LVs. The residual term e10 represents that part of the immune function construct that is not accounted for by the linear influence of depression. The residual term e11 represents that part of the illness construct that is not accounted for by the

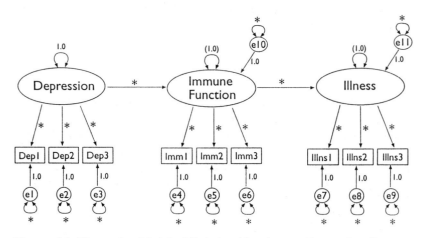

Figure 2.1. Illustrative Model of Relationships Among Depression, Immune Function, and Illness

direct linear effect of immune function, which subsumes the indirect linear effect of depression, through immune function. The influence of each of these error terms on their associated LVs is specified by a single-headed arrow with a fixed weight of 1.0. Each of these residuals is actually an exogenous LV and thus has a variance parameter associated with it. These variance parameters are labeled as * to indicate that they are free parameters whose values are to be estimated.

Let us next consider the relationship of each LV to its indicators. The three indicators of each LV are represented by appropriately labeled rectangles in the path diagram. The depression construct exerts a linear influence on each of its three indicators, as represented by the single-headed paths with associated * labels. Each indicator is specified as containing an error term, with each error term exerting a linear influence on the corresponding indicator, with an associated weight of 1.0, and each error term also having a variance specified as a free parameter and labeled as *. A corresponding structure is specified for the relationship of the immune function and illness constructs to their respective indicators.

The resulting path diagram shows all information about the specified model. Every variable in the system, including error terms, is represented explicitly. Every parameter in the model is shown as having either a free or fixed value, including variances of exogenous variables.

In addition, it is specified that the scales of the two endogenous LVs are established by setting their variances at 1.0. A count of the number of free parameters in this model finds that number to be 22; there are 11 free regression weights and 11 free variances. However, the imposition of two constraints implied by fixing the variances of immune function and illness reduces the effective number of free parameters to 20. The effective number of parameters in a model can be defined as the number of free parameters minus the number of constraints imposed on those parameters.

This model represents a hypothesized pattern of linear relationships among a set of LVs and MVs. The model is intended to account for the relationships among the nine MVs. If we were to conduct a study wherein we gathered data on these nine MVs from an appropriate sample of people, we could compute the variances and covariances among those nine MVs. For p variables, the number of such variances and covariances is $p(p + 1)/2$; in this case, that number would be 45. Thus the specified model can be viewed as an attempt to explain the structure inherent in those 45 variances/covariances using a model containing 20 free parameters. In this sense, the model is substantially simpler than the data whose structure it is trying to explain.

Identification

An important but difficult issue inherent in the process of model specification is the issue of identification. To have a basic understanding of this problem it is necessary first to understand fundamental aspects of the process of parameter estimation. The model shown in Figure 2.1 falls into a general class of linear structural equation models. As mentioned earlier, there are several different but nearly equivalent mathematical frameworks for representing such models. These frameworks simply define the mathematical relationship between the model parameters on the one hand and the variances/covariances of the MVs on the other hand. Thus, if we knew the values of all of the parameters for the model in Figure 2.1, it would be a relatively simple task to compute the true variances/covariances of the nine MVs *as implied by that model and those parameter values*. That is, in a purely theoretical case wherein the model is correct and the parameter values are known, we could compute the true variances/covariances of the MVs. In practice, however, we do not know the parameter values. Instead, we observe a sample of observations on the MVs and obtain sample variances/covariances. We then have the opposite problem. Given the observed variances/covariances for the MVs, and given the specified model, we want to find values of the model parameters that will reproduce the observed variances/covariances. Unfortunately, in practice a solution cannot usually be found so as to yield exact fit of the model to the observed data. Therefore, parameter values are estimated from the sample data so as to obtain a solution wherein the variances/covariances reconstructed from the parameter estimates for the specified model match the corresponding sample values as closely as possible. This is the primary task carried out by SEM computer programs.

During these computations, estimates of model parameters are obtained using complex functions of sample variances/covariances. Thus, for each free parameter, it is necessary that at least one algebraic solution be obtainable expressing that free parameter as a function of sample variances/covariances. Parameters satisfying this condition are said to be identified, and parameters for which there is more than one distinct such solution are said to be overidentified. For these classes of parameters it is possible to find a unique solution. In SEM, models with one or more overidentified parameters are of primary interest because it is only for such models that the issue of correspondence between the model and the data is meaningful. A model with no overidentified parameters will always fit perfectly, thereby making it meaningless to assess model plausibility by evaluating fit. Models containing overidentified parameters generally will not fit data exactly, thus creating the critically important possibility that a model could be found to fit observed data poorly. Only when this possibility exists is a finding of good fit meaningful. This issue is discussed further in the section on disconfirmability.

For a given free parameter, if it is not possible to express the parameter algebraically as a function of sample variances/covariances, then that parameter is said to be unidentified. A model with one or more unidentified parameters cannot be used in practice because estimates of unidentified parameters are arbitrary and cannot be interpreted. Although a mathematical example of this phenomenon is well beyond the scope of this presentation, one can get a sense of the problem by considering the equation, $\beta\phi^2 = 1$. If β and ϕ are parameters to be estimated and this equation represents our entire set of information, then there exists an infinite number of solutions for β and ϕ, thus rendering those parameters unidentified. However, if we had other equations involving β and ϕ (e.g., $\beta = 2$), then the parameters could be identified, or overidentified. To summarize, it is critical that models be specified in such a way that all parameters are identified.

Unfortunately, determination of this property for any particular model can be a very difficult task. There is no simple set of necessary and sufficient conditions that provide a means for verification of identification of model parameters; however, there are two necessary conditions that should always be checked. First, as mentioned earlier, a scale must be established for every LV in the model. If this condition is not satisfied, one or more parameters will be unidentified. (Specifically, for an exogenous LV, the variance of the LV as well as coefficients associated with all paths emitted by the LV would be unidentified; for an endogenous LV, the residual variance and coefficients associated with all paths leading to or from the LV would be unidentified.) Second, the effective number of model parameters, defined earlier, must not exceed the number of sample variances/covariances for the MVs, which is $p(p + 1)/2$. If this condition is violated, the researcher has fewer data values than parameters to be estimated, which will cause lack of identification. These two conditions are necessary but not sufficient. Identification problems can still arise even if these requirements are satisfied. Although a rigorous verification of model identification can be achieved only algebraically, SEM computer programs generally provide a check for identification during the parameter estimation process. If a problem is found, the programs point the user to one or more parameters that are involved in an identification problem. Using this information, the user can attempt to isolate the problem algebraically and determine whether the model can be respecified in a meaningful way so as to eliminate the problem. In no case should one proceed without resolving the problem.

Strategies and Related Issues in Model Specification

DISCONFIRMABILITY

A critical issue in the specification and evaluation of any model in this class is the degree of disconfirmability of the model. A model is disconfirmable to the degree that it is possible for the model to be inconsistent with observed data. If a model can fit any set of MV variances/covariances perfectly, then the model is not disconfirmable at all. Such a model will generally have as many or more parameters than there are MV variances/covariances. A model of this type is not very interesting scientifically. It is as complex as the observed data and thus serves no useful purpose in terms of explaining the structure underlying the data in a parsimonious way. For a model to be disconfirmable to any degree, the effective number of parameters must be less than the number of MV variances/covariances, meaning that the model will have positive degrees of freedom (df), because df equals the number of MV variances/covariances minus the effective number of parameters. Reasonably specified models with lots of parameters and relatively low df often tend to fit data quite well and thus tend to be not very disconfirmable. On the other hand, models with low numbers of parameters relative to the number of MV variances/covariances will be highly disconfirmable. For such models, bad fit to observed data is entirely possible. Thus when good fit is found one can be more confident in drawing a conclusion that the model is a plausible representation of the structure of the data. On the other hand, if a model is not disconfirmable to any reasonable degree, then a finding of good fit is essentially useless and meaningless. Therefore, in the model specification process, researchers are very strongly encouraged to keep in mind the principle of disconfirmability and to construct models that are not highly parameterized. In addition, it is essential in the assessment of model fit that one use fit measures that take into account in some fashion the degree of disconfirmability of a model. Unless such indexes are used, one will simply conclude that more highly parameterized models are better because they fit data better. Researchers are thus strongly urged to consider an index such as the root mean square error of approximation (RMSEA; Browne & Cudeck, 1993; Steiger & Lind, 1980), which is essentially a measure of lack of fit per degree of freedom.

EQUIVALENT MODELS

Another important issue in model specification is the problem of equivalent models. Essentially, two models are equivalent if they fit any set of data equally well. Such models cannot be distinguished mathematically, differing only in terms of their substantive meaning and the interpretability of solutions obtained when they are fit to data. The issue of equivalent models can and should be addressed during model construction. For a given model of interest, it is possible to construct alternative equivalent models by following some simple rules developed by Lee and Hershberger (1990), who expanded on earlier work of Stelzl (1986). These rules indicate conditions under which one can replace one path with a different path without affecting goodness of fit. (For example, in the simplest case of a model of the association between two variables, one cannot distinguish among the following models in terms of fit to the data: A → B; B → A; A ↔ B. Fortunately, when such relationships are embedded in larger overidentified models, the direction of each such path is generally not arbitrary.) By following these procedures, one can construct and consider the substantive meaningfulness of alternative equivalent models. Ideally, one would find that relatively few such models exist and that those that do are not substantively meaningful. On the other hand, if one finds that it is possible to generate a substantial number of such models, and if many of those models seem substantively plausible, then there is relatively little point in conducting a study of one's original model and arguing for its validity.

As noted by MacCallum, Wegener, Uchino, and Fabrigar (1993), the existence of equivalent models raises a problem similar to a confound in an experimental design. In the presence of such a confound there are alternative equally good explanations of observed phenomena. One is not free to ignore one explanation and support another without further study. Likewise, in SEM one is not free to ignore the presence of equivalent models and to assume that one's specified model provides the valid explanation of the data. The problem must be confronted. MacCallum et al. (1993) show that the problem is a severe one in practice, with equivalent models occurring routinely and often in very large numbers, and they provide some recommendations on how to address and manage the problem.

STRATEGIES

In empirical applications of SEM there are various strategies that researchers employ for model construction and development. Jöreskog and Sörbom (1993a) describe three distinct strategies: strictly confirmatory, model generation, and model comparison. In the strictly confirmatory strategy, the researcher constructs one model of interest and evaluates that model by fitting it to appropriate data. If the model yields interpretable parameter estimates and fits the data well, it is supported and considered a plausible model. If not, the model is not supported and no further steps are taken. This procedure is probably not used very often in practice because it leaves little flexibility or opportunity to address a negative outcome.

It is much more common for researchers to use a model generation strategy. In this approach, a researcher begins with a specified model and fits that model to appropriate data. The obtained solution is then evaluated for the purpose of modifying the model to improve its parsimony and/or its fit to the observed data. It might be possible to simplify the model by deleting selected parameters without significantly altering its fit to the data. More commonly, researchers might seek to improve goodness of fit to the data by introducing additional parameters to the model. Bollen (1989b) provides an excellent presentation of methods available for achieving such objectives. Given a solution for the original model, one can employ the Wald test to determine the degree to which fit would deteriorate if any selected subset of free parameters were deleted from the model (i.e., converted into fixed parameters with values of zero). If one can determine a subset of free parameters that, when deleted from the model, would produce little decrement in fit, one could simplify the model accordingly. The result would be a simpler model that would fit the data nearly as well as the original model. Alternatively, one can employ the Lagrange Multiplier (LM) test to determine the degree to which fit would improve if any selected subset of fixed parameters were converted into free parameters. From this perspective it might be possible to determine a subset of fixed parameters that, when converted to free parameters, would substantially improve model fit. One could introduce this set of free parameters into the model and thereby obtain a model with more parameters than the original model that would fit the data much better.

A very commonly used special case of the LM test is represented by the modification index (MI). Some SEM computer programs provide a value of the MI for each parameter in the model that is fixed at zero (i.e., each potential path that is not present in the path diagram); the MI represents the improvement in the overall χ^2 test of model fit that would be achieved if that specific parameter were set free. A large MI indicates that if the corresponding parameter were introduced to the model, the fit of the model would improve significantly. MIs are routinely used in practice to modify models so as to improve their fit to data. Breckler (1990) and MacCallum, Roznowski, and Necowitz (1992) reviewed a total of 100 published applications of SEM and found that 37 of them contained acknowledgments of having modified an initial model primarily using MIs alone. Furthermore, it is not unusual for this procedure to be used to introduce a fairly substantial number of new parameters to a model. MacCallum et al. (1992) cite several papers wherein more than eight parameters were added to a model.

Although the model generation procedure is used widely in practice, responsible researchers will approach it with caution. The methodological literature provides many warnings that are too often ignored in practice. In particular, it is of utmost importance that any modifications made to an original model must be substantively meaningful and justifiable. Of the 37 applications mentioned earlier that used the model generation strategy, only six offered any substantive justification of specific modifications. In the remaining 31, the model was altered purely to improve its fit with no apparent effort to interpret specific modifications. Another critical issue involves the necessity of validating modified models using new data. Because the model generation process is data driven, with models modified to fit a particular set of data better and then refit to the same data, a modified model must be validated using data from a new sample. This warning is also routinely ignored in practice. Of the 37 studies mentioned earlier, only four were found to provide any information about validation of the model on new data. If the model generation strategy is employed without attending to these warnings, the generated model has relatively little meaning or value. Some parameters in the model may have no substantive meaning, and the model will have been evaluated using the same data employed to modify it. It is imperative that researchers using this strategy begin to attend to these issues. It would be appropriate for editors of journals publishing applications of SEM to reject papers employing the model generation strategy if authors ignore these concerns.

There are still other reasons to be concerned about use of the model generation strategy in practice. Consider the ideal case in which a true model exists that exactly accounts for the variances/covariances of the MVs in the population of interest, but suppose that the model that is evaluated in the sample is misspecified by the omission of one or more parameters. Ideally, if model generation using the MI statistic works well, MIs should lead the researcher to add the appropriate parameters to the original model so as to lead to the true model. MacCallum (1986) investigated this issue using simulated data. Using different models, sample sizes, and strategies in a total of 160 sample data sets analyzed, the model generation procedure using MIs led from the misspecified model to the correct model in only 22 cases. Thus, even under ideal conditions, model modification procedures may routinely yield invalid results.

An even more serious issue in model generation involves the problem of capitalization on chance. As noted earlier, model modifications are based on results obtained from analysis of sample data, and modified models are evaluated by refitting them to the same data. Thus specific modifications may well be determined in part by chance characteristics of the observed sample, implying that modifications might not generalize beyond the sample at hand. If the same model generation strategy were followed beginning with the same model using a different sample, or using the entire population, different modifications might be made. MacCallum et al. (1992) studied this issue by conducting a sampling study using two large empirical data sets. They drew repeated subsamples of various sizes from the data sets, fit hypothesized models in each sample, and then modified those models using MIs, following procedures commonly used in practice. Model modifications were then compared across subsamples. Results showed that the specific modifications that were selected were highly unstable from sample to sample with sample sizes less than 400 and were not completely stable even with sample sizes of 1200. Thus the outcome of the model modification process appears to be very sensitive to characteristics of the sample at hand, and generalization beyond that sample is highly suspect unless sample size is extremely large.

Given the findings of these studies, researchers must be concerned about use of the model generation strategy in practice. Users of this strategy must acknowledge that they are engaging in exploratory model development. There is not necessarily anything wrong with exploratory model development as long as it is acknowledged in practice that that is what is being done and that the outcome is a model that cannot be supported without being evaluated using new data. Serious problems arise when the model generation strategy is applied without any effort to attach substantive meaning to model modifications and when the resulting model is treated as if it has been confirmed because it fits the observed sample data well. The model generation strategy is a legitimate approach to model development if it is used responsibly, but such use seems to be the exception rather than the rule in much of the applied literature.

A third strategy for model specification is the model comparison strategy. In this approach a researcher specifies a number of alternative a priori models and fits each model to the same set of data. The multiple models may represent competing theoretical positions or may be constructed based on conflicting research findings. In the early stages of model development in a particular domain, multiple models may simply be a result of uncertainty about the anticipated pattern of relationships among variables and may therefore reflect the exploratory character of the research effort. In such circumstances it may be useful to construct a variety of models ranging from relatively simple to relatively complex.

After each model is fit to an appropriate set of data, results are evaluated and compared with respect to several characteristics. The most obvious is goodness of fit, keeping in mind, as mentioned earlier, that it is important to employ procedures for evaluating fit that take into account model complexity. Researchers must not focus solely on fit, however, because the model that fits the best might exhibit some unattractive qualities. It is critical to examine parameter estimates for interpretability and meaningfulness. A model that fits well but yields nonsensical parameter estimates is of little value. It is also useful to compare models based on cross-validity. Browne and Cudeck (1989) and Cudeck and Henly (1991) encourage the use of a cross-validity index for model comparison that provides an indication of how well a solution obtained from a sample of a given size would fit in an independently drawn sample. This approach to model comparison takes into account the issue of sample size, and findings indicate that simpler models tend to cross-validate best in small samples, with more complex models cross-validating best in large samples (Browne & Cudeck, 1989).

To summarize issues related to these three strategies for model specification and evaluation, the strictly confirmatory strategy is probably overly rigid in most settings and is not used much. The model generation strategy appears to be heavily used but has very serious shortcomings that are routinely ignored in practice. The model comparison strategy circumvents these shortcomings to a great extent and provides a mechanism that is useful in a range of settings, from confirmatory study of a small number of models to more exploratory study of a larger range of models.

Conclusion

In empirical research in which SEM is to be employed, researchers must carefully choose a strategy and specify one or more models in a fashion that is consistent with the objectives of the research. The model comparison strategy, in particular, could probably be used to great benefit much more frequently than it is currently applied. If the model generation strategy is used, researchers must be mindful and actively responsive regarding the warnings and problems discussed earlier. In the specification of the particular model(s) to be evaluated, it is wise to avoid highly parameterized models that tend to be not very disconfirmable, and it is also wise to avoid trying to fit any models to data for very large numbers of variables. The structure of the variances/covariances for a large set of MVs is commonly too complex to be fit well by any parsimonious linear model. Finally, the process of the mechanical specification of a particular model must be conducted with care so that the model represented by the resulting path diagram and computer program instructions corresponds accurately to the intended model.

3 Estimates and Tests in Structural Equation Modeling

CHIH-PING CHOU

PETER M. BENTLER

In this chapter, we review the intimately related concepts of estimation and testing of structural equation models. We also make recommendations about the usefulness of some of the alternatives that are available. Because the existing literature on these topics is not very thorough and is ambiguous in its results, we conducted our own study to provide a solid foundation for our recommendations.

The structural equation model represents a series of hypotheses about how the variables in the analysis are generated and related. The parameters of the model are the regression coefficients and the variances and covariances of independent variables, as will be seen below. These parameters are fundamental to interpreting the model, but they are not known and need to be estimated from the data. Thus estimation is a logical first step in the modeling process after model specification. The statistical test of the adequacy of a model, or the goodness-of-fit test statistic, is obtained simultaneously with the estimation. A goodness-of-fit test statistic indicates the similarity between the covariance matrix based on the estimated model, $\Sigma(\hat{\theta})$, and the population covariance matrix, Σ, from which a sample has been drawn. On the basis of this

AUTHORS' NOTE: This research was supported by grants DA03976, DA01070, and DA00017 from the National Institute on Drug Use. We would like to acknowledge the comments of M. A. Pentz, R. Hoyle, and two anonymous reviewers.

definition, it is apparent that testing is a prerequisite to interpreting modeling results. If a model cannot be considered consistent with the population covariance matrix, as represented via sample data, there is not much point to interpreting the model parameters.

The estimates of parameters as well as the goodness-of-fit χ^2 test statistic depend on the estimation procedure chosen. Different estimation methods typically will yield somewhat different results for estimates and model tests, and it would be desirable to have some guidance about which methods tend to work well under various conditions encountered by researchers in practice. In Chapter 5, Hu and Bentler concentrate on various approaches to the overall evaluation of a model. Although we discuss model testing as well, we also address the important problem of obtaining estimates that have good statistical properties. In particular, the estimates should be close to the true population values of the parameters when the model analyzed is the true model, and tests of the significance of a particular parameter should yield adequate conclusions.

Because real psychological data are almost never normally distributed, we are particularly concerned with selecting an adequate estimation and testing method when the observed variables are not multivariate normally distributed. Although there are many varieties of estimation and testing methods, to keep matters manageable we concentrate on the three most commonly used estimation procedures: maximum likelihood (ML), generalized least squares (GLS) derived under normal distribution assumptions, and the asymptotic distribution free (ADF) method. Each method provides estimates, standard error estimates for the free parameters, and a χ^2 model test; any of these components may prove to be adequate or inadequate in practice.

Maximum likelihood estimation has been the most commonly used approach in structural equation modeling (SEM). The ML method can be inadequate, however, because it is developed under the multivariate normality assumption, which is usually violated in practice. Extensive research has focused on the robustness of ML and other estimation methods to investigate the impact of the violation of the distributional assumption (Anderson & Gerbing, 1984; Boomsma, 1983; Browne, 1982, 1984a; Chou, Bentler, & Satorra, 1991; Harlow, 1985; Hu, Bentler, & Kano, 1992; Muthén & Kaplan, 1985, 1992; Tanaka, 1984). ML estimates have been found to be quite robust to the violation of normality. That is, the estimates are good estimates, even when the data are not normally distributed. The GLS method, in contrast, has not been as intensively studied. Comparing the ML and GLS methods, Jöreskog and Goldberger (1972) and Browne (1974) found that the GLS estimates are likely to be negatively biased. The results reported for the ADF approach have not been consistent. The ADF estimates were found to be biased by Browne (1984a), Chou et al. (1991), Harlow (1985), and Tanaka (1984), but not by Muthén and Kaplan (1992).

To extend results of previous studies on the quality of estimates, we report on extensive computer comparisons of the ML, GLS, and ADF estimation methods in terms of test statistics, parameter estimates, and standard errors under several nonnormal distribution conditions. In addition, the scaled test statistic of Satorra and Bentler (1988a, 1994) and robust standard errors are selected for comparison. These two new statistics provided promising results under some nonnormal conditions (Chou et al., 1991). We extend the work by Chou et al. (1991) and Harlow (1985) as well as make broader comparisons on various estimation methods. These estimation methods are compared in terms of the accuracy of the estimates that they generate, in addition to the associated test statistics, under violation of distributional assumptions.

Basic Concepts in Estimation

IDENTIFICATION

The purpose of estimation is to obtain numerical values for the unknown parameters. In order to obtain appropriate parameter estimates, the issue of parameter identification must be addressed. Identification (Bollen, 1989b; Johnston, 1984) involves the study of conditions to obtain a unique solution for the parameters specified in the model. One of the conditions required to obtain a solution is that the number of free parameters, say q, needs to be equal to or smaller than the number of nonredundant elements in the sample covariance matrix, usually known as p^*, which is equal to $p(p + 1)/2$, with p being the number of variables in the covariance matrix. The requirement that $q \leq p^*$ is, however, only a necessary condition for a model to be identified. The sufficient condition to obtain an identified model is that each and every free parameter is identified. This condition is, however, not as simple to evaluate in practice as an examination of $q \leq p^*$ for the necessary condition, and can become very complicated when the model is large (i.e., contains many free parameters). It can be more easily detected using the computer programs for SEM, such as LISREL (Jöreskog & Sörbom, 1993b) or EQS (Bentler, 1992a; Bentler & Wu, 1993). These programs provide error messages such as that linear dependency exists among parameters, or a matrix is not positive definite. Linear dependency describes the situation in which a parameter is a function of other parameters. More specifically, the solution of that parameter can be determined once the solutions of other parameters are obtained. Consequently, matrices associated with that parameter are no longer positive definite, and their inverse cannot be computed.

The sufficient condition for obtaining a unique solution can be easily demonstrated using the concepts of simultaneous equations in which we solve for the unknown parameters in the equations. Assume that there are three independent equations with two unknown parameters, x and y:

$$x + y = 5 \tag{3.1}$$

$$2x + y = 8 \tag{3.2}$$

$$x + 2y = 9 \tag{3.3}$$

With only one equation, say Equation (3.1), one may obtain infinite sets of solutions for x and y. The x parameter can take any value whereas the y parameter is $(5 - x)$. The solutions for (x, y) can therefore be expressed as $(c, 5 - c)$, with c being any constant. This demonstrates a linear dependency condition in which the solution of y is totally dependent on the solution of x. The above condition in which there are more unknown parameters than the number of equations is called *underidentified*. This situation occurs most frequently in modeling with latent variables, in which the scale of a factor may not have been set. Further restrictions are needed to obtain a unique solution for both x and y.

With two equations, say Equations (3.1) and (3.2), a unique solution of (3, 2) can be obtained for (x, y). In the situation in which the number of linearly independent equations is the same as the number of unknown parameters, we have a *just identified* situation, and a unique and exact solution that satisfies the equations can be obtained. Multiple regression models, and simple path analysis models with measured variables only, are often just identified. This means we can get unique parameter estimates, but the model itself cannot be tested.

Overidentification is the condition in which there are more equations than unknown independent parameters, say Equations (3.1), (3.2), and (3.3) to solve for (x, y). With overidentification, there is no exact solution. This condition at first seems unfortunate, but it is actually a blessing in disguise. Although we may not obtain an exact solution, we may define a criterion and obtain the most adequate solution as an alternative. For example, we can have a criterion that yields the smallest absolute difference from the constants. Under this criterion, we obtain a solution of (2.333, 3.333) for (x, y) ranged between 2 and 4. A different criterion of smallest squared difference yields a solution of (2.273, 3.273). The advantage of the overidentification condition in the context of SEM is that we can have a model test when we have an overidentified model.

TESTING

The concepts of simultaneous equations are easily transferred to the estimation procedures in SEM. The just identified or overidentified conditions need to be satisfied for every parameter to obtain a proper solution. With all q parameters able to be estimated, the number of degrees of freedom (df) for model testing is $(p^* - q)$. When df is positive, we have a testable model. The test is usually based on a χ^2 distribution. Different estimation procedures can be selected for model evaluation, but they will all have the same df. The estimation procedures ML, GLS, and ADF are different in terms of the criteria that are used to obtain the most appropriate solution when a model is overidentified, as shown below.

PRACTICAL PROBLEMS

In addition to the issues of model identification, there are other issues frequently encountered in practice that may still cause problems in estimation procedures. Assume that the empirical data collected have satisfied the fundamental statistical requirement that observations are independently and identically distributed. One of the most commonly encountered problems is that the sample covariance matrix is not positive definite (Wothke, 1993). This problem usually is caused by linear dependency among observed variables; that is, some variables are perfectly predictable by others. Because the inverse of the sample covariance matrix is needed in the process of computing estimators, no solutions can be obtained from the estimation procedure when variables are linearly dependent. To avoid dependencies, variables need to be carefully selected to eliminate redundancies before the model can be estimated and tested.

Nonconvergence is another common problem encountered in estimation. The estimation procedure consists of an iterative process of computational cycles beginning with a set of starting values for the parameters. The starting values can be either provided by the researcher or generated by a computer program. Within each cycle, an improved set of estimates can be obtained. The results from the current cycle are then compared to those obtained from the previous cycle, and this iterative process continues until some predetermined criteria have been satisfied. The basic statistical criteria that must be met in order to stop the iterative process will be discussed in the following section. In practice, most computer programs automatically stop the iterative process after a certain number of cycles to avoid excessive consumption of computer time, which can be very expensive. Nonconvergence occurs when the iterative process is terminated because of the practical consideration of excessive computer time rather than any statistical consideration. Consequently, nonconvergent results cannot be trusted.

Usually, nonconvergence is caused either by poor model specification or by poor starting values. Starting values can be easily modified, for example, randomly. If the model is a good one for the data, only in rare circumstances will choice of start values make much difference. If the model is poor, that is, if even the best estimates do not reproduce the sample data well, start values may be important, in which case improvement of the model is advisable. Discussions of other problems commonly encountered in estimation can be found in Bentler and Chou (1987), Bollen (1989b), or Bollen and Long (1993).

Statistical Theory

SEM is used to evaluate a substantive theory with empirical data through a hypothesized model. The vast majority of structural equation models are covariance structure models (Bollen, 1989b), in which the empirical data to be studied consist of the $p \times p$ sample covariance matrix, S, which is an unstructured estimator of the population covariance matrix, Σ. A structural equation model can be specified by a vector of q unknown parameters, θ, which in turn may generate a covariance matrix $\Sigma(\theta)$ for the model. The SEM null hypothesis is that $\Sigma = \Sigma(\theta)$. Each estimation method, such as ML, GLS, or ADF, has its own criterion to yield an estimator $\hat{\theta}$ for the parameters and a test statistic to evaluate the null hypothesis.

In the sections that follow, the complicated statistical theories and computational procedures in SEM are linked to the more understandable process of solving simultaneous equations summarized earlier. An illustration is provided using the EQS program (Bentler, 1992a). Manipulation of matrices instead of individual equations will be presented to offer a more complete picture of the process. The manipulation of matrices is equivalent to dealing with a set of individual equations.

MODELS

The EQS program uses the Bentler-Weeks (1980) model. Every variable in the model, whether observed or latent, is classified as either an independent or a dependent variable. A dependent variable is a variable in a path diagram that has a one-way arrow aiming at it. The set of such variables is collected into the vector η. All the remaining variables are called independent variables, which are collected in the vector ξ. Then the Bentler-Weeks model can be expressed as

$$\eta = \beta\eta + \gamma\xi, \tag{3.4}$$

where ξ is the vector for the independent variables, η is the vector of the dependent variables, and the coefficient matrices β and γ contain the unknown path coefficients, or regression weights, represented by one-way arrows in the path diagram of the model. In addition to β and γ, parameters can also be defined in φ, the covariance matrix of ξ.

The EQS program does not confront the user with the matrix Equation (3.4) above; rather, the idea of simultaneous equations has been adopted, and equations are individually specified for each variable using a language involving V (measured variable), F (factor), E (error residual), and D (disturbance, or factor residual) variables. Assume that a confirmatory factor analysis (CFA) model has two factors and three indicators for each factor. Each observed variable (V) considered as dependent variable, therefore, has two variables aiming at it: a factor (F) and a measurement error (E). In this CFA model, there are six Vs in η and two Fs and six Es in the ξ vector. The β matrix is a zero matrix and can be ignored, the γ matrix contains basically factor loadings and

1s as coefficients associated with error residuals, and the φ matrix consists of variances and covariances of Fs and Es that are independent variables.

Based on the simultaneous equations in Equation (3.4), the covariance matrix of the measured variables (Vs) can be computed. This can be done symbolically as follows. With all the observed variables treated as dependent variables in the model, the covariance matrix based on the model is

$$\Sigma(\theta) = G(I - \beta)^{-1} \gamma \varphi \gamma' (I - \beta)^{-1}{}' G' , \qquad (3.5)$$

where G is a selection matrix containing 0 and 1 elements to select the observed variables from all the dependent variables in η. Equation (3.5) can be expanded to p^2 equations, or one for each element in $\Sigma(\theta)$. By considering only the nonredundant elements in $\Sigma(\theta)$, which is a symmetric matrix, we can derive the p^* independent equations containing q parameters. Simultaneous equations such as Equations (3.1), (3.2), and (3.3) can be defined by lining up the corresponding elements in $\Sigma(\theta)$ as the functions of unknown parameters, and S as the constant. The identification problem is to ensure that the unknown parameters θ, here contained in matrices β, γ, and φ, can be uniquely solved for when the structural equations specified in Equation (3.4) are transformed into the p^* equations shown in Equation (3.5). Using a predetermined criterion, the q parameter estimates $\hat{\theta}$ can be obtained by solving these p^* simultaneous equations. The LISREL program follows a similar procedure, but involves more matrices (Jöreskog & Sörbom, 1993b).

FITTING FUNCTIONS

Once the identification conditions have been satisfied for the p^* equations mentioned above, a criterion can be selected to obtain a unique solution for the parameters. The criterion selected for parameter estimation is also known as the discrepancy function, $F = F(S, \Sigma[\hat{\theta}])$. The discrepancy function in SEM is conceptually similar to the criterion defined for Equations (3.1), (3.2), and (3.3) to obtain the most appropriate solution. It provides a guideline to minimize the difference between the population covariance matrix, Σ, as estimated by the sample covariance matrix, S, and the covariance matrix derived from the hypothesized model, $\Sigma(\theta)$.

Different estimation methods in SEM have different distributional assumptions and have different discrepancy functions to be minimized. For example, the discrepancy function to be minimized for the ML method is

$$F_{ML} = \log|\Sigma(\theta)| + \text{Trace}\,[\Sigma(\theta)^{-1}S] - \log|S| - p . \qquad (3.6)$$

Forgoing further discussion of the statistical theory for ML, the above function provides a way to measure the discrepancy between the $\Sigma(\hat{\theta})$ and S. The solution for the parameters, θ, yielded by minimizing F_{ML}, implies that the smallest difference between S and $\Sigma(\hat{\theta})$ has been obtained under that specific criterion.

GOODNESS-OF-FIT TEST

The goodness-of-fit test statistic, T, is used for hypothesis testing to evaluate the appropriateness of an application of SEM and is equal to the product of minimized F and $(N - 1)$, where N is the sample size. If the sample size is large enough, the minimized discrepancy function times $(N - 1)$ converges to a χ^2 variate with $(p^* - q)$ degrees of freedom. This asymptotic goodness-of-fit χ^2 test statistic can then be used to evaluate the SEM null hypothesis, H_0: $\Sigma(\theta) = \Sigma$. It should be noted that the test statistic is only χ^2 distributed if the assumptions of large sample, model specification, and distributions of variables are correct. For each estimation procedure, the most appropriate parameter estimates and standard errors are obtained at the minimum of the discrepancy function for that specific procedure.

Hu et al. (1992) showed that these standard ML, GLS, and ADF test statistics did not behave as well under violation of assumptions as had previously been assumed. A scaled test statistic proposed by Satorra and Bentler (1988a, 1994) performed even better than the standard statistics (Chou et al., 1991; Hu et al., 1992). Both ML and GLS have multivariate normal distributional assumptions. Their test statistics may not have the χ^2 distribution if the distributional assumption is false. The idea of the scaled statistic is to modify the standard test statistics to make them more approximately χ^2 distributed. As a function of the standard goodness-of-fit χ^2 statistic T, the scaled test statistic can be expressed as

$$\text{SCALED } T = c^{-1}T, \tag{3.7}$$

where the scaling constant c is an estimate of the average element of a certain matrix. The computation of the scaling constant c is complicated. Conceptually, it is a product of two matrices containing fourth-order moment information used to compute kurtosis; it represents the deviation of the distribution of the data from the normal distribution. Basically, if the data are normally distributed, $c = 1$, whereas heavier-tailed distributions tend to have $c > 1$. In practice, T is taken as T_{ML}. If T_{ML} is too large because of heavier than normal distributions, c^{-1} will make the test statistic smaller. In Chapter 5, Hu and Bentler discuss the performance of these statistics but do not discuss standard errors.

STANDARD ERRORS

Typically, standard errors can be derived from the parameter estimates and the discrepancy function. These standard error estimates are good estimates when the sample size is large, the model is correct, and the distributional assumptions are satisfied. Thus the ADF standard errors should be correct regardless of distribution, but this is not necessarily true of ML and GLS standard errors. ML and GLS standard errors may be substantially off the mark, typically underestimating sampling variability when distributions have heavy tails.

Robust standard errors can be derived as a function of the usual normal theory covariance matrix and the fourth-order moments of the variables. The formula is complex but can be found in Arminger and Schoenberg (1989), Bentler (1992a), and Bentler and Dijkstra (1985).

A New Study

To compare the performance of different estimation methods under various distributional assumptions, we carried out a Monte Carlo study, which is basically a computer sampling experiment. A simple confirmatory factor-analytic model containing two correlated factors with three variables marking each factor is used to evaluate the four estimation methods described above. The true covariance matrix for the six variables and their factor loadings and uniqueness obtained from Harlow (1985) are presented in Table 3.1. The 13 distributions considered in

TABLE 3.1 True Values for the Factor Analytic Model and Population Covariance Matrix

Variable	Loadings F1	F2	Uniqueness	Covariance Matrix V1	V2	V3	V4	V5	V6
V1	0.649	0.000	0.579	1.000					
V2	0.709	0.000	0.498	0.460	1.000				
V3	0.373	0.000	0.861	0.242	0.265	1.000			
V4	0.000	0.831	0.309	0.132	0.144	0.076	1.000		
V5	0.000	0.778	0.395	0.123	0.135	0.071	0.647	1.000	
V6	0.000	0.897	0.195	0.142	0.155	0.082	0.746	0.698	1.000

NOTE: Correlation between F1 and F2 is 0.244.

Harlow (1985) are also used in this study to generate the observed variables. The nonnormal distributions are characterized by skewness and kurtosis. The skewness and kurtosis of the 13 conditions are summarized in Table 3.2. Variables with specific covariance matrix, skewness, and kurtosis are generated using the algorithm developed by Vale and Maurelli (1983). Among the 13 conditions, only the first condition assumes a multivariate normal distribution for all the variables. Conditions 2 through 7 are considered moderately nonnormal, whereas Conditions 8 through 13 are considered extremely nonnormal.

Sample size has always been a major concern in the application of SEM because small samples are more likely to yield unreliable results. To avoid an excessive number of tables in this chapter, we concentrate only on the relatively small but practically reasonable sample size of 200. Within each distributional condition, 100 samples were randomly simulated. The overall performance across the 100 replications can then be used for comparisons among different estimation methods and distributions. Consequently, a total of 13 (conditions) × 100 (replications) = 1300 data sets were created. To extend the work of Chou et al. (1991) and Harlow (1985), the two types of models investigated in their research were also evaluated for each sample in this study. Model A assumes that all the nonzero parameters in the true model (six factor loadings, one factor covariance, and six uniqueness) are free parameters, whereas Model B assumes the same except that the six factor loadings are fixed. Model B is a less typical model that might arise because of extensive prior research. There are 13 free parameters in Model A (df = 8) and only 7 free parameters in Model B (df = 14).

TABLE 3.2 Thirteen Distributional Conditions and Values for Skewness and Kurtosis

Nonnormality Conditions		Moderate Nonnormality							Extreme Nonnormality					
		V1	V2	V3	V4	V5	V6		V1	V2	V3	V4	V5	V6
Multivariate normality	1)	0.0	0.0	0.0	0.0	0.0	0.0							
		0.0	0.0	0.0	0.0	0.0	0.0							
Symmetric Distributions														
equal negative kurtosis	2)	0.0	0.0	0.0	0.0	0.0	0.0	8)	0.0	0.0	0.0	0.0	0.0	0.0
		-0.5	-0.5	-0.5	-0.5	-0.5	-0.5		-1.0	-1.0	-1.0	-1.0	-1.0	-1.0
equal positive kurtosis	3)	0.0	0.0	0.0	0.0	0.0	0.0	9)	0.0	0.0	0.0	0.0	0.0	0.0
		1.0	1.0	1.0	1.0	1.0	1.0		6.0	6.0	6.0	6.0	6.0	6.0
unequal kurtosis	4)	0.0	0.0	0.0	0.0	0.0	0.0	10)	0.0	0.0	0.0	0.0	0.0	0.0
		-1.0	0.0	1.0	1.0	2.0	3.0		2.0	5.0	8.0	6.0	7.0	8.0
Nonsymmetric Distributions														
unequal skewness and zero kurtosis	5)	-0.3	-0.4	-0.5	-0.2	-0.3	-0.4	11)	-0.6	-0.7	-0.8	-0.5	-0.6	-0.7
		0.0	0.0	0.0	0.0	0.0	0.0		0.0	0.0	0.0	0.0	0.0	0.0
unequal positive skewness and equal kurtosis	6)	0.2	0.4	0.6	0.5	0.75	1.0	12)	1.2	1.4	1.6	1.5	1.75	2.0
		1.0	1.0	1.0	1.0	1.0	1.0		6.0	6.0	6.0	6.0	6.0	6.0
unequal skewness and unequal kurtosis	7)	0.0	-0.5	1.0	-0.25	0.75	-1.25	13)	-0.5	1.5	-2.0	0.0	-1.0	2.0
		-1.0	0.0	1.0	2.0	3.0	4.0		0.0	4.0	8.0	-1.0	3.0	7.0

NOTE: The twelve entries in each condition correspond to the skewness (top) and kurtosis (bottom).

48

Comparisons are made among the goodness-of-fit χ^2 test statistics, parameter estimates, and standard errors across the different estimation methods. The performance of these estimation methods are evaluated on two criteria of accuracy: unbiasedness and the mean square errors of estimates from the true values. Unbiasedness can be measured by the absolute difference between estimates $\hat{\theta}$ and corresponding true values θ_0. The mean square error (MSE) considers both the unbiasedness and the variances of parameter estimates:

$$MSE = (\hat{\theta} - \theta_0)^2 + Var(\hat{\theta}), \qquad (3.8)$$

where θ_0 is the true parameter value. Both criteria are used for goodness-of-fit χ^2 test statistics and parameter estimates across all 13 distributional conditions. The MSE criterion is not commonly used for the comparisons of standard errors. Therefore, only the unbiasedness criterion is used for comparing standard errors among estimation methods.

Comparisons are made in terms of the rank order of accuracy. For the goodness-of-fit χ^2 test, the four statistics T_{ML}, T_{GLS}, T_{ADF}, and SCALED T are compared to determine which is the most accurate. Comparisons of parameter estimates can be made only among GLS, ML, and ADF methods, but comparisons of standard errors may also include the robust approach. To simplify the comparisons of a set of parameter estimates and standard errors, the estimation methods are compared in terms of the average rank of accuracy of all estimators involved. For example, ML may rank first, or be the most accurate, for parameter estimate 1 (θ_1) and be last in accuracy for parameter estimate 2 (θ_2). An average rank can be computed across the rank of all estimators (13 for Model A and 7 for Model B). Thus the comparisons of estimation methods on parameter estimates and standard errors are based on the average rank. The unbiasedness of parameter estimates is compared in terms of the frequencies of rejecting the null hypothesis that they are equal to the true values.

RESULTS

The mean goodness-of-fit χ^2 test statistics, standard deviations, and frequencies of rejection of the null hypothesis across 100 samples for the four estimation methods (T_{GLS}, T_{ML}, T_{ADF}, and SCALED T) under the 13 conditions were computed. In general, all four test statistics

performed similarly with Model A but yielded very different results
with Model B. The performance of SCALED T was much better than
T_{ML}, T_{GLS}, and T_{ADF}, with T_{ADF} being the worst.

The frequencies of rejection of the null hypothesis were all very
close to the expected frequency of 5, or 5% of rejection for Model A.
The frequencies of rejection by the four test statistics ranged from 2 to
9. The mean χ^2 values for all four methods across all 13 conditions in
general were very close to the expected value of 8, with a minimum of
7.298 and a maximum of 9.040. All the standard deviations were also
close to the expected value of 4. The GLS method was more likely to
underestimate χ^2 values than were other methods. The standard deviations for the χ^2 values also tended to be smaller than expected for GLS.
Both GLS and ML seem to be very robust to the violation of the
multivariate normality assumption under Model A.

Model B, however, showed quite different results for the four estimation procedures. Examination of the test statistics revealed that
Conditions 9, 10, and 12 yielded very unsatisfactory results for GLS
and ML. For those three conditions, the null hypothesis was rejected
from 27 to 32 times by the GLS and ML methods. Means and standard
deviations were close to the expected values of 14 and 5.292, respectively, across the 13 distributional conditions, except for Conditions 9,
10, and 12. This is an indication that both estimation methods are not
robust under all conditions. Results depend on the model as well as the
degree of nonnormality, especially with observed variables containing
extremely large kurtosis.

The method that should perform well under nonnormality, the ADF
method, did not perform well in general under all 13 conditions, rejecting the true null hypothesis more than 10 times for each of the 13
conditions. For conditions 7, 9, 10, 12, and 13, rejection frequencies
exceeded 20. The χ^2 values were consistently overestimated with larger
standard deviations.

The scaled test statistic, on the other hand, demonstrated very promising results. It did not seem to be affected by the nonnormal distribution of the variables. The frequencies of rejection of the null hypothesis
ranged from 3 to 9. The means for the 13 conditions were between 13.715
and 14.935 (with 14 as the expected value), and the standard deviations
were between 5.030 and 7.028 (with 5.292 as the expected value).

Further comparisons were made of the accuracy of the χ^2 test statistics across the four estimation methods. Both MSE and unbiasedness
were used as the criteria of accuracy to compare these methods. The

TABLE 3.3 Rank Order of Accuracy of χ^2 Test Statistics Among Estimation Methods

| | *Moderate Nonnormality* | | | | *Extreme Nonnormality* | |
	MSE	*Unbiasedness*			*MSE*	*Unbiasedness*
1)	G,S,M,A	M,S,G,A				
	M,S,G,A	S,G,M,A				
2)	G,S,M,A	M,S,G,A	8)		G,M,S,A	M,S,G,A
	M,S,G,A	S,G,M,A			M,S,G,A	S,G,M,A
3)	G,S,M,A	M,S,G,A	9)		S,G,A,M	G,S,M,A
	S,M,G,A	S,M,G,A			S,M,G,A	S,M,G,A
4)	G,S,M,A	S,M,G,A	10)		G,S,A,M	M,S,G,A
	M,S,G,A	S,M,G,A			S,M,G,A	S,M,G,A
5)	G,S,M,A	G,M,S,A	11)		G,S,M,A	G,S,M,A
	M,S,G,A	M,S,G,A			M,S,G,A	S,M,G,A
6)	G,S,M,A	S,M,A,G	12)		S,A,G,M	S,G,A,M
	S,M,G,A	S,M,G,A			S,M,G,A	S,M,A,G
7)	G,S,M,A	A,S,M,G	13)		G,S,M,A	G,M,S,A
	S,M,G,A	S,M,G,A			S,M,G,A	S,M,G,A

NOTE: Methods are rank ordered from the most accurate to the least accurate. The names of estimation methods are shortened: G = GLS, M = ML, A = ADF, S = SCALED. The two rows for each cell are for Models A and B, respectively.

four methods were rank ordered in terms of accuracy for each model across all 13 distributional conditions. Results of the comparisons are summarized in Table 3.3. The sequence of characters at each entry represents the accuracy of each method, with the first one being the most accurate and the last one the least accurate. Under the MSE criterion, the GLS method consistently demonstrated its accuracy with the goodness-of-fit test statistic with Model A, except in Conditions 9 and 12. This, however, could be due to the fact that GLS, in general, underestimated the χ^2 values and also yielded smaller dispersion for the χ^2 variates. The unbiasedness criterion, which does not use the information of dispersion, indicates that the ML and SCALED estimation methods also provided very accurate test statistics. The ADF method again showed relatively poor performance in estimating χ^2 values and yielded only one most unbiased χ^2 test statistic under Condition 7. For Model B, the ML and SCALED estimation methods are superior to the GLS and ADF methods in terms of the criterion of the mean square error. Using the unbiasedness criterion, the SCALED method consistently outperformed all other methods, except in Condition 5 where it was ranked second.

TABLE 3.4 Rank Order of Accuracy of Parameter Estimates ($\hat{\theta}$) and Standard Errors (SE) Among Estimation Methods

	Moderate Nonnormality				Extreme Nonnormality		
	MSE for $\hat{\theta}$	Unbiasedness for $\hat{\theta}$	Unbiasedness for SE		MSE for $\hat{\theta}$	Unbiasedness for $\hat{\theta}$	Unbiasedness for SE
1)	M,G,A	M,A,G	G=M,R,A				
	M,G,A	M,A,G	M,G=R,A				
2)	M,G,A	M,A,G	R,A,G,M	8)	M,G,A	M,A,G	R,A,G,M
	M,G,A	M,A,G	R,G,M=A		M,A,G	M,A,G	R,G,A,M
3)	M,G,A	M,G,A	M=R,G=A	9)	A,G,M	M,G,A	R,A,M,G
	M,G,A	M,G,A	R,M,A,G		A,G,M	M,G,A	R,A,M,G
4)	M,G,A	M,G,A	R,A,M,G	10)	A,G,M	M,G,A	R,A,M,G
	M,G=A	M,G=A	R,M,A,G		A,G,M	M,G,A	R,A,M,G
5)	M,G,A	M,G,A	M,G,R,A	11)	M,G,A	M,G,A	R,M,G,A
	M,G,A	M,A,G	M,R,G,A		M,G,A	M,G,A	R,M,G,A
6)	G,M,A	M,G,A	R,M,A,G	12)	A,G,M	M,G,A	R,A,M,G
	M,G,A	M,G,A	R,A,M,G		A,G,M	M,G,A	R,A,M,G
7)	M,A,G	M,G,A	R,A,M,G	13)	G,M,A	M,G,A	R,M,A,G
	M,A,G	M,G,A	R,A,M,G		A,G=M	M,G,A	R,M,A,G

NOTE: Methods are ordered in terms of average rank of accuracy across all θ or SE. The names of estimation methods are shortened: G = GLS, M = ML, A = ADF, R = Robust. The two rows at each cell are for Models A and B, respectively. The "=" indicates that there is a tie between two methods.

Comparisons of the parameter estimates and standard errors are more complicated than the comparisons of χ^2 values because each model has only one χ^2 value but q parameter estimates and q standard errors. The comparisons reported in Table 3.4 for parameter estimates and standard errors are based on the average ranks of accuracy. The estimates of the same parameter were first compared and rank ordered among the three estimation methods: GLS, ML, and ADF. The average ranks across all q parameters were then computed to decide the ranking of each method summarized in Table 3.4. Similar steps were carried out for the comparisons of the standard errors. The robust standard errors were also computed for comparison. The true values for the evaluation of the accuracy of parameter estimates are those used for data simulation. For standard errors, ML and ADF have been found to be downward, or negatively, biased under extremely nonnormal conditions (Arminger & Schoenberg, 1989; Chou et al., 1991). Expected standard errors are derived from the population robust standard errors, estimated from the "population" containing all 100 samples with $N = 200$ (subjects) × 100 (replications) and rescaling to the sample size of 200.

TABLE 3.5 Percentages of Rejecting True Values by the Parameter Estimates

	Moderate Nonnormality					Extreme Nonnormality			
	Model A		*Model B*			*Model A*		*Model B*	
1)	4.08	1.46	7.57	1.14					
	2.92	1.92	4.00	1.57					
	5.92	2.38	10.43	2.43					
2)	3.54	1.38	6.57	0.86	8)	3.15	1.38	4.57	0.71
	2.54	1.46	3.00	1.57		2.38	1.69	2.71	1.29
	4.85	2.77	9.29	2.43		4.00	2.69	7.71	2.29
3)	5.46	1.69	11.57	1.71	9)	13.00	5.77	23.14	7.29
	4.31	2.85	6.71	3.43		11.62	6.85	17.00	11.00
	7.31	1.77	13.14	1.71		14.46	0.77	21.29	2.00
4)	6.08	1.92	11.00	2.29	10)	12.54	5.62	21.71	7.00
	4.92	2.62	7.00	4.14		10.77	6.38	16.00	10.29
	7.08	1.77	11.71	2.29		13.62	1.15	20.00	2.14
5)	4.92	1.69	9.29	1.14	11)	5.62	2.15	9.29	0.86
	3.23	2.08	5.14	1.43		4.15	2.62	5.43	2.00
	5.92	2.23	11.00	2.00		6.23	2.38	12.86	2.00
6)	5.15	2.38	10.71	2.86	12)	12.77	6.00	21.71	7.57
	4.69	3.15	5.57	3.57		10.62	6.69	15.00	11.71
	6.92	2.23	11.86	2.57		13.38	1.23	20.71	2.86
7)	7.38	2.62	13.14	2.57	13)	8.85	3.85	18.71	6.86
	6.38	3.08	9.00	5.14		7.23	4.46	14.57	9.29
	8.23	2.08	12.57	2.57		11.08	1.54	16.86	3.57

NOTE: Percentages are reported considering all parameter estimates (13 in Model A and 7 in Model B). Each cell contains three rows for GLS, ML, and ADF, respectively. The two entries at each row are the percentages of upward rejection (negatively biased estimates) and downward rejection (positively biased estimates) of the true values.

Comparisons based on the criterion in Equation (3.8) indicated that ML seemed to have performed better than both the GLS and ADF methods with both Models A and B. The ML method performed even better with the unbiasedness criterion and consistently provided the most unbiased estimates across all 13 distributional conditions.

In addition to the three estimation methods (GLS, ML, and ADF) the robust standard errors are also included in the comparisons of standard errors. Using unbiasedness as the criterion, the robust standard errors seemed to yield the most unbiased standard errors, especially when the distributions of the observed variables were extremely nonnormal.

Significance tests of the parameter estimates as deviations from the corresponding true values are summarized in Table 3.5 at $\alpha = .05$ level. For simplicity, percentages of upward and downward rejection of true values are reported for all parameters considered, instead of for each parameter separately. Upward rejection indicates that true values are rejected because they are above the upper end of the confidence interval and parameter estimates are negatively biased. In downward rejection, on the other hand, the true values are smaller than the lower end of the confidence interval, and estimates are positively biased. The confidence interval is computed based on the parameter estimates and standard errors obtained from each method for significance tests. If the parameter estimates are asymptotically multivariate normally distributed with true values as the means, we would expect 2.5% of upward rejection and 2.5% of downward rejection. In general, the results indicate that the distributions of parameter estimates for all three methods are not symmetric and are more likely to have heavier tails at the left end. The distributions of the parameter estimates obtained from the GLS and ADF methods depart more from the normal distribution than those obtained for ML.

Summary and Recommendations

In this chapter, we used the concepts of simultaneous equations to explicate the complicated process of the estimation procedure in SEM. The issues of identification, model specification, hypothesis testing, discrepancy function, and goodness-of-fit test statistics involved in the estimation procedure were demonstrated using simultaneous equations. Problems frequently encountered in practice also were mentioned, and recommendations were made to deal with these problems.

It was pointed out in this chapter that researchers cannot simply choose a default estimation method from their favorite computer program and be assured that model tests, standard error estimates, and tests of the significance of parameters are performing well. Performance of the various estimation methods depends on the nature of the model and the data. When the data are multivariate normally distributed and when the sample size is large enough, the ML and GLS methods are certainly preferred because of computational simplicity, accuracy, and correctness of statistical results, but when data are nonnormal, the situation changes completely. Our empirical study extended the efforts of Chou et al. (1991) and Harlow (1985) to evaluate the performance of some frequently used estimation methods, namely ML, GLS, and ADF, in terms of accuracy of estimates, standard errors, and z test statistics. In addition, we evaluated both the Satorra-Bentler scaling correction for the χ^2 test and the robust standard errors.

In general, the commonly used ML and GLS methods performed quite well in generating reliable statistical results. The ADF method did not perform as well as expected, even though it was developed specifically for nonnormally distributed data. Both the scaled test statistic and the robust standard errors yielded the most satisfactory results, regardless of the distribution of the variables and the specific model type. They should be more seriously considered when data are not multivariate normal; they are routinely available in EQS (Bentler, 1992a; Bentler & Wu, 1993).

Although our results are consistent with the recent literature, we caution that the results obtained in our empirical study might be limited in terms of generalizability. Researchers usually deal with additional types of nonnormally distributed data and more complicated models. Furthermore, the empirical results in this study also were obtained under the null hypothesis. In practical application, model misspecification could affect analytic processes and results in ways that might not be consistent with the discussions or recommendations presented in this chapter.

4 Structural Equation Models With Nonnormal Variables

Problems and Remedies

STEPHEN G. WEST

JOHN F. FINCH

PATRICK J. CURRAN

Over the past 15 years, the use of structural equation modeling has become increasingly common in the social and behavioral sciences. Enthusiastic recognition by researchers of the advantages of the structural equation modeling approach and an eagerness to implement this potentially powerful methodology has also brought with it inappropriate use of the technique. One major source of inappropriate usage has been the failure of investigators to satisfy the scaling and normality assumptions upon which estimation and testing are based. The commonly used approaches to estimating the parameters of structural equation models, maximum likelihood and normal theory generalized least squares, assume that the measured variables are continuous and have a multivariate normal distribution. In practice, current applications of the structural equation modeling approach to real data often involve violations of these assumptions.

AUTHORS' NOTE: S. G. West was supported by NIMH grant P50MH39246 during the writing of this chapter. We thank Leona Aiken, William L. Cook, William R. Shadish, Jr., and Rick Hoyle for their comments on an earlier version of this chapter.

In some substantive areas, the measured variables used by researchers are dichotomous or ordered categories (e.g., "agree," "no preference," "disagree") rather than truly continuous. In other areas, the measured variables are continuous but their distributions depart dramatically from normality (e.g., measures of amount of substance use). Micceri (1989) analyzed over 400 large data sets, finding that the great majority of data collected in behavioral research do *not* follow univariate normal distributions, let alone a multivariate normal distribution. Yet researchers often ignore these assumptions. For example, Breckler (1990) identified 72 articles in personality and social psychology journals that had used structural equation modeling and found that only 19% acknowledged the normal theory assumptions, and fewer than 10% explicitly considered whether these assumptions had been violated.

Given that real data often fail to satisfy the underlying scaling and normality assumptions, there has been growing interest in determining the robustness of structural equation modeling techniques to violations of the scaling and normality assumptions and in developing alternative remedial strategies when these assumptions are seriously violated. These topics are the focus of the present chapter.

Overview of Normal Theory Estimation

As discussed in Chapters 1 and 3, the objective of estimation is to minimize the magnitude of the set of differences between each element in S and the corresponding element in $\Sigma(\hat{\theta})$. Recall that S is the sample covariance matrix calculated from the observed data and $\Sigma(\hat{\theta})$ is the covariance matrix implied by a set of parameter estimates $\hat{\theta}$ for the hypothesized model. Throughout the presentation below, all parameters that are estimated will be grouped in a vector θ.

The two most commonly used estimation techniques are maximum likelihood (ML) and normal theory generalized least squares (GLS). Both techniques are based on the same set of assumptions, yield very similar estimates, and have the same desirable statistical properties. These techniques are discussed in more detail in Chapter 3 and by Bollen (1989b); here we briefly review the assumptions and properties of the GLS estimator to set the stage for our later discussion of nonnormality.

The generalized least squares fitting function, F_{GLS}, can be expressed as

$$F_{\text{GLS}} = \frac{1}{2}\text{tr}\left[([S - \Sigma(\hat{\theta})]W^{-1})^2\right]. \tag{4.1}$$

In this equation, S represents the observed covariance matrix, $\Sigma(\hat{\theta})$ represents the covariance matrix implied by the hypothesized model, W^{-1} represents a weight matrix, and "tr" is the trace operator, which takes the sum of the elements on the main diagonal of the matrix, here the matrix resulting from the operations within the large brackets. Minimization of this fitting function involves minimization of the weighted squared discrepancies between S and $\Sigma(\hat{\theta})$. Like other members of the class of weighted least squares procedures, GLS requires the selection of the weight matrix. The most common choice for W^{-1} is S^{-1}, which weights the squared discrepancies between S and $\Sigma(\hat{\theta})$ according to their variances and covariances with other elements. This choice is based on two assumptions. First, $E(s_{ij})$, the expected value of the sample covariance between x_i and x_j, is assumed to equal σ_{ij}, the corresponding covariance in the population. Second, the large sample distribution of the elements of S is assumed to be multivariate normal. If these assumptions are satisfied, GLS estimates have several desirable statistical properties.

1. The parameter estimates are asymptotically unbiased: On average, in large samples, they neither overestimate nor underestimate the corresponding population parameter (i.e., $E[\hat{\theta}] = \theta$, where $E[\hat{\theta}]$ is the expected value of the estimate of θ).

2. The parameter estimates are consistent: They converge in probability to the true value of the population parameter being estimated as sample size increases.

3. The parameter estimates are asymptotically efficient: With increasing N, they have minimum variance.

4. $(N - 1)F_{\text{GLS}}$ approximates a chi-square distribution in large samples, permitting tests of the fit of the model to the data.

Recall, however, that these desirable statistical properties of the GLS estimator (and the ML estimator; see Bollen, 1989b) are contingent on meeting several assumptions. These assumptions include that a very large (asymptotic) sample size is employed, the observed variables are continuous, the measured variables have a multivariate normal distribution, and the model estimated is a valid one. When these assumptions are *not* met, there is no guarantee in statistical theory that the desirable properties will continue to hold. Consequently, the robustness of the estimators to violations of assumptions becomes an important issue for empirical study.

Effects and Detection of Nonnormality

THEORETICAL BASIS FOR THE PROBLEM

Potential problems in estimation of structural equation models are introduced when the distribution of the observed variables departs substantially from multivariate normality. As can be seen from Equation 4.1, the parameter estimates are derived from information in S, the sample covariance matrix, and W^{-1}, the optimal weight matrix. When the observed variables are (a) continuous but nonnormal, (b) dichotomous, or (c) ordered categories, the information in S or W^{-1} or both may be incorrect. As a result, estimates based on S and W^{-1} may also be incorrect.

Continuous, Nonnormal Variables. As we saw in the discussion of estimation, the variation in the measured variables is completely summarized by the sample covariances only when multivariate normality is present. If multivariate normality is violated, the variation of the measured variables will not be completely summarized by the sample covariances; information from higher-order moments is needed. In this situation, S^{-1} is no longer the correct estimator of W^{-1}. The parameter estimates do remain unbiased and consistent (i.e., as sample size grows larger, $\hat{\theta}$ converges to θ), but they are no longer efficient. These results suggest that theoretically two important problems will occur with normal theory estimators (ML, GLS) when the observed variables do not have a multivariate normal distribution. (a) The χ^2 goodness-of-fit test is not expected to produce an accurate assessment of fit, rejecting too many (> 5%) true models. (b) Tests of all parameter estimates are expected to be biased, yielding too many significant results.

Coarsely Categorized Variables. Investigations of the effects of coarse categorization of continuous variables (e.g., Bollen & Barb, 1981) have found that the Pearson correlation coefficient between two continuous variables is generally higher in magnitude than the correlation between the same variables when they have been divided up into a set of ordered categories. The greatest attenuation occurs when few categories are employed (i.e., fewer than five) for either variable involved in the correlation and when the categorized variables are skewed, particularly in opposite directions. These findings imply that coarse categorization of continuous variables can theoretically be expected to lead to biased χ^2 tests of model fit, parameter estimates, standard errors, and tests of parameter estimates.

DETECTING DEPARTURES FROM NORMALITY

Skewness and Kurtosis, Univariate and Multivariate. A number of procedures are available for assessing the univariate and multivariate normality of the measured variables. These procedures depend on the calculation of higher order moments: A moment is defined as $(1/N)\sum(x - \mu)^k$, where N is sample size, x is an observed score, μ is the population mean, and k is the order of the moment ($k = 1$ for the first-order moment; $k = 2$ for the second-order moment, etc.). When univariate normality is satisfied, only the first- and second-order moments (mean and variance) are needed to describe fully the distribution of the measured variables—the standardized third-order moment is 0 and the standardized fourth-order moment is technically 3 for a normal distribution. Univariate distributions that deviate from normality, however, possess significant nonzero skewness and kurtosis that are reflected in the standardized third- and fourth-order moments, respectively. Nonzero skewness is indicative of a departure from symmetry. Negative skewness indicates a distribution with an elongated left-hand tail; positive skewness indicates a distribution with an elongated right-hand tail (relative to the symmetrical normal distribution). Kurtosis, which is particularly important for statistical inference, indicates the extent to which the height of the curve (probability density) differs from that of the normal curve. Positive kurtosis is associated with distributions with long, thin tails, whereas negative kurtosis is associated with shorter, fatter tails relative to the normal curve. To simplify interpretation, many computer packages subtract 3 from the standardized fourth-order moment so that kurtosis will be 0 for a normal curve. We follow this convention in reporting values of kurtosis in this chapter.

Examinations of the skewness and kurtosis of the univariate distributions provide only an initial check on multivariate normality. If any of the observed variables deviate substantially from univariate normality, then the multivariate distribution cannot be multinormal. However, the converse is *not* true: Theoretically, all of the univariate distributions may be normal, yet the joint distribution may be substantially multivariately nonnormal. Consequently, it is also important to examine multivariate measures of skewness and kurtosis developed by Mardia (1970; see also D'Agostino, 1986).

The Mardia measures construct functions of the third- and fourth-order moments, which possess approximate standard normal distributions, thereby permitting tests of multivariate skewness and multivariate kurtosis. The Mardia measure of multivariate kurtosis, which is particularly important for structural equation modeling (Browne, 1982), is available in the EQS (Bentler, 1992a) and PRELIS (Jöreskog & Sörbom, 1993c) computer software packages.

Outliers. Outliers are extreme data points that may affect the results of structural equation modeling, even when the remainder of the data are well distributed. Outliers typically occur because of errors in responding by subjects or data recording errors, or because a few respondents may represent a different population from the target population under study. Outliers can potentially have dramatic effects on the indices of model fit, parameter estimates, and standard errors. They can also potentially cause improper solutions, in which estimates of parameters are outside the range of acceptable values (e.g., Heywood cases in which estimates of error variance are < 0; see Dillon, Kumar, & Mulani, 1987). Possible corrective actions for outliers include checking and correction of the data for the extreme case, dropping the extreme case, redefinition of the population of interest, or respecification of the model, with the appropriate remedy depending on the apparent source of the outlier.

Two general approaches can be used to detect outliers in the context of structural equation models. The first, a model-independent approach, is to identify any deviant cases whose values diverge sharply from the mass of data points. Univariately, this can be accomplished by visual examination of the plots of each measured variable, identifying cases that are several standard deviations from the mean of the distribution and not close to other observations. Multivariately, leverage statistics, such as Mahalanobis distance available in major regression diagnostic packages, identify extreme points in multivariate space (see Chatterjee & Yilmaz, 1992). Alternatively, Bentler (1989) has proposed identifying the cases that have the greatest contribution to Mardia's measure of multivariate kurtosis. Typically, all measured variables would be considered together in these analyses.

The second approach is to identify observed data points that are extreme relative to their predicted value based on a specific model. Bollen and Arminger (1991) have proposed a method based on factor scores, which represent each case's predicted score on the hypothetical factor. These factor scores, in turn, are used to estimate a set of predicted scores on the measured variables for each case. Raw residuals representing the difference between the predicted and the observed scores for each case on each measured variable are calculated. The residuals are standardized ($M = 0$; $SD = 1$), using procedures described in Bollen and Arminger (1991), and then plotted and visually examined to detect possible outliers.

RESULTS OF EMPIRICAL STUDIES OF NONNORMALITY

Continuous, Nonnormal Variables. Several simulation studies have assessed the performance of the normal theory ML and GLS estimators for a variety of CFA models under diverse conditions of nonnormality and sample size (Browne, 1984a; Curran, West, & Finch, 1994; Finch, Curran, & West, 1994; Hu, Bentler, & Kano, 1992). In these studies, the value of each parameter is set to a known value in the population. This value is then compared with the mean of a large number of empirical estimates to study the effects of specified levels of nonnormality. The following conclusions have been reached:

1. ML and GLS estimators produce χ^2 values that become too large when the data become increasingly nonnormal. For example, Curran et al. (1994) investigated a three-factor, nine-indicator confirmatory factor analysis model in which each measured variable was highly nonnormal (skewness = 3; kurtosis = 21). Compared to the expected χ^2 of 24, the mean of χ^2 from 200 simulations was 37.4 (approximate 50% overestimate) when sample size was 1000 in each simulation. Compared to the expected Type 1 error rate of 5%, 48% of the true models in the population were rejected under these conditions.

2. The GLS and particularly the ML estimator produce χ^2 values that are slightly too large when sample sizes are small, even when multivariate normality is present. For example, in the Curran et al. (1994) study, when the sample size was 50 and the observed variables were

multivariate normal, the mean χ^2 of 200 simulations was 26.7 (10% overestimate) and 12% of the true models in the population were rejected. Simulations by Anderson and Gerbing (1984) and Boomsma (1983) have also found that decreasing sample size and increasing nonnormality lead to increases in the proportion of analyses that fail to converge or that result in an improper solution (Heywood case).

3. Nonnormality leads to modest underestimation of fit indexes such as the Normed Fit Index (NFI; Bentler & Bonett, 1980), the Tucker and Lewis (1973) Index (TLI), and the Comparative Fit Index (CFI; Bentler, 1990). (See Tanaka, 1993, for an overview of fit indexes.) For example, Curran et al. (1994) found that when using maximum likelihood estimation with a sample size of 100, the mean CFI for a correctly specified model was .97 (3% underestimate), compared to the expected value of 1.00 when each of the measured variables was highly nonnormal (skewness = 3; kurtosis = 21). The TLI and the CFI are modestly underestimated, whereas the NFI is severely underestimated at low sample sizes (e.g., mean NFI = .81 vs. 1.00 expected at $N = 50$ under multivariate normality; see also Marsh, Balla, & McDonald, 1988).

4. Nonnormality leads to moderate to severe underestimation of standard errors of parameter estimates. For example, Finch et al. (1994) studied the standard errors of parameter estimates in confirmatory factor analysis models. When the measured variables were highly nonnormal (skewness = 3; kurtosis = 21), the standard errors of correlations between factors (ϕ) were underestimated by about 25%, whereas the standard errors of factor loadings (λ) and the specific factors (error variances; θ) were underestimated by approximately 50%. Such substantial underestimates in standard errors imply that tests of parameter estimates will not be trustworthy under conditions of nonnormality.

Coarsely Categorized Variables. Several simulation studies (Babakus, Ferguson, & Jöreskog, 1987; Boomsma, 1983; Muthén & Kaplan, 1985) have evaluated the performance of the normal theory ML and GLS estimators when continuous normally distributed measured variables are divided into ordered categories. Once again, a variety of CFA models and rules for categorizing the continuous variables have been utilized. These studies have led to the following conclusions:

1. The number of categories per se has relatively little impact on the χ^2 goodness-of-fit test when the distribution of the categorized variables is approximately normal. As the distributions of the categorized

variables become increasingly and particularly differentially skewed (e.g., variables skewed in opposite directions), the χ^2 values become inflated.

2. Factor loadings and factor correlations are only modestly underestimated as long as the distribution of the categorized variables is approximately normal. However, underestimation becomes increasingly serious as (a) there are fewer categories (e.g., two or three), (b) the magnitude of skewness increases (e.g., > 1), and (c) there is a differential degree of skewness across variables.

3. Estimates of error variances (specific factors) are more severely biased than other parameter estimates by each of the influences noted under (2). Relatedly, correlations may be spuriously obtained between the error variances associated with items having similar degrees of skewness. When there are only a small number (e.g., two) of categories, the degree of skewness is determined by the percentage of subjects in the study agreeing with (or passing) the item. Thus a set of items with similar agreement rates (e.g., 15% to 20%) can give rise to a spurious factor (so-called "difficulty factor") reflecting only the common degree of skewness among the items.

4. Estimated standard errors for all parameters are too low, particularly when the distributions are highly and differentially skewed. This means that tests of parameter estimates may not be trustworthy.

Remedies for Multivariate Nonnormality

ALTERNATIVE ESTIMATION TECHNIQUES

As we saw above, the problem of nonnormality can arise in two different contexts: poorly distributed continuous variables or coarsely categorized continuous variables. Estimation-based remedies to these two problems differ. However, these techniques share the common goal of yielding χ^2 tests and estimates of standard errors that more closely approximate their true values.

The Asymptotically Distribution Free Estimator. Browne (1984a) developed an alternative estimator that does not assume multivariate normality of the measured variables. His "asymptotically distribution free" (ADF) estimation procedure is based on the computation of a general weight matrix, W, and GLS estimation. The key to ADF estimation is the use of an optimal weight matrix that consists of a combination of second- and fourth-order terms. W is a covariance matrix of the elements in S, which contains both variances and covariances. Thus the ADF weight matrix has many more elements than the normal theory GLS weight matrix (S^{-1}); however, it has the desirable property of simplifying to the normal theory matrix (S^{-1}) under conditions of multivariate normality (i.e., fourth-order moments = 0). Because of the link to the normal theory GLS fitting function, the ADF estimator is sometimes referred to as the arbitrary generalized least squares (AGLS) estimator.

The ADF estimator produces asymptotically (large sample) unbiased estimates of the χ^2 goodness-of-fit test, parameter estimates, and standard errors. These are major theoretical advantages relative to the normal theory-based ML and GLS estimators, which, as was shown above, produce biased test statistics and standard errors under conditions of multivariate nonnormality. However, the ADF estimator is associated with two important practical limitations. First, the ADF estimator is computationally demanding. The calculation of the ADF fitting function requires the inversion of the ADF optimal weight matrix. In CFA with p measured variables, W is a $p^* \times p^*$ matrix, where p^* is $\frac{1}{2}p(p + 1)$, the number of unique elements in S. For example, with 15 measured variables it is necessary to invert a 120 by 120 weight matrix consisting of 14,400 unique elements. With more than 20 to 25 measured variables, implementation of the methodology becomes impractical, even given modern high speed computers (Bentler, 1989). Second, the calculation of the matrix of fourth-order moments requires a large sample size to produce stable estimates (Jöreskog & Sörbom, 1992). This sample-size based limitation is a serious one, as we will see below.

SCALED χ^2 Statistic and Robust Standard Errors. Although the normal theory χ^2 statistic does not follow the expected χ^2 distribution under conditions of nonnormality, it can be corrected or rescaled to approximate the referenced χ^2 distribution. Satorra and Bentler (see Satorra, 1990) have developed the statistical theory underlying this rescaling. The normal theory χ^2 (from ML or GLS) is divided by a constant k, whose value is a function of the model-implied residual weight matrix, the observed multivariate kurtosis, and the degrees of freedom for the model. As the degree of multivariate kurtosis increases, so does k, subsequently leading to a greater downward adjustment of the normal theory χ^2. The same theory underlying the SCALED χ^2 statistic can also be applied to the computation of robust standard errors. These standard errors can theoretically be considered to be adjusted for the degree of multivariate kurtosis. The SCALED χ^2 and robust standard errors are available in the EQS program.

Bootstrapping. Modern, computationally intensive statistical methods provide a completely different approach to tests of goodness-of-fit and parameter estimates. Rather than relying on the theoretical distributions of classical test statistics (e.g., χ^2, normal), we can imagine taking repeated samples from a population of interest. For each sample, we calculate the parameter estimates of interest resulting in an *empirical* sampling distribution. In cases in which the assumptions of the classical test statistics are severely violated, the empirical distribution that describes the actual distribution of the estimates from this population will be substantially more accurate than the theoretical distribution.

Efron and his coworkers (e.g., Efron & Tibshirani, 1986; see Mooney & Duval, 1993) have shown that the empirical sampling distribution can often be reasonably approximated based on data from a single sample. In the bootstrapping procedure, repeated samples of the same size are taken from the original sample *with replacement* after each case is drawn. To illustrate, imagine that the original sample consists of cases (1, 2, 3, 4). Three possible bootstrap samples from this original sample are (1, 4, 1, 1), (2, 3, 1, 3), and (4, 2, 2, 4). Note that the elements can be repeated in the bootstrap samples and that they are of the same size as the original sample. By taking a large number of bootstrap samples from the original sample, the mean and variance of the empirical bootstrap sampling distribution can be determined.

The bootstrap approach is simple conceptually and computationally, given the increasing availability of software to implement bootstrap resampling, including some of the structural equation modeling packages. Two related complexities arise in application. First, as Bollen and Stine (1992, p. 207) emphasize: "The success of the bootstrap depends on the sampling behavior of a statistic being the same when the samples are drawn from the empirical distribution and when they are taken from the original population." Conditions under which this assumption appears to hold are discussed in Efron and Tibshirani (1986). Second, the bootstrap is often more usefully applied to understand a portion or a transformation of the statistic of interest. Bollen and Stine (1992) have shown that the simple bootstrap approach to the χ^2 goodness-of-fit test for a properly specified model in CFA often produces inaccurate results under conditions of multivariate normality. Even with a properly specified model in the population, the original sample will reflect some sampling fluctuation (e.g., s_{ij} in the sample will not, in general, equal σ_{ij}). The expected value of the χ^2 for the set of bootstrap samples constructed from the original sample will typically *not* be equal to the expected value of the χ^2 (i.e., the df for the model) for a set of samples taken from the population. Consequently, the bootstrap distribution will follow a noncentral χ^2 distribution (which reflects the fluctuation present in the original sample), rather than the usual central χ^2 distribution specified by statistical theory. Bollen and Stine (1992) present a transformation that is a complex function of the original data in the sample and its covariance matrix that minimizes this problem. Evaluations of Bollen and Stine's approach have also shown reasonable performance compared to the values expected from statistical theory for the χ^2 test statistic and the standard errors of direct effects and indirect effects under conditions of multivariate normality.

Empirical Studies of Alternative Estimation Procedures. A number of simulation studies have examined the performance of the ADF estimator, the SCALED χ^2 statistic and robust standard errors, or both (Chou & Bentler in Chapter 3, this volume; Chou, Bentler, & Satorra, 1991; Curran et al., 1994; Finch et al., 1994; Hu et al., 1992; Muthén & Kaplan, 1985, 1992). To date, no large simulation studies have investigated the performance of the bootstrapping approach with diverse nonnormal distributions. The following conclusions may be reached about the ADF and rescaling approaches:

1. All studies have found that the ADF procedure produces χ^2 statistics that are far too high when sample sizes are small to moderate. For example, in the Curran et al. (1994) study, in which the expected χ^2 was 24, when the sample size was 100, the ADF-based χ^2 was 36.4 (50% overestimate) when the distribution was multivariate normal and 44.8 (approximate 90% overestimate) when all measured variables were highly nonnormal (skewness = 3; kurtosis = 21). In contrast, the corresponding values of the SCALED χ^2 statistics were 25.2 (5% overestimate) and 26.8 (10% overestimate), respectively. Under these conditions, the ADF estimator rejected 68% of models that were true in the population, whereas the SCALED χ^2 statistic rejected only 10% of models that were true in the population.

All studies have shown that very large samples are required for adequate performance of the ADF-based χ^2 statistic. Sample sizes of 1000 appear to be necessary with relatively simple models under typical conditions of nonnormality (Curran et al., 1994). Perhaps 5000 cases are necessary for more complex models, less favorable nonnormal conditions, or both (Hu et al., 1992). The SCALED χ^2 statistic appeared to provide good estimates of χ^2 for samples of size 200 and higher.

2. Finch et al. (1994) found that when sample size was 100 and the data were highly nonnormal (skewness = 3; kurtosis = 21), the ADF estimates of the standard error underestimated the empirical standard errors of the factor correlations by 25% and the standard errors of the factor loadings and error variances (specific factors) by approximately 35%. The performance of the Satorra-Bentler robust standard errors was only modestly better under these conditions, with the standard errors being underestimated by approximately 20% for the factor correlations and 25% for the factor loadings and specific factors. The robust standard errors provided generally accurate estimates beginning at a sample size of 200 for moderately nonnormal (skewness = 2; kurtosis = 7) and 500 for highly nonnormal observed variables.

Coarsely Categorized Variables. As we saw earlier, coarse categorization of continuous variables produces bias not only in the χ^2 test-of-fit and standard errors of parameter estimates, but also in the parameter estimates themselves. Muthén (1984) has developed an alternative estimator, which he termed the CVM (for continuous/categorical variable methodology) estimator. The CVM estimator permits the analysis of any combination of dichotomous, ordered polytomous, and interval-scaled measured variables. Unlike traditional normal theory methods, the CVM estimator can yield unbiased, consistent, and efficient parameter estimates when observed variables are dichotomous or ordered categories.

The CVM approach to estimation is based on a strong assumption: A continuous normally distributed ($M = 0$, $\sigma^2 = 1.0$) latent response variable, y^*, is assumed to underlie each measured variable, y. For dichotomous variables, a response of "yes" would be observed if the individual's standing on the underlying normally distributed y^* dimension is greater than a threshold value. A response of "no" would be observed if the individual's standing was below the threshold. Generalizing to ordered categorical variables, the observed response category is assumed to depend on the individual's standing on the normally distributed underlying y^* variable, relative to a set of response thresholds. In the case of a continuous measured variable, y and y^* are assumed to be equivalent.

Because the categorical and/or nonnormally distributed y variables are assumed to be only approximations of the underlying normally distributed y^*s, a distinction is drawn between the covariance structure of the ys and the covariance structure of the underlying y^*s. When one or more observed variables are categorical, the covariance structure of the ys will differ from the covariance structure of the y^*s in important respects. In general, measures of association between categorical variables will be attenuated relative to the underlying, continuous y^*s. A solution in this case is to calculate measures of association between the y^*s based on tetrachoric, polychoric, and polyserial correlations between the measured y variables. The objective of the CVM approach, then, is to reproduce this estimated covariance structure of the y^* variables.

Note that this approach will be theoretically reasonable only in some cases. For example, for many attitude items, the researcher will be more interested in the relationships among the normally distributed, continuous underlying latent variables than in the simple relationships between the observed "agree" versus "disagree" responses on the items. For other continuously distributed variables such as current drug use ("yes" vs. "no"), it is difficult to conceive of a *normally distributed* underlying latent variable. Finally, some variables such as gender are inherently categorical, so no continuous underlying variable could exist.

The CVM approach once again utilizes a weighted least squares estimator (Muthén, 1984). The fitting function minimized by this estimator is of the form

$$F_{\text{WLS}} = [S - \sigma(\hat{\theta})]' \, W^{-1} \, [S - \sigma(\hat{\theta})], \qquad (4.2)$$

where p is the number of measured variables, S is a $p^* \times 1$ vector containing the nonredundant elements of the sample covariance matrix, $\sigma(\hat{\theta})$ is the corresponding $p^* \times 1$ vector from the model implied covariance matrix $\Sigma(\hat{\theta})$, and W^{-1} is a $p^* \times p^*$ weight matrix. Here p^* is defined as $\frac{1}{2}p(p + 1)$. When S contains Pearson correlations (or covariances) for normally distributed interval scaled measured variables, the fitting function simplifies to the normal theory GLS estimator discussed previously. Muthén's CVM approach is very general and can be applied to ordered categories through the use of polychoric correlations and continuous variables that have been censored or truncated through the use of tobit correlations (Muthén, 1991). Combinations of these types of variables can also be addressed.

Muthén's CVM approach also has some significant limitations. Like the ADF estimator, the estimation of the weight matrix places severe practical limits on the number of variables that can be considered (maximum is about 25). The use of the CVM estimator also requires that large samples be used (at least 500-1000 cases, depending on the complexity of the model). Nonetheless, simulation studies to date (see, e.g., Muthén & Kaplan, 1985; Schoenberg & Arminger, 1989) have shown good performance of the CVM estimator relative to ML, GLS, and ADF estimators. The differences in performance are most apparent under the conditions identified above when ML and GLS perform poorly: The observed variables have a small number (two to three) of categories and are highly (> 1 in magnitude) and differentially skewed.

REEXPRESSION OF VARIABLES

An alternative approach is to reexpress nonnormally distributed continuous variables so as to produce distributions that more closely approximate normality. The reexpressed variables can then be analyzed using normal theory estimation techniques (e.g., GLS) without producing biased estimates of model fit or the standard errors of the relationships between the reexpressed variables.

Item Parcels. A commonly used simple method of reexpression is the construction of item parcels by summing or taking the mean of several items that purportedly measure the same construct (e.g., Marsh, Antill, & Cunningham, 1989). These parcels will typically exhibit distributions that more closely approach a normal distribution than the original items. Another perhaps less obvious advantage of item parcels is that fewer parameters will need to be estimated in the measurement model, implying that the estimates will be more stable in small samples.

Note, however, that the construction of item parcels is not without its potential drawbacks (Cattell & Burdsal, 1975). Of most importance, the construction of parcels may obscure the fact that more than one factor may underlie any given item parcel. This problem leads to considerable potential complication in the interpretation of relationships and structure in models using item parcels. Moreover, the use of too few measured variables (parcels) as indicators of a construct yields less stringent tests of the proposed structure of confirmatory factor models. Identification problems are also more likely to occur if too few item parcels are used per factor (i.e., < 3). In such cases, if the correlation between factors is near 0, the model will not be identified.

Transformation of Nonnormal Variables. A transformation performs an operation on observed scores that preserves the order of the scores but alters the distance between adjacent scores. Linear transformations (e.g., standardization) have no effect on either the distributions of variables or the results of simple structural equation models that do *not* impose equality constraints (see Cudeck, 1989). Nonlinear transformations potentially alter the distribution of the measured variables as well as the relationships among measured variables, potentially eliminating some forms of curvilinear effects and interactions between variables. In the presentation below, we assume that all observed values of the variable being transformed are greater than 0, a condition that can be achieved by adding a constant to each observation.

Two classes of approaches to selecting an appropriate transformation are available. First, a power function of the variable may be identified that produces a new (transformed) variable that more closely approximates normality. Several sources (e.g., Daniel & Wood, 1980) offer rules of thumb for selecting power transformations. Given positively skewed distributions, taking logarithmic, square root, or reciprocal transformations (or, more generally, raising the scores on the measured variable to a power less than 1.0) will typically result in distributions that more closely approximate normality. Given negatively skewed distributions, raising raw scores to a power greater than 1.0 will often result in a more normally distributed transformed variable. Daniel and Wood (1980) present plots that are highly useful in selecting a potential transformation. Emerson and Stoto (1983) present a useful technique, the transformation plot for symmetry, in which simple functions of scores associated with specified percentile ranks are plotted. The slope of the resulting graph helps identify the optimal power transformation.

A second class of approaches is useful when scatterplots suggest a possible nonlinear relationship between pairs of variables. Box and Cox (1964) suggested framing this as a nonlinear regression problem: The slope (b_1) and intercept (b_0) of a linear regression equation, $y^\lambda = b_0 + b_1 x + e$, are estimated simultaneously with the optimal power transformation (λ) for the dependent variable. In practice, several regression equations representing values of λ over the range -2 to $+2$ (with the logarithmic transformation representing a value of 0) may be computed, selecting the value of λ for which R^2 is maximized as the optimal power transformation. A more recent exploratory approach, the Alternating Conditional Expectation (ACE) algorithm (see de Veaux, 1990), goes one step further, finding the transformation of each variable that produces the maximum *possible* R^2 between y and x (or even a set of predictors). The ACE algorithm finds optimal transformations that maximize the linear relations between two variables, even when power transformations are unsuccessful.

The Box-Cox and ACE approaches have considerable power when applied to single regression equations; however, structural equation analysts must recall that they are seeking a single transformation that is applicable across a series of regression equations, some of which involve latent variables. Consequently, Box-Cox and ACE must be viewed as providing guidance, rather than a definitive solution in the search for a single transformation that will improve the linearity of the set of relations involving an initially problematic variable.

Several observations should be made about transformations. First, the univariate skewness and kurtosis of the transformed data should always be examined to assess the improvement, if any, in the distribution of the new variable. These indices are also useful in choosing between competing transformations. Note that for some distributions of observed variables, there will be no simple power transformation that will substantially reduce the skewness and kurtosis. Second, the Mardia measures of multivariate skewness and kurtosis for the original and transformed variables should be compared for the set of original and transformed variables. Recall that well-behaved univariate distributions are only a necessary and not a sufficient condition for multivariate normality. Third, although the second approach to transformation, increasing the linearity of relationships, does not directly address normality, linearizing transformations often have the additional benefit of improving the distribution and homoscedasticity of errors of measurement. Fourth, transformation of the data changes the original measure y to a new measure y^*. The new correlations or covariances are computed between the y^* transformed variables, not between the original variables. Reflecting this change, fit statistics, parameter estimates, and standard errors will be based on the y^* variables and may differ, perhaps substantially, from those based on the original variables. Fifth, the application of the ACE algorithm to any measured variable or of different power transformations to each measured variable can potentially result in considerable confusion in the interpretation of the trans-formed results. Even more severe interpretational problems result when different transformations are applied to the *same* measured variable across studies. This is particularly problematic in the use of the ACE algorithm because of its strong tendency to capitalize on chance rela-tionships that cannot be expected to replicate across studies. In general, the loss of metric associated with the transformation is an issue to the extent that researchers wish to compare results across variables or across studies. In addition, the original metrics of the measured vari-ables may represent important units in some areas of social science (i.e., income in dollars). However, in other areas of social science, measures are more often assessed in arbitrary metrics (e.g., seven-point Likert scales), so it is less crucial to preserve the scale of measurement.

Conclusion and Recommendations

The effect of nonnormality on structural equation modeling depends on both its extent and its source (poorly distributed continuous vari-ables, coarsely categorized variables, or outliers). In general, the greater the extent of nonnormality, the greater the magnitude of the problem. Our presentation above has detailed the statistical effects of each of the sources of nonnormality on χ^2 goodness-of-fit statistics, parameter estimates, and standard errors. These problems also have important practical implications. Researchers obtaining inflated χ^2 goodness-of-fit statistics because of nonnormal data will be tempted to make inap-propriate, nonreplicable modifications in theoretically adequate models to achieve traditional standards of fit (MacCallum, Roznowski, & Necowitz, 1992; Chapter 2, this volume). Underestimated standard errors will produce significant paths and correlations between factors, even though they do not exist in the population. Such "findings" can be expected to fail to be replicated, contributing to confusion in many research areas.

The choice among the remedial measures again depends on the extent and source of the nonnormality, as well as the sample size. Considering first the measures of goodness of fit and standard errors for continuous, nonnormally distributed variables, both the ADF esti-mator and the Satorra-Bentler SCALED χ^2 and robust standard errors have shown very good performance, regardless of the degree of non-normality in large samples when the model has been correctly specified.

What is meant by "large samples" has varied across studies, but it is clearly of the range of 1000 to 5000 cases. For sample sizes in the range of approximately 200 to 500 cases, depending on the extent of nonnormality, the Satorra-Bentler statistics appear to have the best properties. For smaller sample sizes, we recommend normal theory ML or GLS estimates when the distributions are not substantially nonnormal, and the Satorra-Bentler statistics as the distributions begin to depart substantially from normality (e.g., skewness = 2; kurtosis = 7). Under these conditions, the use of a more stringent level of α for tests of parameters might also be considered. Particularly for smaller sample sizes, we also recommend inspection of the CFI or Bollen's (1989a) IFI, which have only a small downward bias (3% to 4%), even under severely nonnormal conditions. Note that these recommendations assume that the model has been correctly specified.

For small sample sizes in particular, the two methods of reexpression considered here may improve normal theory estimation techniques. The construction of item parcels usually produces composite variables that more closely approximate normality. The data reduction accomplished in the process also yields a more favorable parameter-to-subject ratio, which is likely to be particularly important in small samples (Bentler & Chou, 1988). Transformations can also often yield new variables that more closely approximate normal distributions. Identification of the optimal normalizing transformation is less certain in small than in large samples. The identification of an adequate transformation that is satisfactory for normal theory estimation can be achieved in some, but not all, data sets. Each of the reexpression methods has its own disadvantages: Item parcels may obscure multifactorial structures; the loss of the original metric from transformation may complicate the interpretation of the results. To date, little empirical work has been done specifically investigating the effect of reexpression techniques on the results of structural equation modeling analyses.

Finally, the CVM estimator appears to provide the most appropriate estimates of the model χ^2, parameter estimates, and standard errors with coarsely categorized, skewed data. The primary advantage of the CVM estimator over the competing normal theory and the Satorra-Bentler statistics occurs as the number of ordered categories decreases. With five or more categories, there is little or no benefit to using CVM; with two categories, there is a substantial advantage given poorly distributed observed variables. The CVM estimator appears to produce good results for ordered categories only with large samples (e.g., at least

500-1000 depending on the complexity of the model being estimated). In addition, the relationships provided by the CVM estimator are between latent, normally distributed variables rather than the original measured variables, potentially complicating interpretation of the results. Coarsely categorized variables that cannot be conceptualized as having an underlying normal distribution, or for which latent variables cannot be constructed that have joint normal distributions, are not appropriate candidates for the technique and are likely not appropriate candidates for structural equation modeling.

The remedies prescribed here address the majority of situations in which nonnormality arises in practice. Most of the remedies are easy to program and are increasingly available as options in the standard computer packages for structural equation modeling (see Chapter 8, this volume). These advances will make it easier for researchers to check the distributional assumptions underlying normal theory estimation and to select and implement alternative approaches when they are not met.

5 Evaluating Model Fit

LI-TZE HU

PETER M. BENTLER

Despite the availability of various measures of model fit, applied researchers often have difficulty determining the adequacy of a structural equation model because different aspects of the results point to conflicting conclusions about the extent to which the model actually matches the observed data. The two most popular ways of evaluating model fit are those that involve the χ^2 goodness-of-fit statistic and the so-called fit indexes that have been offered to supplement the χ^2 test. Both types of indexes can be used to evaluate a priori models or models developed empirically through procedures of model modification. Our discussion will concentrate on evaluating a priori models.

In this chapter, we consider the following issues: (a) the usefulness of the χ^2 statistic based on various estimation methods for model evaluation and selection; (b) the conceptual elaboration of and selection criteria for fit indexes; and (c) identifying some crucial factors that will affect the magnitude of χ^2 statistics and fit indexes. We review previous research findings as well as report results of some new, unpublished research. It will be seen that a certain amount of care must be used when

AUTHORS' NOTE: This research was supported by a grant from the Division of Social Sciences and by a Faculty Research Grant from the University of California, Santa Cruz, and by USPHS Grants DA00017 and DA01070.

evaluating models with the χ^2 test and fit indexes. We conclude with a brief summary of additional aspects of model fit.

The χ^2 Test

The conventional overall test of fit in covariance structure analysis assesses the magnitude of the discrepancy between the sample and fitted covariance matrices. Let S represent the unbiased estimator, based on a sample of size N, of a $p \times p$ population covariance matrix Σ, whose elements are hypothesized to be functions of a $q \times 1$ parameter vector θ: $\Sigma = \Sigma(\theta)$. The parameters are estimated so that the discrepancy between the sample covariance matrix S and the implied covariance matrix $\Sigma(\hat{\theta})$ is minimal. A discrepancy function $F = F[S, \Sigma(\theta)]$ can be considered to be a measure of the discrepancy between S and $\Sigma(\theta)$ evaluated at an estimator $\hat{\theta}$ and is minimized to yield F_{min}. Under an assumed distribution and the hypothesized model $\Sigma(\theta)$ for the population covariance matrix Σ, the test statistic $T = (N - 1)F_{min}$ has an asymptotic (large sample) χ^2 distribution. The statistic T is often called "the χ^2 test." A large T statistic relative to the degrees of freedom associated with the model indicates that the model may not be a good representation of the process that generated the data in the population. In general, the H_0: $\Sigma = \Sigma(\theta)$ is rejected if the value of the T statistic exceeds a T_α in the χ^2 distribution at an α level of significance. The T statistics derived from maximum likelihood (ML) and generalized least squares (GLS) estimation methods under the assumption of multivariate normality of variables are the most widely employed summary statistics for assessing the adequacy of a structural equation model, but other T statistics are available as well.

The χ^2 test enjoyed substantial popularity at first, because it seemed as if its use could make confirmatory factor analysis (Jöreskog, 1969) become free of the many subjective decisions that were historically associated with exploratory factor analysis (e.g., the number of factors or the choice of rotational method). An objective test could thus replace subjective judgment. This is not necessarily the way modeling is described today; for instance, Jöreskog (1993) considers model generating analyses far more typical than model testing analyses despite the fact that model testing is what generated enthusiasm for the techniques.

However, problems associated with goodness-of-fit χ^2 tests were recognized quite early (e.g., Bentler & Bonett, 1980; Steiger & Lind,

1980) and have attracted continuing discussion (e.g., Bentler, 1990; Jöreskog & Sörbom, 1988; Kaplan, 1990). One of the concerns has centered on the sample size issue. The statistical theory for T is asymptotic; that is, it holds as sample size gets arbitrarily large. So T may not be χ^2 distributed in a small sample and, therefore, it may not be correct for model evaluation in practical situations. Also, with the increased statistical power of the test afforded by a large sample, a trivial difference between the sample covariance matrix S and the fitted model $\hat{\Sigma}$ may result in the rejection of the specified model. Furthermore, T may not be χ^2 distributed when the typical underlying assumption of multivariate normality is violated. Therefore, the standard χ^2 test may not be a good enough guide to model adequacy, because a significant goodness-of-fit χ^2 value may be a reflection of model misspecification, power of the test, or violation of some technical assumptions underlying the estimation method.

PERFORMANCE OF χ^2 TESTS
AS TESTS OF MODEL FIT

Because there are really many χ^2 tests, each depending on the choice of F and hence T, some may perform better than others. Hu, Bentler, and Kano (1992) examined the adequacy of six χ^2 goodness-of-fit tests under various conditions. We mention these test statistics and how they perform.

As noted above, ML and GLS statistics assume multivariate normality of the data (e.g., Browne, 1974; Jöreskog, 1969). A violation of this assumption can seriously invalidate normal-theory test statistics (see Chapter 4). The recent theory of asymptotic robustness has found that normal-theory based methods such as ML or GLS possibly can correctly describe and evaluate a model with nonnormally distributed variables (e.g., Amemiya & Anderson, 1990; Anderson & Amemiya, 1988; Browne & Shapiro, 1988; Satorra & Bentler, 1990, 1991). This requires that the latent variables (common factors, unique factors, or errors) that are typically considered as simply uncorrelated must actually be mutually independent, and common factors, when correlated, must have freely estimated variance/covariance parameters. There is no practical test of such assumptions.

Browne (1984a) introduced multivariate elliptical theory with distributional assumptions that are more general than normal. Elliptical distributions are symmetric, with tails that can be identical to those of a normal distribution as well as heavier or lighter. In these distributions, a kurtosis parameter, reflecting the assumed common kurtosis of the variables, in addition to the usual normal-theory model parameters, is needed to yield asymptotically optimal estimators and simple χ^2 goodness-of-fit tests.

Kano, Berkane, and Bentler (1990) found that a simple adjustment of the weight matrix of normal theory, using univariate (marginal) kurtosis estimates of the variables, can result in optimal statistical properties. Their heterogeneous kurtosis (HK) statistics specialize to elliptical and normal-theory statistics when the variables have homogeneous kurtoses or no excess kurtosis, respectively.

When the assumptions underlying normal, elliptical, or heterogeneous kurtosis theory are false, the test statistics, T, based on these assumptions can be corrected using a scaling factor developed by Satorra and Bentler (1988a, 1988b, 1994). The Satorra-Bentler corrected test statistic, called here the SCALED statistic, is computed on the basis of the model, estimation method, and sample fourth-order moments, and it holds regardless of the distribution of variables. Similarly, asymptotic (large-sample) distribution-free (ADF) methods (e.g., Bentler, 1983; Browne, 1984a) make the promising claim that the test statistics for model fit are insensitive to the distribution of the observations when the sample size is large.

Hu et al. (1992) evaluated the performance of the above six goodness-of-fit test statistics when (a) distributional, (b) assumed independence, and (c) asymptotic sample size requirements were violated. The dependence condition is one in which two or more variables are functionally related, even though their linear combinations may be exactly zero. In contrast, with relative normal data, linear relations of zero implies independence. A confirmatory factor-analytic model based on 15 observed variables with three common factors was studied. The results, based on the Monte Carlo procedure, revealed several important implications for practice. Consistent with previous findings (e.g., Chou, Bentler, & Satorra, 1991; Muthén & Kaplan, 1992), the theoretical expectation that the ADF method would work well for any arbitrary distribution was correct only when the sample size was extremely large (at a sample size of 5000). With small sample sizes, ADF performed poorly under all the conditions studied and therefore is not recommended for practical application. With data generated to yield asymptotic robustness, normal-theory methods (ML, GLS) performed adequately; however, at smaller sample sizes, ML rejected the true model too frequently, and it required a sample size of 2500 for the rejection rate to approach nominal levels, whereas GLS seemed to perform much better at the smaller sample sizes. Unfortunately, the practitioner cannot trust normal-theory test statistics when there might be a dependence among latent variates, because the normal-theory methods (ML, GLS) essentially always rejected true models under that condition.

Both elliptical and heterogeneous kurtosis methods tended to accept models more frequently than expected when the latent common and error variates were independently distributed. When the latent variates were dependent, the elliptical method tended to reject models more frequently than expected, whereas the HK method accepted models too often.

The Satorra-Bentler SCALED statistic, based on a correction to the ML χ^2 statistic, performed better than all other methods examined under the dependence condition. It performed as well as the normal-theory methods under the independence condition. Generally, it performed well overall, but it had a tendency to overreject true models at smaller sample sizes.

In a recent follow-up study, Hu and Bentler (1993) studied the Satorra-Bentler scaling correction applied to the GLS χ^2 statistic rather than the ML χ^2 statistic (using METHOD = GLS, ROBUST in a special version of EQS; Bentler, 1989). The results revealed that this SCALED test statistic performed adequately even at smaller sample sizes and seemed to be the most adequate test statistic for evaluating model fit when sample size is small. With a relatively large sample size, both ML- and GLS-based SCALED statistics performed about equally well, and when sample size is extremely large, the ADF statistic also was an appropriate statistic for model evaluation and selection.

NONCENTRAL χ^2 DISTRIBUTION

Suppose $\Sigma \neq \Sigma(\theta)$, that is, the null hypothesis is not true. Then T will not be χ^2 distributed, but it may still be distributed as a "noncentral" χ^2 variate. A noncentrality parameter (λ) and degrees of freedom (df) are required for the specification of a noncentral χ^2 distribution, which can be denoted by $\chi^2(df, \lambda)$. The noncentrality parameter λ represents a measure of the discrepancy between Σ and $\Sigma(\theta)$ and can be considered as a "population badness-of-fit statistic" (Steiger, 1989). Thus, the larger the λ, the farther apart the true alternative hypothesis from the null hypothesis. The usual central χ^2 distribution is a special case of the noncentral χ^2 distribution for which $\lambda = 0$.

Cudeck and Henly (1991) classified several types of error involved in fitting a model based on discrepancies among different matrices. For example, the overall error is defined as the discrepancy between Σ and $\Sigma(\hat{\theta})$, and error of approximation refers to the discrepancy between lack of fit of the Σ and $\Sigma(\theta)$. So, the noncentrality parameter is a measure of the error of approximation. Because the measure of error of approximation can be estimated only from a sample, Steiger and Lind (1980; also Steiger, 1989) have suggested that constructing a confidence interval on a population noncentrality parameter will allow one to assess (a) the badness-of-fit of a model in the population and (b) the precision of the population badness-of-fit determined from the sample data. As will be seen below, the noncentrality parameter also can be used to generate noncentrality-based fit indexes.

Fit Indexes

In practice, only the central χ^2 distribution is used to test the sharp null hypothesis $\Sigma = \Sigma(\theta)$, and the Satorra-Bentler SCALED statistic seems to perform quite well, as noted earlier. Nevertheless, even if evaluating models with this statistic, the problem of excess power to reject models because of very large sample size will remain. That is, even if the discrepancy between estimated model and data is very small, if the sample size is large enough, almost any model will be rejected because the discrepancy is not statistically equal to zero. Stated differently, the strict null hypothesis $\Sigma = \Sigma(\theta)$ almost surely will not be exactly true, because the researcher surely will not know *everything* there is to know about the data. Moreover, a χ^2 test offers only a dichotomous decision strategy implied by a statistical decision rule and cannot be used to quantify the degree of fit along a continuum with some prespecified boundary.

Thus many so-called fit indexes have been developed to assess the degree of congruence between the model and data (Akaike, 1974, 1987; Bentler, 1983, 1990; Bentler & Bonett, 1980; Bollen, 1986, 1989a; James, Mulaik, & Brett, 1982; Jöreskog & Sörbom, 1981; Marsh, Balla, & McDonald, 1988; McDonald, 1989; McDonald & Marsh, 1990; Steiger & Lind, 1980; Tanaka & Huba, 1985; Tucker & Lewis, 1973). Although there has been some discussion of using a fit index to test the null hypothesis $\Sigma = \Sigma(\theta)$ (e.g., Maiti & Mukherjee, 1991), in our opinion this defeats the purpose of fit indexes. Like R^2 in multiple regression, these indexes are meant to quantify something akin to variance accounted for, rather than to test null hypotheses. In particular, these indexes generally quantify the extent to which the variation and covariation in the data are accounted for by a model. As noted by Bentler and Bonett (1980), who introduced several of the indexes and popularized the ideas, fit indexes were designed to avoid some of the problems of sample size and distributional misspecification in the evaluation of a model. Initially, it was hoped that these fit indexes would more unambiguously point to model adequacy as compared to the χ^2 test. This optimistic state of affairs is, unfortunately, also not true. Issues such as sample size and complexity of the model also may affect the magnitude of the fit indexes (e.g., Browne & Cudeck, 1993; Gerbing & Anderson, 1993; Kaplan, 1990; Tanaka, 1993).

In this section, we review the adequacy of four types of fit indexes derived from various estimation methods across different sample sizes. We also reevaluate their adequacy under conditions such as violation of underlying assumptions of multivariate normality and asymptotic robustness theory, providing evidence from our own unpublished research regarding the efficacy of the oft stated idea that a model with a fit index greater than .90 should be acceptable (e.g., Bentler & Bonett, 1980).

TYPES OF FIT INDEXES

One of the most widely adopted dimensions for classifying fit indexes is the absolute versus incremental distinction of fit indexes (Bollen, 1989a; Gerbing & Anderson, 1993; Marsh et al., 1988; Tanaka, 1993). An absolute fit index directly assesses how well an a priori model reproduces the sample data. Although no reference model is employed to assess the amount of increment in model fit, an implicit or explicit comparison may be made to a saturated model that exactly reproduces the observed covariance matrix. As a result, this type of fit index is analogous to R^2 by comparing the goodness of fit to a component that is similar to a total sum of squares. In contrast, an incremental fit index measures the proportionate improvement in fit by comparing a target model with a more restricted, nested baseline model. Incremental fit indexes are also called comparative fit indexes. A null model in which all the observed variables are uncorrelated is the most typically used baseline model (Bentler & Bonett, 1980), although other baseline models have been suggested (e.g., Sobel & Bohrnstedt, 1985).

Further distinctions can be made among incremental fit indexes. We shall define three groups of indexes, types 1, 2, and 3. The terminology of type-1 and type-2 indexes follows Marsh et al. (1988), although our specific definitions of these terms are not identical to theirs.[1] A type-1 index uses information only from the optimized statistics T used in fitting baseline (T_B) and target (T_T) models. T is not necessarily assumed to follow any particular distributional form, although it is assumed that the fit function, F, is the same for both models. Type-2 and type-3 indexes are based on an assumed distribution of variables and other standard regularity conditions. A type-2 index additionally uses information from the expected values of T_T under the central χ^2 distribution. A type-3 index uses type-1 information but additionally uses information from the expected values of T_T and/or T_B under the relevant noncentral χ^2 distribution. When the assumed distributions are correct, type-2 and type-3 indexes should perform better than type-1 indexes because more information is being used; however, note also that type-2 and type-3 indexes may use inappropriate information, because any particular T may not have the distributional form assumed. For example, type-3 indexes make use of the noncentral χ^2 distribution for T_B, but one could seriously question whether this is generally its appropriate reference distribution. A type-4 index, not studied further here, could use expectations under various other distributional forms; an example might be noncentral mixture distributions ($1 - $ df) based on prior work of Satorra and Bentler (1988a, 1994).

Type-1 Incremental Fit Indexes. Incremental fit indexes assess the adequacy of a target model (T_T) in relation to a baseline model (T_B), using the nonnegative statistic T in each case (presumably based on the same statistical and mathematical assumptions). Bentler and Bonett's (1980) normed fit index (NFI) is the classic example:

$$\text{NFI} = (T_B - T_T)/T_B. \tag{5.1}$$

T_B will usually be large. If T_T is only a trivial decrement to T_B, the fit index is close to 0, but if T_T is very small, the fit index is close to 1. More generally, NFI represents the proportion of total covariance among observed variables explained by a target model when using the null model as a baseline model (Mulaik, James, Van Alstine, Bennett, Lind, & Stillwell, 1989). As developed by Bentler and Bonett (1980), NFI can be computed even when the fit measures T_B and T_T are not presumed to be test statistics that have χ^2 distributions, and, because $T_B \geq T_T$ for optimized indexes, it is "normed"—it has a 0-1 range.

A related type-1 index, which we shall call BL86, was developed by Bollen (1986). It can be obtained by replacing each T in NFI by the ratio of that T to its degrees of freedom (df). That is,

$$BL86 = [(T_B/df_B) - (T_T/df_T)]/(T_B/df_B). \qquad (5.2)$$

Type-2 Incremental Fit Indexes. The classic index first developed by Tucker and Lewis (1973) under assumed normality and ML estimation uses information from the expected value of T_T. In its final form, it is similar to BL86, but one subtracts 1 in the denominator of BL86. That is,

$$TLI = [(T_B/df_B) - (T_T/df_T)]/[(T_B/df_B) - 1]. \qquad (5.3)$$

Tucker and Lewis' original purpose for developing their index was to quantify the degree to which a particular exploratory factor model is an improvement over a zero factor model when assessed by maximum likelihood. Generalizing Tucker and Lewis' definition to all types of covariance structure models under various estimation methods, Bentler and Bonett called the generalized TLI the "nonnormed" fit index (NNFI), because it need not have a 0-1 range, even if $T_B \geq T_T$. Another type-2 index was developed by Bollen (1989a), called here BL89, which modifies the denominator of NFI by subtracting degrees of freedom:

$$BL89 = (T_B - T_T)/(T_B - df_T). \qquad (5.4)$$

We do not have space to summarize the rationales advanced for these various indexes by their authors. In general, these rationales did not involve first defining a population fit index parameter and then using estimators of this parameter to define sample fit indexes. The more recent noncentrality fit indexes use this more rational approach (Bentler, 1990; McDonald, 1989; McDonald & Marsh, 1990; Steiger, 1989).

Type-3 Incremental Fit Indexes. As noted above, with true or not extremely misspecified null hypotheses, the errors of approximation are small relative to the sampling errors in the matrix S, and a test statistic T can be approximated in large samples by the noncentral $\chi^2(df, \lambda)$

distribution (e.g., Satorra, 1989). The noncentrality parameters associated with a sequence of nested models (i.e., $M_B, \ldots, M_j, \ldots, M_T, \ldots,$ M_S) representing the degree of model misspecification are ordered λ_B $\geq \lambda_j \geq \lambda_T \geq \lambda_S = 0$, with the parameter for the baseline model the largest and that for the saturated model the smallest. Thus the population counterpart to NFI is obviously (Bentler, 1990) given by

$$\delta = (\lambda_B - \lambda_T)/\lambda_B. \tag{5.5}$$

For a given baseline model, the smaller the misspecification of M_T (i.e., the smaller the λ_T), the larger the δ. Thus a noncentrality fit index assesses the reduction in the amount of misfit of a target model (M_T) relative to a baseline model (M_B).

Of course, δ is not operational unless consistent estimators of the population λs are used. Using a test statistic T to estimate the λs would bring us back to the NFI, but T is not a good estimator of λ. Bentler's (1989, 1990) fit index (BFI) and McDonald and Marsh's (1990) relative noncentrality index, which are identical, estimate each noncentrality parameter by the difference between its T statistic and the corresponding degrees of freedom, that is,

$$\text{BFI} = [(T_B - df_B) - (T_T - df_T)]/(T_B - df_B). \tag{5.6}$$

A problem with BFI is that it can lie outside the 0-1 range. Bentler proposed to modify BFI to avoid this problem, calling the resulting index the comparative fit index,

$$\text{CFI} = 1 - \max[(T_T - df_T), 0]/\max[(T_T - df_T), (T_B - df_B), 0]. \tag{5.7}$$

Whenever BFI is in the 0-1 range, BFI = CFI. See Goffin (1993) for further details. Historically, the EQS program (Bentler, 1992a) has favored evaluating model fit with incremental or comparative fit indexes. In contrast, the LISREL program (Jöreskog & Sörbom, 1988) has favored absolute fit indexes, although the newest version of the program (Jöreskog & Sörbom, 1993a) provides both types.

Absolute Fit Indexes. Jöreskog and Sörbom (1984) proposed an absolute fit index for ML methods:

$$\text{GFI}_{ML} = 1 - [\text{tr}(\hat{\Sigma}^{-1}S - I)^2/\text{tr}(\hat{\Sigma}^{-1}S)^2]. \tag{5.8}$$

They further developed a corresponding adjusted fit index to incorporate a penalty function for the inclusion of additional parameters:

$$AGFI_{ML} = 1 - [p(p + 1)/2df](1 - GFI_{ML}). \qquad (5.9)$$

Jöreskog and Sörbom (1984) define GFI as a measure of the relative amount of variances and covariances in S that are accounted for by the implied model $\hat{\Sigma}$. When $S = \hat{\Sigma}$, GFI_{ML} and $AGFI_{ML}$ have their maximum value of 1. Their typical values are greater than zero, but it is possible for them to be less than zero. The GLS versions of GFI and AGFI were given by Tanaka and Huba (1985). These indexes have a general form, first developed by Bentler (1983, eqs. 3.5, 3.8) and studied by Tanaka and Huba (1985, 1989).

Akaike's Information Criterion (AIC; Akaike, 1987) was developed to adjust for the number of parameters estimated. Cudeck and Browne (1983) developed a rescaled version of AIC (called CAK here):

$$CAK = [T_T/(N - 1)] + [2q/(N - 1)]. \qquad (5.10)$$

It is expected to be valid at all sample sizes. Based on a single calibration sample, Browne and Cudeck (1989) further developed a single sample cross-validation index (called CK here):

$$CK = [T_T/(N - 1)] + [2q/(N - p - 2)]. \qquad (5.11)$$

CK is expected to be a good approximation to a fit index that one could obtain on cross-validation to a new sample. CAK and CK are intended to be used to select one or more models from a set of plausible models, and the goal is to identify models that will perform optimally in future samples. In general, the smaller the values of CAK and CK, the better the fit of the implied models.

McDonald's (1989) Centrality Index (MCI, as called here) transforms the rescaled noncentrality parameter:

$$MCI = \exp\{-\tfrac{1}{2}[(T_T - df_T)/(N - 1)]\}. \qquad (5.12)$$

MCI typically ranges from 0 to 1, but it may exceed 1 because of sampling error.

In an effort to develop a fit index that will be independent of sample size, Hoelter's (1983) CN has been proposed to estimate an adequate sample size for accepting the fit of a given model for a χ^2 test. Hoelter (1983) suggested that a CN value exceeding 200 indicates that a given model is an adequate representation of the sample data. That is,

$$CN = \{(z_{crit} + \sqrt{2df - 1})^2/[2T_T/(N - 1)]\} + 1. \qquad (5.13)$$

Note that z_{crit} is the critical z-value at a selected probability (α) level.

Given the availability of these various types of fit indexes, the decision of choosing one or more appropriate fit indexes requires careful consideration of some critical factors that might influence the performance of fit indexes on evaluating model fit. Thus we examine these issues and evaluate some of the most well-known fit indexes, based on the criteria identified in the previous research and our own unpublished research.

ISSUES IN ASSESSING FIT BY FIT INDEXES AND SELECTION CRITERIA

There are three major problems involved in using fit indexes for evaluating goodness of fit: (a) small sample bias, (b) estimation effects, and (c) effects of violation of normality and independence. These are a natural consequence of the fact that these indexes typically are based on χ^2 tests. It does not seem profound to expect that a fit index will perform better, generally speaking, when its corresponding χ^2 test performs well. Because, as noted earlier, these χ^2 tests may not perform adequately at all sample sizes, and also because the adequacy of a χ^2 statistic may depend on the particular assumptions it requires about the distributions of variables, these same factors can be expected to influence evaluation of model fit.

Small Sample Bias. Estimation methods in structural equation modeling are developed under various assumptions. One is that the model is true (i.e., $\Sigma = \Sigma[\theta]$). We shall assume this is the case and not study misspecification here. Another is the assumption that estimates and tests are based on arbitrarily large samples, which will not be true in practice. The adequacy of the test statistics is thus likely to be influenced by sample size, perhaps performing more poorly in smaller samples that are considered to be not "asymptotic" enough. In fact, the relation between sample size and the adequacy of a fit index when the model is true has long been recognized; for instance, Bearden, Sharma,

88 STRUCTURAL EQUATION MODELING

and Teel (1982) found that the mean of NFI is positively related to sample size and that NFI values tend to be far less than 1.0 when sample size is small. Their early results pointed out the main problem: possible systematic fit index bias. Bollen (1990) also noted that it may be important to determine whether sample size N directly enters the calculation of a fit index. This feature has not turned out to be especially important.

If the mean of a fit index, computed across various samples under the same condition when the model is true, varies systematically with N, such a statistic will be a biased estimator of the corresponding population parameter. Or, stated differently, the decision for accepting or rejecting a particular model may vary as function of sample size, which is certainly not desirable.

Estimation Method Effects. Not much is known about estimation effects. Even if the distributional assumptions are met, as noted above different estimators yield χ^2 statistics that perform better or worse at various sample sizes. This may translate into differential performance of fit indexes based on different estimators; however, the overall effect of mapping from χ^2 to fit index, while varying estimation method, is unclear.

In pioneering work, Tanaka (1987) and La Du and Tanaka (1989) found that given the same model and data, the NFI behaved erratically across ML and GLS, whereas GFI behaved consistently across the two estimation methods. Their results must be due to the differential quality of the null model χ^2 used in the NFI computations because the GFI maps the hypothesized model into an approximate 0-1 range. Based on these results, Tanaka and Huba (1989) suggest that estimation-specific fit indexes (e.g., GFI) are more appropriate than estimation-general fit indexes (e.g., NFI) in finite samples. Tanaka and Huba's (1989) findings are based on normal-theory based estimation methods under limited conditions. Hu and Bentler (1993) further tested the generalizability of such a suggestion.

Effects of Violation of Normality and Independence. An issue related to the adequacy of fit indexes that has not been studied is the potential effect of violation of assumptions underlying estimation methods—specifically, violation of distributional assumptions and the effect of dependence of latent variates. Nothing is known about the adequacy of fit indexes under conditions such as dependency among common and unique latent variates, along with violations of multivariate normality, at various sample sizes. Using Monte Carlo methods, Hu and Bentler (1993) examined the four types of goodness-of-fit indexes (described in the previous section) derived from ML, GLS, and ADF estimation methods under conditions in which the assumptions of multivariate normality and asymptotic robustness theory are violated. An attempt was made to evaluate the "rule of thumb" conventional cutoff criterion of .90 (Bentler & Bonett, 1980) that has been used in practice to evaluate the adequacy of models. Considering any model with a fit index above .90 as acceptable, and one with an index below this value as unacceptable, we evaluated the rejection rates for most of the fit indexes (except CAK, CK, and CN; a cutoff value of 200 was used for CN). One might hope that about 5% of true models would be rejected with this criterion by chance alone. The findings are used as a basis for evaluating the fit indexes discussed here.

Reevaluation of Fit Indexes
As Alternative Measures of Model Fit

TYPE-1 INCREMENTAL FIT INDEXES

Bentler and Bonett's Normed Fit Index (NFI). It has long been documented that the mean of the sampling distribution of NFI (Equation 5.1) is positively associated with sample size and that NFI substantially underestimates its asymptotic value at small sample sizes (e.g., Bearden et al., 1982; Bollen, 1986, 1989a; Hu & Bentler, 1993). As was found by Tanaka (1987) and La Du and Tanaka (1989), Hu and Bentler (1993) reported that NFI behaved erratically across estimation methods under conditions of small N. The mean values obtained from ML were substantially greater than those of GLS and ADF across various conditions. NFI based on GLS and ADF tended to overreject models even at moderate sample sizes. These effects became even more substantial when the latent variates were dependent. NFI is not a good indicator for evaluating model fit when N is small.

Bollen's Fit Index (BL86). Like NFI, the sampling distributions of BL86 (Equation 5.2) tended to increase with sample size (e.g., Bollen, 1986, 1989a; Hu & Bentler, 1993). Several findings also emerged in Hu and Bentler's (1993) study. BL86 obtained from ML behaved substantially differently from its counterpart obtained from GLS and ADF at sample sizes of 1000 or less in various conditions. The asymptotic value of BL86 was underestimated under dependence conditions to a greater extent than under the independence conditions. At sample sizes of 1000 or less, the values of BL86 based on GLS and ADF rejected the true models much too frequently in all seven conditions. This index is thus not recommended as a good indicator for evaluating model fit.

TYPE-2 INCREMENTAL FIT INDEXES

Tucker-Lewis Index (TLI, Also NNFI). Although Anderson and Gerbing (1984) and Marsh et al. (1988) found that the association between TLI (Equation 5.3) and sample size is not substantial, this finding holds only when the ML method is used and there is independence among the latent variates (Hu & Bentler, 1993). Hu and Bentler found that at sample sizes of 1000 or less, TLI based on GLS was below its asymptotic value to a great extent. Under independence, only the mean value of TLI based on ADF was related to the sample size. At sample sizes of 250 or less, TLI based on ADF overrejected the true model. At a sample size of 150, TLI from GLS rejected true models too frequently. Under dependence, the mean values based on all three estimations were related to sample size. TLI based on GLS and ADF rejected models too frequently (85% to 95%) at sample sizes of 500 or less. At a sample size of 150, TLI based on ML rejected 30% of the models. When the latent common and error variates were independently distributed, TLI performed relatively consistently across ML and GLS methods at sample sizes of 250 or greater, but the mean values based on ADF tended to be much smaller than those based on ML and GLS at sample sizes of 250 or less. When the latent variates were dependent, TLI behaved erratically across the three estimation methods at sample sizes of 500 or less.

Bollen's Fit Index (BL89). Bollen (1989a) reported a weak association between the mean of the sampling distribution of BL89 (Equation 5.4) and the sample size. Hu and Bentler (1993) further reported that the mean values based on GLS were more likely to be influenced by sample size than those based on ML when latent variates are dependent. The mean value of BL89 based on ADF was substantially related to sample size in all seven conditions. BL89 behaved consistently across ML and GLS methods at sample sizes of 250 or greater under independence, and it behaved erratically across ML, GLS, and ADF methods under dependence conditions.

TYPE-3 INCREMENTAL FIT INDEXES

Bentler's Fit Index and McDonald and Marsh's Relative Noncentrality Index. Using the ML method, Bentler (1990) found no systematic bias of BFI/RNI (Equation 5.6) and CFI (Equation 5.7) when sample size was small. Hu and Bentler (1993) reported that although the mean values and standard deviations were different between CFI and BFI, with CFI being trivially smaller on average but sometimes substantially less variable, the CFI and BFI behaved similarly across various conditions. CFI (and BFI) performed only slightly inconsistently across ML, GLS, and ADF at sample sizes of 250 or less when the latent common and error variates were independently distributed. When the latent variates were dependent, CFI (and BFI) behaved inconsistently across three estimation methods at sample sizes of 500 or less. The mean value of CFI (and BFI) based on ML was substantially greater than those based on GLS and ADF at sample sizes of 250 or less under dependence conditions. A relatively large percentage of fit indexes based on GLS and ADF fell below the .90 cutoff value when the latent variates were dependent. CFI (and BFI) based on ADF tended to overreject the true models at sample sizes of 250 or less in all seven conditions.

Under independence, the mean values of CFI (and BFI) based on ML and GLS were not associated with the sample size, but the mean value derived from ADF was related to sample size. The sample size effect on the values of CFI (and BFI) based on GLS and ADF was much greater than that based on ML.

ABSOLUTE FIT INDEXES

Goodness-of-Fit Index (GFI) and Adjusted Goodness-of-Fit Index (AGFI). Several studies have reported a positive association between the means of the sampling distributions of GFI (Equation 5.8) and AGFI (Equation 5.9) and sample size (e.g., Anderson & Gerbing, 1984; Marsh et al., 1988; Bollen, 1986, 1989a, 1990). In spite of these findings, Marsh et al. (1988) found that GFI appeared to perform better than any other absolute index (e.g., AGFI, CAK, CN, RMR, etc.) studied by them. GFI also underestimated its asymptotic value to a lesser extent than the NFI. Hu and Bentler (1993) further found that GFI underestimated its asymptotic value at small sample sizes in each of the estimation methods. The tendency of underestimation was greater when the latent variates are dependent. Under the independence conditions, all the models were accepted by GFI at a sample size of 250 or greater. Evidently, the cutoff value of .90 is inadequate under these circumstances to assess adequately a model fit. Under dependency conditions, GFI based on ML and GLS behaved poorly at sample sizes of 250 or smaller. The cutoff tended to reject the true model far too frequently than at an expected rejection rate of .05. GFI from ADF required a sample size greater than 500 to ensure that its rejection rate approached the nominal value.

When common and unique variates were distributed independent of each other regardless of the form of the distribution of observed variables, GFI behaved consistently across ML and GLS at all sample sizes. This finding is consistent with those of Tanaka (1987) and La Du and Tanaka (1989). At a sample size of 250 or greater, GFI behaved consistently across all three estimation methods. When the latent variates were dependent, GFI behaved inconsistently across three estimation methods at sample sizes of 250 or smaller. The values of ML and GLS converged at a sample size of 500 or greater; however, a minimum sample size of 5000 was required for the value from ADF to converge with those of ML and GLS.

When the latent variates were independent, AGFI performed consistently across ML and GLS methods. At $N \geq 250$, AGFI behaved consistently across all three estimation methods. When the latent variates were dependent, AGFI behaved relatively consistently across ML and GLS at $N \geq 500$. The value from ADF did not converge with those of ML and GLS even at a sample size of 5000. Using the cutoff value of .90 resulted in an underrejection of true models (except for the smallest sample size) when latent variates were independent; however, at small sample sizes it resulted in a overrejection of true models when latent variates were dependent.

Information Criterion Indexes. Sample size was found to be substantially associated with CAK (Equation 5.10) and CK (Equation 5.11; see also Browne & Cudeck, 1989; Cudeck & Browne, 1983). CAK and CK performed relatively consistently across ML and GLS at all sample sizes when the latent variates were independently distributed. They behaved inconsistently at sample sizes of 500 or less when the latent variates were dependent. The values of CAK and CK from ADF were inconsistent with those based on ML and GLS when sample size was 500 or less across all seven conditions (Hu & Bentler, 1993).

McDonald's Centrality Index. Under the independence conditions, the means of MCI (Equation 5.12) based on ML and GLS were not associated with sample size (Hu & Bentler, 1993; McDonald, 1989; McDonald & Marsh, 1990); however, Hu and Bentler (1993) reported that sample size was related to the mean of MCI based on ADF under independence and was also related to the mean of MCI based on all the three estimation methods under dependence. MCI behaved consistently across ML and GLS methods at various sample sizes under independence conditions. It behaved erratically across the two methods at sample sizes less than or equal to 500 under the dependency conditions. The mean values of MCI from ADF were substantially different from those based on ML and GLS in all seven conditions when sample size was equal to or less than 250.

Using the .90 criterion for model acceptance, MCI from ML and GLS tended to reject the true model far too frequently at sample sizes of 500 or less when the latent variates were dependent. On the other hand, the .90 cutoff was useless for MCI from ML and GLS under dependence conditions when $N \geq 250$; all models were accepted. MCI from ADF rejected true models too frequently at sample sizes equal to or less than 250 in all seven conditions.

Hoelter's Critical N (CN). The mean of the sampling distribution of CN (Equation 5.13) for a given model was positively related to the sample size (e.g., Bollen & Liang, 1988; Hu & Bentler, 1993). Hu and Bentler's (1993) recent study revealed that, under independence conditions, CN behaved less inconsistently across ML and GLS. At sample sizes of 250 or less, CN based on ADF behaved quite differently from those based on ML and GLS. Under dependence, CN behaved erratically across all three estimation methods at all sample sizes. At a sample size of 150, CN performed poorly because the sample means across replications substantially underestimated its asymptotic value, leading to rejection of the true models far too often. CN accepted almost all the models under the independence conditions with a sample size of 250 or greater, as well as under dependence conditions with a sample size of 500 or greater. A cutoff value that is substantially greater than 200 would be required to evaluate appropriately the fit of the model.

OVERALL SUMMARY AND RECOMMENDATIONS

When common and error variates are distributed independently of each other, all the fit indexes behaved less consistently than expected across ML, GLS, and ADF at small sample sizes. Type-2 and type-3 incremental, as well as absolute, fit indexes behaved consistently across ML and GLS. GFI performed rather consistently across all three estimation methods. When common and error variates were dependent, however, the performance of all four types of fit indexes was inconsistent at even moderate sample sizes (Hu & Bentler, 1993).

The general finding seems to be a positive association between sample size and the goodness-of-fit fit index size for type-1 incremental fit indexes. Obviously, type-1 incremental indexes will be influenced by the badness of fit of the null model as well as the goodness of fit of the target model, and Marsh et al. (1988) as well as Hu and Bentler (1993) reported a strong effect. On the other hand, the type-2 and type-3 incremental indexes seem to be substantially less biased. The results for absolute indexes are mixed. The type-2 and type-3 incremental fit indexes, in general, perform better than either the absolute or type-1 incremental indexes. This is true for the older indexes such as TLI, as noted above, but appears to be especially true for the newer indexes based on noncentrality (e.g., Bentler, 1990; Hu & Bentler, 1993). For example, Bentler (1990) reported that BFI (RNI), CFI, and BL89 performed essentially with no bias, though by definition CFI must be somewhat downward biased to avoid out of range values greater than 1 that can occur with RNI. This bias, however, is trivial, and it results in lower sampling variability in the index.

Type-1 incremental fit indexes tended to underestimate their asymptotic values and overreject true models at small sample sizes. This was especially true for indexes obtained from GLS and ADF, which, therefore, are not recommended for model evaluation. Although the performance of NFI was substantially better than that of BL86 under most of the conditions, it should be used with caution when sample size is small.

In most cases, all the fit indexes obtained from ML performed much better than those obtained from GLS and ADF and should be preferred indicators for model selection and evaluation. Specifically, when the latent variates are distributed independently of one another, the following ML-based fit indexes are recommended: MCI, BFI (or RNI), CFI, BL89, and TLI (or NNFI). However, it should be noted that at extremely small sample sizes (e.g., $N = 50$), the range of TLI (and NNFI) tends to be so large that in many samples one would suspect model incorrectness and, in many other samples, overfitting (Bentler, 1990). Thus TLI (and NNFI) is less preferred when sample size is extremely small. All four types of fit indexes based on ADF, except GFI under independence, are not recommended for model evaluation when sample size is relatively small, because they tend to reject models far too frequently.

When the latent variates are dependent, most of the four types of fit indexes overreject models at a sample size of 250 or less. When $N \geq$ 250, GLS-based GFI, as well as ML-based BFI, CFI, BL89, and TLI performed relatively adequately in all seven conditions and are recommended as alternative measures of model fit when sample size is large; however, a cutoff criterion greater than .90 is required for model evaluation or selection.

Although some of the ML-based fit indexes performed extremely well under independence conditions, practitioners should be aware of the possible existence of dependence of latent variates in their data. Because the data-generating process is unknown for real data, one cannot generally know whether the independence of factors and errors, or the errors themselves, hold.

Finally, the rule-of-thumb to consider models acceptable if a fit index exceeds .90 is clearly an inadequate rule. It does not work equally well with various types of fit indexes, sample sizes, estimators, or distributions. In fact, we are hardly able to point to a condition for which it yields appropriate results.

Factors That May Affect the Magnitude of χ^2 Statistics and Fit Indexes

Previous studies and our two Monte Carlo studies revealed that factors such as sample size, assumptions regarding the independence of latent variates, and estimation methods may influence the adequacy of performance of χ^2 goodness-of-fit statistic and fit indexes. Violation of the multivariate normality assumption alone seems to exert less impact on the performance of χ^2 statistic and fit indexes.

THE EFFECT OF SAMPLE SIZE AND LATENT VARIATE DEPENDENCE

Sample size is a crucial factor in determining the extent to which currently existing model evaluation procedures can be trusted. Of course, there is the predictable effect of power (see Chapter 6). At smaller sample sizes, there may not be enough power to detect the differences between several competing models using the χ^2 statistic for model selection or evaluation. On the other hand, at larger sample sizes power is so high that even models with only trivial misspecifications are likely to be rejected.

Furthermore, the effect of sample size depends on the dependence/ independence of latent variates for some, but not all, estimators as shown by Hu et al. (1992) and Hu and Bentler (1993). Normal theory statistics such as the ML and GLS χ^2 statistics break down when the assumption of independence among common and error variates is violated. On the other hand, whereas the Satorra-Bentler SCALED χ^2 statistic continues to perform acceptably whether based on the ML or GLS estimator, its best performance under various conditions is with the GLS χ^2 correction, especially when sample size is small. Disappointingly, sample size has a substantial effect on the χ^2 statistic based on the ADF estimation regardless of the form of distribution of the observed variables. ADF can be trusted only at the largest (> 5000) sample sizes.

Sample size also has an important effect on the magnitude of many of the fit indexes. Especially when the latent variates are dependent, none of the fit indexes behaved adequately at small sample sizes. Sample size exerts greater effect on the magnitudes of fit indexes when the asymptotic assumption of independence among latent variates is violated. A substantially larger sample size is required for the fit index to behave adequately for a dependence condition than for an independence condition.

THE EFFECT OF ESTIMATION METHODS

The performance of χ^2 statistics and fit indexes varies as a function of estimation methods. The estimation method effect is greater when the latent variates are dependent on each other. For example, the χ^2 statistics based on ML and GLS are inaccurate under the dependence conditions, whereas the Satorra-Bentler SCALED test statistic proved to be relatively adequate. A substantially larger sample size is required for the χ^2 statistic based on ADF to be appropriate.

All ADF-based fit indexes behave poorly except GFI. In contrast, fit indexes obtained from ML underestimate their asymptotic values to a lesser extent. All fit indexes behave inconsistently at small sample sizes across ML, GLS, and ADF when the common and error variates are dependent on each other. When the common and error variates are independently distributed, type-2, type-3, and absolute fit indexes perform consistently across ML and GLS, whereas type-1 indexes behave erratically across ML, GLS, and ADF at small sample sizes.

Conclusions

Although our discussion has been focused on the issues regarding overall fit indexes, consideration of other aspects such as the adequacy and interpretability of parameter estimates, model complexity, and many other issues remain critical in deciding the validity of a model. Thus we conclude with a brief discussion of three additional points that are important in evaluating the validity of a model.

PENALTY OF MODEL COMPLEXITY

As noted by many researchers, for a given set of data and variables, the goodness of fit of a more complex, highly parameterized model tends to be greater than for simpler models because of the loss of degrees of freedom of the complex model (e.g., Akaike, 1987; James et al., 1982; Jöreskog & Sörbom, 1981, 1984; Mulaik, 1990; Steiger & Lind, 1980). Thus a good model fit indicated by fit measures may result from (a) a correctly specified model that adequately represents the sample data or (b) a highly overparameterized model that accounts for the fit of the model in the sample, regardless of whether there is a match between the specified model and the population covariance matrix. Jöreskog and Sörbom (1984) thus developed AGFI to adjust for the bias of fit indexes resulting from model complexity. James et al. (1982; Mulaik et al., 1989) also suggested penalizing complex models by multiplying the fit indexes by a parsimony ratio. A parsimony ratio is defined as the degrees of freedom of the target model relative to the total number of relevant degrees of freedom in the data. Akaike's (1987) information criterion was developed to adjust the statistical goodness of fit for the number of parameters estimated in the model. Based on Akaike's (1987) work, Browne and Cudeck (1989) and Cudeck and Browne (1983) developed information criterion indexes to allow researchers to select the less complex models for small sample sizes and increasingly more complex models for larger sample sizes. Mulaik et al.

(1989) described a type-2 parsimonious normed-fit index for examining the relationship among the observed variables. They also developed an incremental normed-fit index and a corresponding relative parsimony ratio to assess the goodness of fit for a nested sequence of models (i.e., a series of covariance matrix-nested models; Mulaik et al., 1989).

It may be desirable to use model parsimony in addition to other information such as the adequacy of parameter estimates, sampling variability, and violation of assumptions when selecting the "best" model from a set of alternative models.

EVALUATION OF RESIDUALS

If we consider the χ^2 test as a statistical method for evaluating models, and the fit indexes as more descriptive than statistical, it is seen that both approaches can work well and be trusted under some conditions; however, they also break down and can be misleading. If, in spite of a best attempt to work with these indexes, the researcher still has difficulty in trusting these quantifications of the extent of model adequacy, we suggest that a more traditional method also be used. This method existed in exploratory factor analysis for many years before structural equation modeling became popular: Namely, describe and evaluate the residuals that result from fitting a model to the data. It is best done in the metric of the correlation matrix, not the covariance matrix, because correlations are always in the range of +1 to −1 and, therefore, are easily interpreted. If the discrepancy between the observed correlations and the model-reproduced correlations are very small, clearly the model is good at accounting for the correlations, no matter what the χ^2 test or fit indexes seem to imply. For example, if the average of the absolute values of the discrepancy between observed and reproduced correlations is .02, it is simply a fact that the model explains the correlations to within an average error of .02. This is true whether the correlations are large or small and whether the χ^2 test is large or small. If the largest discrepancy between observed and reproduced correlations, among all the correlations, is also small, say .10, the model is only marginally wrong for some variables. Of course, if the largest discrepancy is quite large, say .40, clearly the model is not explaining some of the correlations well at all. We suggest that this descriptive information always accompany reports of model fit, to round out the more popularly used χ^2 and fit indexes. Of course, it might be that the size of such residuals also can depend on sample size and method of estimation, as has been found for the related RMR statistic (e.g., Marsh et al., 1988), but that raises another complex topic that is best left for another time.

DISCLAIMER ON MODEL MODIFICATION

Our discussion of statistical and descriptive measures of model fit assumes that the estimates of model fit are large-sample consistent estimates of their population counterpart definitions. That is, if the sample size N were to increase without limit, the statistics we have discussed would be appropriate measures of model adequacy. This condition is met when any a priori model is evaluated by the procedures described above. It is not met when procedures are used that empirically modify a model to make it look as good as possible in a particular sample. In such a case, all of the indexes discussed in this chapter will appear unduly optimistic about the quality of a model (see Bentler & Chou, 1987; MacCallum, 1986; Chapters 2 and 6, this volume).

Note

1. Their type-2 index has some definitional problems, and its proclaimed major example is not consistent with their own definition. They define type-2 indexes as $(T_T - T_B)/(E - T_B)$, where T_T is the value of the statistic for the target model, T_B is the value for a baseline model, and E is the expected value of T_T if the target model is true. Note first that E may not be a single quantity: Different values may be obtained depending on additional assumptions, such as on the distribution of the variables. As a result, the formula can give more than one type-2 index for any given absolute index. In addition, the absolute values in the formula have the effect that their type-2 indexes must be nonnegative; however, they state that an index called TLI (see below) is a type-2 index. This is obviously not true because TLI can be negative.

6 Statistical Power in Structural Equation Modeling

DAVID KAPLAN

In the standard practice of structural equation modeling, it is often the case that a proposed model is not consistent with the data as evidenced by such standard tests as the likelihood ratio χ^2. When the null hypothesis implied by the model is rejected, usually an attempt is made to modify the model. The most common strategy of model modification involves inspection of the modification index (MI; Sörbom, 1989) or, equivalently, the Lagrange multiplier (LM) test (Bentler, 1986). Sometimes these statistics are used in combination with the expected parameter change (EPC) statistic (see e.g., Kaplan, 1989a). Typically, the maximum MI or LM is employed, both indicating the largest drop in the overall value of the test statistic when the fixed parameter associated with that index is freed. If the model is not consistent with observed data, then further modifications are considered.

In addition to modifying models by freeing fixed parameters, analysts often attempt to simplify models by removing (fixing) parameters that are judged to be statistically or substantively nonsignificant. The statistical judgment to fix a parameter is typically based on a test statistic associated with the free parameter. In LISREL, the test statistic is referred to as the "T-Value" (Jöreskog & Sörbom, 1989), whereas in EQS, the square of the "T-Value" is used and is referred to as the "Wald Test" (Lee, 1985). When a parameter is fixed, the result is an increase in the overall model test statistic, and this increase is measured by the Wald test. The Wald test is known to be asymptotically equivalent to other related test statistics such as the LM and likelihood ratio (LR) tests (see, e.g., Buse, 1982; Engle, 1984; Satorra, 1989).

Regardless of how model modifications are conducted, an underlying issue that pervades model assessment is that of statistical power. Power enters into issues of model assessment in two related ways. First, an analyst may be concerned that the model was rejected because of the known sample size sensitivity of the likelihood ratio test and other asymptotically equivalent tests such as generalized least squares (see, e.g., Bollen, 1986; Chapter 5, this volume). This is a reasonable concern because, if a model fits the data perfectly, the minimum of the fitting function will be zero, and sample size will have no effect. But models never fit data perfectly and will always contain specification errors of varying magnitude. When a model contains small specification errors, large sample sizes will magnify their effects, leading to rejection of the null hypothesis. When a model contains large specification errors, small sample sizes will mask their effects, leading to acceptance of the null hypothesis. Later I will consider how one judges the size of specification errors.

A second but somewhat less recognized problem in structural equation modeling is the increase in the probability of committing Type II errors resulting from extended sequences of model modifications (see, e.g., Kaplan, 1989b; MacCallum, Roznowski, & Necowitz, 1992). Typically, the a priori specification of fixed and free parameters implied by the null hypothesis is guided by theoretical considerations. Therefore, the investigator is initially concerned with not rejecting the null hypothesis, as rejecting the null (perhaps simply because the sample size was "large") would imply that the model is wrong and that some new specification is required. The new specification, as discussed above, would be based on the sequential use of the MI or LM statistic. It can be seen then that the problem is one of inflating the probability of accepting the null hypothesis implied by the model when it is false—the probability of a Type II error. This issue is analogous to following up main effects in analysis of variance with uncontrolled post-hoc comparisons, only in that case the concern is with inflation of Type I errors. Thus, to address the problem of capitalization on chance in finding a well-fitting model, one needs to minimize Type II errors. One way to do this is to choose modifications that have maximum power. This strategy is discussed later in the chapter.

The purpose of this chapter is to present an overview of the issue of power as it pertains to the practice of structural equation modeling. Naturally, a discussion of power is intimately connected to other issues of model testing and evaluation. Thus, for completeness, the relevant literature on model testing and evaluation will need to be included (see also Chapter 5, this volume). The chapter is organized as follows. First, I discuss the manner in which power can be evaluated. I examine how power is calculated for the overall model test as well as for associated tests of individual parameters. Next, I discuss power on several restrictions simultaneously. This section will be followed by a discussion of the expected parameter change statistic, which has been suggested as useful in supplementing power evaluations and judging the size of misspecifications. Following the discussion on expected parameter change, I explore the empirical evidence on power. In this section, recent research into the factors that influence power beyond those of sample size and specification error will be discussed. This is followed by a discussion of power in multisample situations. The chapter will close with some observations on the role of power in model assessment.

Calculation of Power

To begin, it is useful to review briefly hypothesis testing, parameter estimation, and power in the structural equation modeling framework. I focus on maximum likelihood estimation for simplicity and without loss of generality. Structural equation models belong to a general class of covariance structure models of the form $\Sigma = \Sigma(\theta)$, where Σ is a population covariance matrix that can be expressed as a matrix valued function of a parameter vector θ. In the typical practice of structural equation modeling, a researcher specifies a null hypothesis, H_0, to be tested against a general unrestricted alternative hypothesis, H_1. The specification of H_0 yields a partitioning of θ into $(\theta'_{fi}, \theta'_{fr})$, where θ_{fi} and θ_{fr} are vectors of fixed and free parameters, respectively. Estimation of the parameters of the model under H_0 involves minimizing a specified discrepancy function $F(\theta) \equiv F[S, \Sigma(\theta)]$, where S is the unbiased sample covariance matrix. The most common discrepancy function is maximum likelihood (ML).

Nearly a decade ago, Satorra and Saris (1985; see also Matsueda & Bielby, 1986) recognized that the power associated with the likelihood ratio test could be obtained in a relatively straightforward fashion. Specifically, the power of the LR test is defined as $\text{Prob}\{LR > K_\alpha \mid \theta_a\}$ where K_α is the critical value of the test at a nominal significance level, α, and where the probability depends on the alternative parameter vector θ_a, which is assumed not to be far from the null hypothesis. The procedure for assessing the power of the test outlined by Satorra and Saris (1985; see also Saris & Stronkhorst, 1984) is to specify an alternative model, say H_a (to distinguish it from the unrestricted alternative H_1 above), which consists of H_0 with the implied restriction dropped and replaced with a "true" alternative value to be tested. This population covariance matrix contains the parameter estimates obtained under H_0 fixed at their estimated values plus the restriction to be tested. This covariance matrix, say $\Sigma(\theta_a)$, is tested under the original H_0 specification. If the resulting value of the test statistic differs from zero, it is because of the misspecification. The obtained value of the χ^2 test statistic corresponds to the noncentrality parameter (NCP), λ, of the noncentral χ^2 distribution. The noncentral χ^2 distribution is the distribution of χ^2 when the null hypothesis is false. With λ and the degrees of freedom of the model in hand, the power of the test can be easily obtained from tables such as those given in Saris and Stronkhorst (1984).

One disadvantage of the approach developed by Satorra and Saris (1985) is that it requires the researcher to specify an alternative value to be tested. Specifying an alternative value taken to be the "true" alternative for the purposes of calculating power may be difficult to carry out in practice. More recently, Satorra (1989) found that one could calculate power without the need for specifying an alternative value. Specifically, Satorra found that the MI could be used to approximate the noncentrality parameter for each restriction in the model. This finding was based on the known asymptotic equivalence between the LM and LR tests (see, e.g., Buse, 1982) and the fact that the MI is asymptotically equivalent to the LM test. Because there is an MI associated with each fixed parameter, a unit degree-of-freedom assessment of power can be obtained for each univariate restriction in the model. In this case, one is asking whether, for a given fixed parameter, the test is powerful enough to reject the null hypothesis, given that it is false. Satorra (1989) has shown that approximating power using the MI as the noncentrality parameter and approximating power using the Saris-Satorra procedure are asymptotically equal.

Although it is typically the case that power is assessed for restrictions in the model, it is possible to assess the power for tests of free parameters as well. Recall that for each free parameter estimated under the null hypothesis there is an associated test statistic referred to as the T-Value in LISREL and the Wald test in EQS. For each of these free parameters, the null hypothesis is, by definition, false. Therefore, the Wald test (or, equivalently, the squared T-Value) also approximates the noncentrality parameter of the noncentral χ^2 distribution and can be used to obtain a unit degree-of-freedom assessment of the power associated with the test for that parameter (Satorra, 1989). In this case, interest might center on whether a test could not reject the null hypothesis, because of a small estimated value or because of small sample size. These issues are discussed later in the chapter.

Simultaneous Power Analysis

The approaches just discussed involve examining power for a single parameter at a time. However, in multiparameter systems such as structural equation models in which there are numerous restrictions, multiple specification errors are to be expected. The aim, then, would be to evaluate power simultaneously for restrictions on many parameters. Recently, Saris and Satorra (1993) developed an approach for assessing power for many parameter misspecifications simultaneously, using what they referred to as isopower contours. They define an isopower contour as a "set of (alternative) parameter values at which the power of the test is constant" (p. 195). The procedure requires that the researcher specify the power level of interest and the probability of a Type I error. It then calculates an isopower contour via a quadratic expression for the noncentrality parameter (Wald, 1943) and provides points of low power sensitivity and high power sensitivity. Low sensitivity is represented by the major axis of the contour because the point at which the ellipse is cut by the major axis is the point farthest from the null model. Similarly, high sensitivity is represented by the minor axis because the point at which the ellipse is cut by the minor axis is the point closest to the null model.

To take an example, suppose an investigator wishes to obtain the low sensitivity points associated with high power. In this case, if the estimated point is close to the null hypothesis for that parameter (say, zero), then the test has high power because it was associated with the low sensitivity direction. By comparison, if one obtained the high sensitivity points associated with low power and found that the values were substantively far from the null hypothesis, then one would conclude that the test has low power because the points were obtained in the high sensitivity direction.

Saris and Satorra (1993) raised two important issues with respect to this procedure. First, they noted that what constitutes high and low power is a matter of judgment related to the precision of the theory under consideration. Second, they noted that for a given set of restrictions under investigation, their approach requires that the investigator be confident that the remaining restrictions are correct. They point out that their power calculations depend heavily on the validity of the remaining restrictions, unless complete separability (independence) holds for the restrictions under investigation and the remaining restrictions. Later, I discuss the issue of independence and separability as it pertains to power.

Unfortunately, isopower contours are not currently available in standard computer software packages such as LISREL or EQS. Nevertheless, Saris and Satorra (1993) indicate that all the available components are present in those software packages and could easily be implemented if so desired.

Power and Expected Parameter Change

Returning to the single parameter case, Saris, Satorra, and Sörbom (1987) found that one can approximate the size of a misspecified parameter by examining the MI for the fixed parameter and conducting a sensitivity analysis. In particular, they found that by calculating power for a variety of alternative values of the misspecified parameter and comparing the obtained noncentrality parameter associated with each value with the MI for that parameter, the size of the misspecified parameter could be approximated. They found that an examination of the MI alone might lead to freeing a parameter that was small in absolute value. In combination with a sensitivity analysis, however, they were able to determine which parameter would yield a large value if freed. Thus they argued for the importance of assessing the size of a misspecified parameter.

To estimate the size of a misspecified parameter, Saris, Satorra, and Sörbom (1987) developed an index of the expected change in the value of a parameter if that parameter was freed. Following their discussion, let θ_i be a parameter that takes on the value θ_0 (usually zero) under H_0, and let $d\theta_i = \partial \ln L(\theta)/\partial \theta_i$ evaluated at $\hat{\theta}_i$, where $\ln L(\theta)$ is the log likelihood function. Saris, Satorra, and Sörbom show that the expected change or shift in the parameter can be derived as

$$\theta_i - \theta_0 = \text{MI} / d\theta_i . \tag{6.1}$$

The proof of Equation (6.1) is given in Saris, Satorra, and Sörbom (1987). Asymptotic theory for the EPC is given in Satorra (1989). The EPC is now available in LISREL and EQS.

Saris, Satorra, and Sörbom (1987) discussed four possible outcomes that might occur using the EPC statistic. First, a large MI might be associated with a large EPC. In this case, one would be justified in freeing the parameter, especially if there is a sound theoretical rationale for doing so. Second, a large MI might be associated with a small EPC. Here, Saris, Satorra, and Sörbom argue that it does not make sense to free this parameter despite the large drop in χ^2, because the obtained parameter estimate is likely to be trivial. As is discussed later, this case can also occur because of sample size sensitivity. In the third situation, a small MI might be associated with a large EPC. In this case, the situation is ambiguous and might be due to sampling variability or the fact that the test statistic is not sensitive to this parameter. A more detailed power analysis might be necessary. Finally, the fourth outcome might be a small MI associated with a small EPC. Clearly, there would be little interest in freeing this parameter.

Clearly, the EPC statistic represents a shift of focus away from improving model fit in terms of χ^2 alone and toward removing large, and perhaps theoretically important, misspecifications. However, because the metric of the observed variables is often arbitrary, it is necessary to standardize the EPC in order to allow valid comparisons. In the context of ML estimation of path analysis models using correlation matrices, the EPC is in a standardized metric. In structural models among latent variables, however, the metric problem is not removed by simply using correlation matrices.

A standardized version of the EPC was originally proposed by Kaplan (1989a). To standardize the EPC, it is necessary to recognize that the same logic applies as when standardizing any free parameter. For a general structural equation model, standardization of the EPC requires the standard deviations of the endogenous and exogenous constructs associated with the parameter of interest. For example, using LISREL notation, the standardized expected parameter change (hereafter referred to as SEPC) associated with a fixed element of Γ (the coefficient matrix relating endogenous variables to exogenous variables), say θ_γ^{sepc}, would be calculated as $[\mathrm{Var}(\xi)/\mathrm{Var}(\eta)]^{\frac{1}{2}} \theta_\gamma^{epc}$, where $\mathrm{Var}(\xi)$ is an appropriate diagonal element of Φ and $\mathrm{Var}(\eta)$ is expressed in terms of other model parameters. It should be noted that, even though the variances of the endogenous constructs are themselves functions of other model parameters (see Chapter 2), the information is directly obtainable from the output of LISREL. Thus SEPCs for the regression of endogenous constructs on other endogenous constructs (contained in B) can be easily obtained.

Having obtained the SEPC statistic, it is possible to compare values for all fixed parameters of the model. Recently, however, Chou and Bentler (1990) noted that the SEPC proposed by Kaplan (1989a) was only partially standardized and thus sensitive to arbitrary scaling of constructs. Chou and Bentler (1990) extended Kaplan's work by offering a fully standardized version of the EPC and generalizing it to a multivariate SEPC. An empirical study conducted by Chou and Bentler (1990) demonstrated the utility of their expanded statistics.

Power-Based Model Evaluation

Recently, Kaplan (1990) argued for the evaluation of structural equation models based on power considerations. Kaplan argued that the typical approach to model evaluation in the presence of large sample sizes and specification error has been to assume that a significant χ^2 was the result of a *main effect* of sample size. The standard response has been the application of numerous alternative measures of model fit now available in structural modeling software packages. If one can rule out or explicitly model other factors that contribute to misfit such as nonnormality and/or missing data (see Allison, 1987; Muthén, 1984; Muthén, Kaplan, & Hollis, 1987), then the difficulty with the standard response is that, in the presence of misfitting models, sample size *interacts* with the degree of the specification error to affect the size of the test statistic. To again borrow from ANOVA logic, main effects cannot be unambiguously interpreted in the presence of interactions. In other words, without a clear understanding of the single cause of the misfit, the standard χ^2 statistic should be taken seriously as a sign of some complex problem with the model. This sentiment has been echoed by Saris, den Ronden, and Satorra (1987).

By taking the value of the test statistic seriously, Kaplan argued for a model modification strategy that would provide the investigator with the information needed to choose modifications with power in mind. Specifically, recall the four scenarios of model modification presented by Saris, Satorra, and Sörbom (1987) and discussed earlier. Clearly, one would want to free a parameter associated with a large MI and large SEPC, provided there is sufficient theoretical justification for doing so. After modifications of this type are exhausted, it is possible that one may be left with large MIs associated with small SEPCs. An example of this was found by Kaplan (1989a) in the reanalysis of the total sample of the Sewell, Haller, and Ohlendorf (1970) model. In this case, it could be argued that the sensitivity of the test statistic is primarily due to sample size rather than to some fundamental *internal* specification error. That is, large MIs associated with small SEPCs may be taken as an indicator of a main effect of sample size sensitivity. Continuing to free parameters in this case would lead to an increase in Type II errors.

The rationale underlying this approach rests on the fact that the EPC gives the expected size of the misspecification (i.e., the probable size of the distance between H_0 and H_a for that parameter). If specification errors are small and MIs are large, then, all other things being equal, the misfit is due to sample size sensitivity. Kaplan (1990) suggested that at this point in the modeling process an investigator may wish to use a sample size independent alternative fit index (see Chapter 5).

Three caveats were noted by Kaplan (1990) when engaging in the type of power-based model evaluation and modification outlined in this section. First, one-step modifications dictated by the MI-EPC approach have been found to change the correlational structure of the parameter estimates. The manner in which parameter estimates are correlated moderates the effects of specification error and is known to be highly model dependent (Kaplan & Wenger, 1993). This issue is discussed in more detail later. Thus one must be confident that all of the important *internal* errors have been removed before assessing the effects of sample size. Second, *external* specification errors, in the sense of omitted variables, are not addressed by this method. Theoretical developments in one's substantive area should dictate what are the appropriate set of variables. Third, what constitutes a large EPC is, naturally, a matter of judgment. The SEPC is helpful in this regard but does not replace substantive knowledge. Nevertheless, Kaplan (1990) argued that this approach to model evaluation, which takes into account specification error and sample size sensitivity, offers the user a statistically grounded, power-analysis based alternative for evaluating and modifying covariance structure models.

Studies of the Power Characteristics of
Structural Equation Models

Since the introduction of methods for calculating power for structural equation models by Satorra and Saris (1985), numerous studies have been designed to examine power characteristics of prototype models under typical conditions. Saris and Satorra (1987), for example, studied how various model characteristics affect the power approximation procedure. They found that the LR test has unequal power for the same size misspecification in different places within a model. This means that only some misspecifications will be detected. Saris, Satorra, and Sörbom (1987) replicated this finding and argued that, because the overall model test examines multiple hypotheses, only a very elaborate power study of many possible misspecifications could give enough information to draw any conclusions. A power study of that scope could become tedious for large models. Later in the chapter, I discuss the underlying mechanism that explains some of the findings of Saris and Satorra (1987).

In addition to the studies by Saris and his colleagues, Kaplan (1989c) studied, among other things, the behavior of the power for the test of single parameters as a function of different degrees of misspecification. Utilizing a Monte Carlo methodology and a prototype structural equation model, Kaplan found results similar to those of Saris and his colleagues—namely, that power depended quite heavily on the size of the misspecified parameter, the sample size, and the location of the parameter in the model.

It is not surprising to find that power is affected by the size of the misspecified parameter and the sample size. These are known to be the factors that influence power in other statistical procedures as well. What is unusual, or at least unique to multiparameter systems such as structural equation modeling, is that power depends on the location of the parameter of interest within the model. It has been suggested by Kaplan (1988, 1989a, 1989b) as well as Saris, Satorra, and Sörbom (1987) that an explanation for this phenomenon resides in the pattern of zero and nonzero elements in the estimated covariance matrix of the estimates. These patterns, which are determined by the initial specification of the model, appear to regulate the effects of specification error as well as standard errors and ultimately power probabilities. Consideration of the covariance matrix of the estimates and its role in model testing leads back to the classic study by Aitchison (1962) of asymptotically independent (AI) test statistics and separable hypotheses in restricted maximum likelihood theory. Satorra (1989) alluded to the importance of AI test statistics and separable hypotheses in the structural equation modeling setting, and Saris and Satorra (1993) noted that their isopower contour approach discussed above also depends on asymptotic independence and separability.

Recently, Kaplan and Wenger (1993) attempted to provide an empirical demonstration of the role of AI test statistics and separable hypotheses and, specifically, the role of the covariance matrix of the estimates as it pertained to specification error, power, and model modification. Kaplan and Wenger studied the problem from the viewpoint of an investigator wishing to assess, among other things, the post-hoc power associated with a test of a free parameter. In this case, the investigator would make use of the fact that the Wald test is distributed as a noncentral χ^2 statistic with 1 degree of freedom. This value, as was noted above, can be used to assess the power associated with having rejected the null hypothesis that the parameter in question is zero.

From this viewpoint, Kaplan and Wenger (1993) showed that the simultaneous test of the hypothesis that two parameters are zero (via a multivariate Wald test) would decompose into the sum of two univariate Wald tests only if the covariance between the two parameters was zero. This condition results in tests that are asymptotically independent, which in turn implies that the associated hypotheses are separable (Aitchison, 1962; Satorra, 1989).

Kaplan and Wenger (1993) extended this basic finding to testing sequences of multivariate hypotheses. They considered the case in which one may be interested in restricting two parameter vectors, say θ_1 and θ_3, on the basis of the multivariate Wald test. They allowed the parameters in θ_1 to have zero asymptotic covariance with the parameters in θ_3, yet share nonzero asymptotic covariances with the elements of some other parameter vector, say θ_2. In this case, Kaplan and Wenger found that the test statistics associated with θ_1 and θ_3 are asymptotically independent, but the value of the multivariate Wald test of the joint hypothesis that θ_1 and θ_3 are zero would not asymptotically decompose into the sum of the individual multivariate Wald test values, unless the conditions of mutual asymptotic independence held—namely, all three parameter vectors would have to have zero asymptotic covariances.

Kaplan and Wenger (1993) further noted that although AI could hold for individual parameters within and between vectors θ_1 and θ_3, a restriction in θ_1 would manifest its effects in θ_3 because of its shared nonzero covariance with θ_2. They defined *transitive hypotheses* as those hypotheses that exhibit the property of being asymptotically independent yet not separable.

The importance of the study by Kaplan and Wenger (1993) for issues of power rests on the fact that specification errors induce bias in standard errors as well as in parameter estimates (Kaplan, 1989c). Because test statistics are formed as ratios of parameter estimates to their respective standard errors, it is not surprising to observe changes in power probabilities as a result of specification error elsewhere in a model. Kaplan and Wenger (1993) empirically demonstrated this by using a prototype model and allowing two parameters to have identical true values but different correlations with a third parameter. They found that the separate restriction of the two parameters with identical true values yielded different power probabilities for the third parameter— even though the specification errors were of exactly the same magnitude. Because different parameters obviously reside in different locations within a model, the study of Kaplan and Wenger (1993) provided empirical evidence for the observations of Saris and his colleagues and of Kaplan.

Studies of Power in
Multisample Structural Equation Models

Up to now, the discussion of power in structural equation models has focused on single-sample situations. Also of interest to the applied investigator are multisample situations wherein group comparisons are desired. Studies of the power characteristics of multisample structural equation models have typically centered on the measurement part of the model—namely on power in the multiple group confirmatory factor analysis setting.

Multigroup confirmatory factor analysis (MGCFA) models have become increasingly popular tools in education and psychology. The methodology for engaging in MGCFA was originally developed by Jöreskog (1971), who provided the statistical framework for estimating and testing multigroup models. His paper also provided a strategy of hypothesis testing that proceeds from simple tests of the equality of covariance matrices to tests of increasingly restrictive hypotheses regarding the structure of the covariance matrix. MGCFA models have also been extended to estimation of factor mean differences (Sörbom, 1974, 1982).

It had been assumed for some time that testing multigroup hypotheses required invariance of factor loadings. Muthén and Christofferson (1981), however, alluded to the possibility of testing hypotheses when only some of the loadings were invariant across groups—what was termed *partial measurement invariance*. This strategy of multigroup modeling allows for the specification of separate baseline models, which may not be identical for both groups. Allowing for these differences, tests of partial measurement invariance can be conducted. Byrne, Shavelson, and Muthén (1989) have illustrated establishing baseline models and testing equality of factor covariance and mean structures under partial measurement invariance in a model of adolescent self-concept.

An issue of importance to the focus of this chapter concerns the power characteristics associated with multigroup models—particularly tests of total and partial invariance under conditions of model misspecification. In the case of MGCFA without a structure on the means, Kaplan (1989c) studied the power of the likelihood ratio test under partial measurement invariance. Using a six-variable, two-factor model with a known specification error in one group, and varying the size of the specification error and size of remaining free parameters, Kaplan found that the power of the test was dependent on the size of the misspecified parameter and the size of the free loadings, as well as on the correlation between the misspecified parameter and the parameter held invariant.

More recently, Kaplan and George (in press) studied the power associated with testing factor mean differences under violations of factorial invariance. Using the Wald test to assess the power asscociated with true factor mean differences, the results showed that power was most affected by the true differences between the factor means. Moreover, the size of the model was found to affect the power of the test, with larger models giving rise to increased power probabilities. However, the results of that study suggested that when sample sizes are equal, the approximate power of the Wald test for factor mean differences is relatively robust against violations of factorial invariance. This finding held across variations in the actual size of the factor mean differences. By contrast, when the sample sizes were unequal, large changes in the approximate power of the test were observed even under conditions of factorial invariance, with power substantially decreasing as the sample sizes become increasingly disparate. This finding was found to hold across conditions in which the group with the larger sample was associated with the larger generalized variance (positive condition), and in which the group with the larger sample was associated with the smaller generalized variance (negative condition). No major differences were observed with respect to positive or negative conditions of sample size, except that the positive condition yielded uniformly higher approximate power probabilities compared to the negative condition. Similar results were observed for the partial noninvariance case.

Two results reported by Kaplan and George (in press) can again be explained by the underlying mechanism discussed by Kaplan and Wenger (1993). The first result concerned the differentiation of the first- and second-factor means in the partial noninvariance case, and the second result concerned the direction of change in power for the total versus partial noninvariance case. With respect to the first issue, for the total noninvariance case, the covariances for the first $p/2$ loadings and the first-factor mean were found to be equal to the last $p/2$ loadings and the second-factor mean. In addition, the cross-covariances were also found to be equal. As a result, equating the loadings for both groups induced a specification error that was absorbed uniformly throughout the means, such that there was no differentiation between the first- and second-factor means. For the partial noninvariance case, the cross-covariances were not equal, thus leading to a differential absorption of the specification error and subsequent separation of the first- and second-factor mean.

With respect to the second issue, the power for the total noninvariance case was found to increase for increasing degrees of noninvariance, whereas for the partial invariance case, the opposite result was observed. For the total noninvariance case, it was observed that as the degree of noninvariance increased, the covariances between the factor loadings and factor means increased (as did the power), whereas for the partial noninvariance case, the covariances between the factor loadings and factor means decreased. It should be noted that these differences were very small and, as such, did not represent a serious constraint on the substantive conclusions of that study.

Framed in terms of decision errors, Kaplan and George (in press) showed that the marginal effect of noninvariance was to slightly decrease the probability of a Type II error. On the other hand, the marginal effect of inequality of sample size led to a dramatic increase in Type II error probabilities, even when the factorial invariance hypothesis was true. This increase appeared to be slightly greater for the negative condition case. This finding held for both the total and partial noninvariance cases. Thus Kaplan and George (in press) concluded that if the null hypothesis of equal factor means was rejected under conditions of unequal sample size, the practitioner could be fairly confident that the hypothesis is probably false. However, if the hypothesis was not rejected, the situation was somewhat ambiguous—owing to either the effect of unequal sample sizes on the power of the test, lack of substantive factor mean differences, or both.

When faced with a multisample problem, Kaplan and George (in press) advised that if sample sizes are unequal, the practitioner may wish to consider the alternative multiple indicator-multiple cause (MIMIC) model approach to multigroup modeling discussed by Muthén (1989). The MIMIC approach requires the formation of dummy variables representing group membership. Estimates of factor mean differences are obtained by regressing the factors on the dummy variables using a regression based approach to structural equation modeling (see, e.g., Muthén, 1984). One advantage of the MIMIC approach over the standard approach examined in this chapter is that it can handle cases in which the sample size in a given group may be too small to ensure stable estimates of variances and covariances. Moreover, by creating dummy variables representing group membership, the MIMIC approach allows one to consider familiar models of main effects and interactions. Kaplan and George (in press) noted, however, that the power characteristics of the MIMIC approach relative to the standard approach are, as yet, unknown. Nor is it clear how the MIMIC approach would fare when group membership is highly unequal. Thus, if the practitioner wishes to stay within the traditional multigroup modeling framework of Jöreskog (1971) and Sörbom (1974, 1982), then he or she is advised to examine the size of the factor mean differences as they pertain to the substantive aspects of the research, as well as to test the hypothesis utilizing a more liberal significance level. Of course, the choice of significance level will depend on the willingness of the researcher to commit Type I errors associated with the test of factor mean differences.

Conclusion

The purpose of this chapter was to present a general discussion of current research on power in structural equation modeling. It is clear that developments in assessing power in structural equation models have important implications for practice. Because power is intimately connected to issues of hypothesis testing and model modification, an immediate implication is that model evaluation must take place with statistical power in mind. For example, the known sensitivity to sample size of the overall goodness-of-fit test as well as single parameter tests is primarily an issue of power. Sample size is not an issue when models fit perfectly. Only when the null hypothesis is false does sample size enter into issues of goodness of fit. Even then, the role of sample size must be weighed against the size of the specification error. Small errors are magnified by large samples and visa versa. Because power is defined to be the probability of rejecting the null hypothesis when it is false, and because a false null means that the alternative is "true" (i.e., a nonzero specification error that can be approximated by the EPC), one must keep issues of power in mind when testing the fit of the model or the statistical significance of individual parameters.

Power must also be kept at the forefront when modifying a model. We have seen that sequential use of the modification index for freeing parameters can result in a capitalization on Type II errors. The modification strategy proposed by Kaplan (1990) was designed to help mitigate Type II errors by basing decisions on power associated with the proposed modifications. The same holds true for fixing parameters on the basis of the Wald test.

An important finding with respect to power is the role of asymptotically independent test statistics and separable hypotheses when evaluating the power characteristics of a model (Kaplan & Wenger, 1993). It must now be recognized that the outcome of any model modification strategy and corresponding power evaluation depends, in a fundamental way, on the initial pattern of zero and nonzero elements in the covariance matrix of the estimates. This pattern is determined once the initial specification of fixed and free parameters is assigned but can change each time the model is modified. Such changes are difficult to anticipate and suggest an unpredictability in the direction model modifications might take, because each time a parameter is restricted (or relaxed) the pattern of zero and nonzero values in the covariance matrix of the estimates changes unless mutual asymptotic independence continues to hold. Moreover, this pattern appears to interact with such factors as sample size and size of specification errors (MacCallum et al., 1992; Silvia & MacCallum, 1988). Because sample size and specification errors are factors that influence power, it is clear that power is also affected by this fundamental feature of structural equation models.

The results of Kaplan and Wenger's (1993) study have direct bearing on model modification strategies available in structural equation modeling computer software packages. For example, the current version of EQS (Bentler, 1992a; see also Bentler, 1986) allows the user to examine multivariate Wald tests in either an a priori or hierarchical a priori fashion. In the latter case, a set of parameters is tested in the order specified by the user. Kaplan and Wenger (1993) found that, unless the tests were mutually asymptotically independent (MAI), the univariate Wald tests did not sum to the multivariate Wald test. In other words, if one were to fix all parameter estimates simultaneously, the result would not be equal to that obtained by incrementally fixing the parameters unless the test statistics were MAI. A similar observation was made by Chou and Bentler (1990) in the context of univariate versus multivariate Lagrange multiplier tests.

A larger issue raised by Kaplan and Wenger (1993) concerns whether one should evaluate univariate versus multivariate Wald tests when contemplating restricting a parameter or set of parameters. The results of their study demonstrated that restrictions in a model can change the initial structure in ways that may have little to do with the substantive theory that led to the specification of the model in the first place. A multivariate approach to model modification would make it difficult to observe artifactual changes among parameter estimates, standard errors, and power probabilities resulting from lack of MAI among univariate tests. It is important to note that this argument also holds for sets of *multivariate* model modifications. That is, two or more sets of multivariate restrictions must be MAI in order to trust that changes in parameter estimates, standard errors, and power probabilities are not artifactually induced by lack of MAI. This result is true even if MAI holds within any given set of restrictions. Thus, in the unlikely event that MAI can be determined from a visual inspection of the covariance matrix of the estimates, Kaplan and Wenger (1993) advocate the more prudent *univariate sequential approach* to model modification, whereby restrictions (or inclusions) are made one parameter at a time, with careful attention paid to changes in substantively important parameters and power probabilities (see also Saris & Stronkhorst, 1984).

In conclusion, the work of Saris and Satorra (1993; Satorra, 1989; Satorra & Saris, 1985) now makes it possible for power analyses to be routinely applied to the structural equation modeling setting. The subsequent investigations by Kaplan (1989a, 1990) and by Chou and Bentler (1990) allow model evaluation and modification to be conducted within a framework that acknowledges the prominent role of statistical power within structural equation modeling. As long as investigators choose to continue to apply Neyman-Pearson hypothesis testing to structural equation models, then it must be recognized that all models are, by definition, approximations to reality, and therefore false. Under these conditions, the conclusions one draws regarding the adequacy of one's model for explaining a phenomenon are dependent on statistical power. Assessing power, therefore, must now become a routine part of establishing the statistical validity of an estimated model.

7 Objectivity and Reasoning in Science and Structural Equation Modeling

STANLEY A. MULAIK

LAWRENCE R. JAMES

There are a number of ways to interpret the meaning of a structural equation model. One way, known from ancient times as the doctrine of "saving the appearances" (Losee, 1980), is to regard a model as simply a procedure for the reproduction of some data having no substantive basis in reality. A more frequently taken alternative approach seeks to establish the objective validity of a substantive model and regards the relations between latent variables in these models as causal rather than merely predictive relations.

Our aim is to develop this alternative approach for the interpretation of structural equation models as objective representations. We shall interpret a structural equation model as a representation of an objective state of affairs that stands in causal and/or criterial relationships with the data, and thereby as a causal explanation of the data. It will not be sufficient in this framework that the structural equation model merely reproduces the data. Something more will be required: evidence supporting the assertion that the state of affairs represented by the model exists as represented, independently of the observer. In developing this approach of models as objective representations, we will argue that it is to be embedded within a conception of science as a social, normative, dialectical, and dynamically changing practice, centered on the evolving concepts of subjectivity and objectivity, which grew out of metaphors in language that made possible the idea of self-consciousness.

Understanding how to reason from empirical evidence to establish the objectivity of a structural equation model will be the major focus of this chapter; however, we will first briefly critically review some philosophical positions that have frequently been inimical to objective and causal interpretations of structural equation models to clear the way for such interpretations.

Preliminary Considerations
From Contemporary Philosophy of Science

THE LEGACY OF LOGICAL POSITIVISM

The period between 1920 and 1965 may be thought of as the era of logical positivism in Western science. Logical positivism was characterized by the verifiability theory of meaning, which held in its extreme forms that to be meaningful, propositions had to be potentially verifiable; that is, they had to be of a kind that, in principle, could be shown to be either true or false. The positivists used this theory to dismiss metaphysical, religious, and ethical propositions as meaningless, because they believed these could not be established as true or false. For positivism, there were only two kinds of meaningful propositions: (a) analytic propositions, such as tautologies, and mathematical and logical propositions, whose truth could be determined by showing that they followed logically from axioms and/or definitions and (b) empirical propositions whose truth is determined either directly by observation, known as *observation statements* (e.g., "The dial shows 190 pounds"), or indirectly by logical deduction from observation statements (e.g., "John weighs more than the average person his size"). The essential ideas of logical positivism were that (a) our knowledge of the world rests ultimately on an incorrigible foundation of self-evidently true observation statements and (b) formal logic ultimately is the medium by which scientific propositions link diverse observation statements together into scientific theories.

Although not a method unique to logical positivism, according to logical positivism, science develops by use of the hypothetico-deductive method. A hypothesis is formulated to explain some phenomenon by showing that the phenomenon follows deductively from the hypothesis. Scientists assess the validity of the hypothesis by empirically testing other deductive consequences of the hypothesis. Science also forms inductive generalizations and tests these against additional observations (Bechtel, 1988; Dancy, 1985).

Carl Hempel (1965), one of the founders of the logical positivist movement, formulated logical positivism's concept of explanation: In science, the explanation of an event is the logical deduction of the specific event from true general laws and background conditions surrounding the occurrence of the event. This form of explanation is known as the deductive-nomological (D-N) concept of explanation. (*Nomological* refers to "law.")

In Hempel's D-N formulation of explanation, the concept of causality as a form of explanation dropped out of consideration, replaced by the logical operation of material implication. Hempel's view of explanation reinforced a negative attitude held by logical positivists and their empiricist followers toward causality. British empiricism, a forerunner of logical positivism, had long regarded causality with suspicion because of Hume's (1739/1968) contention that there is no referent in experience for the causal connection. Causality had also been expelled from science early in the development of logical positivism by the physicist Moritz Schlick (1959), one of the Viennese founders of logical positivism, primarily because, he declared, physics had abandoned determinism (Mulaik, 1987). Thus formal logical deduction was the ideal explanatory form of logical positivism.

THE FALL OF LOGICAL POSITIVISM

Meaning as Use. After the middle 1950s, there developed a gradual ground swell of opposition to logical positivism. First to fall was the verifiability theory of meaning. Wittgenstein (1953), for example, argued that the meanings of propositions are not the things to which they truly or falsely refer but the manner and place in which the propositions are used in language and human social activities, with reference merely one of these uses. So, propositions can be meaningful in other ways than merely by referring to fundamental objects of experience.

Popper's Argument Against the Verifiability of Theories. The verifiability theory of meaning was further undermined by Popper's (1959) observation that theoretical propositions can never be determined to be true on the basis of experience. Most scientists using the hypothetico-deductive method proceed by formulating a hypothesis, H, and testing it against some deduced consequence, C. They seem to argue:

If H is true, then C is true.

C is true

Therefore, H is true.

But this form of argument is fallacious. The fallacy has a name: the fallacy of affirming the consequent. The explanation of the fallacy is that even if the consequence C of the hypothesis H is true, that does not establish the truth of the hypothesis. The consequence C could be true, even though the hypothesis H is false. There could be other reasons for the truth of C.

Popper rejected the verifiability theory of meaning and the verification theory of hypothesis testing. We cannot test theories in science, he argued, to establish their truth. Rather, we can only test to see whether a theory is false by showing consequences of the theory to be false. The form of the argument against a hypothesis would then be

If H is true, then C is true.

C is false

Therefore, H is false.

This is known as the logical form of *modus tollens* or denying the consequent. It is a valid form of inference.

The Falsifiability Criterion. Popper argued further that it is the mark of science to formulate potentially falsifiable propositions and put them to the test. Where propositions cannot be potentially falsified, then science is not present. Popper sought to delimit valid science from pseudoscience and other endeavors by his falsification criterion.

But Popper's falsifiability criterion itself was shown to have shortcomings when it was recognized that one cannot absolutely falsify a hypothesis by experience, either. Hypotheses in science are not tested in isolation. The deduced consequence C often depends on other auxiliary theories, $T_1, T_2, \ldots, T_k$, taken in combination with the hypothesis H. One may regard these other theories to be true (even though, as we have pointed out, they never could have been established to be true). The tests themselves also depend upon the truth of other auxiliary theories about the observing instruments and descriptions, $B_1, B_2, \ldots,$

B_m, of the setup of the experimental apparatus and of the background conditions for the experiment. Thus the inference proceeds as follows:

> If auxiliary theories T_1 and T_2 and . . . and T_k are true, and propositions B_1 and B_2 and . . . and B_m concerning experimental background conditions are true, and H is true, then C is true.
>
> C is false
>
> _____
>
> Therefore, H is false.

But this conclusion does not necessarily follow. This is also a fallacious argument. H could still be true while one or more propositions about a background condition or one or more auxiliary theories are false. It is not possible to determine from the falsity of C which premise on which it is based is false. Although many scientists accept the idea of the falsifiability criterion as essential to science, knowing its limitations, they now modify it to a weakened disconfirmability criterion, which merely presumes that auxiliary theories and background conditions are true, or on firmer ground than the hypothesis. Thus, if C is false, they will doubt first the truth of the hypothesis before doubting the auxiliary theories and background conditions.

With the inability to determine that a theory or hypothesis is absolutely true or false from experience, we have a condition known as the logical underdetermination of empirical theories from experience (Garrison, 1986).

Defeasible Reasoning. How then are we to reason about general theories using the findings of experience if our reasons for accepting or rejecting a theory do not logically entail their conclusions? Pollock (1986) argues that one of the most important discoveries of contemporary epistemology is that we can reason with *defeasible* reasons. "Such reasons," he says, "are defeasible in the sense that, while they can justify our believing their conclusions, that justification can be 'defeated' by acquiring further relevant information" (Pollock, 1986, p. 16). We take this to mean something like the following: Suppose we perform what we believe after careful empirical review is a controlled experiment to test a hypothesis. Suppose we then obtain results supportive of the hypothesis. That gives us a *prima facie* but defeasible reason to believe the hypothesis. This reason is defeasible because someone may next show empirical evidence that an extraneous variable, correlated with the experimental variable and a known cause of the dependent variable, was not controlled for. That evidence defeats the reason to accept the hypothesis, because it could be argued that this other variable caused the differences in the dependent variable, not the experimental variable. On the other hand, in this case it is not sufficient to defeat our belief in the hypothesis by raising a skeptical doubt. "How can you be sure," the skeptic might ask, "that you have not left uncontrolled an important extraneous variable?" Our answer should be, "Do you have empirical evidence for such an extraneous variable in this situation?" Positive evidence must be offered to defeat our reasons for accepting the hypothesis; however, such a treatment of skeptical doubts should not be used to turn away criticisms of the conclusions based on citing prior experience of possible extraneous variables in the given experimental situation. "Did you control for variable x?" the critic might ask, and then cite support in prior experiences for raising the question: "Variable x has turned up as an extraneous variable in similar experimental situations before." To defeat in turn this potential defeater of our conclusion, we must be able to say something like, "We considered that and found no evidence for its presence in this experiment." But even that counterevidence could be defeated by further investigation. Defeasible reasoning is a normative framework for reasoning that closely approximates the way individuals seem empirically to reason informally (Kuhn, 1991). We will shortly show that it is a form of dialectical reasoning (not to be confused with Hegel's or Marx's notions of dialectical reasoning).

The Theory-Laden Nature of Observation. Many followers of logical positivism believed that basic observation statements were simple and free of any theoretical content and hence, self-evidently true or false. This guaranteed a theory-neutral basis in experience for adjudicating between conflicting theories. But even as early as the turn of the 20th century, Gestalt psychologists had observed ambiguities in basic perception. For example, Jastrow (1900) had produced a figure that was interpreted alternatively by the same observers as both a duck and a rabbit. Wittgenstein (1953) used Jastrow's duck-rabbit to illustrate a fundamental ambiguity in interpreting experience. Hanson (1958) argued that we are taught to see what we see. Furthermore, what we see often reflects the theories we have been taught. An aquatic biologist will see in a river things a layman would overlook or ignore. A hydraulic engineer will see something else. Hanson's view was that we do not first see a theory-neutral object and then impose an interpretation upon it. Rather, we see the object directly as this or that kind of object, depending upon our training and theoretical dispositions (Bechtel, 1988).

The Empirical Underdetermination of Theories. In the early 19th century, many scientists believed science would progress by collecting masses of facts and then going over these facts to find commonalities and generalizations. For these scientists, theories were simply inductive generalizations from the particulars. They regarded induction, the process of generalizing from particulars, as a straightforward process, totally driven by experience to determine a unique generalization. Contemporary philosophy of science recognizes the ambiguity of induction, of generalizing from specific items of experience. More than one curve may be constructed to pass through a given set of points.

This can be illustrated in the mathematical and statistical realm by Figure 7.1, where one is given five data points and presented with the task of finding some curve that passes through these points to serve as a way of generalizing beyond these points. There is no unique way to fit a curve to a given set of data points (Hempel, 1965). Thus more than one mathematical theory might be formulated to represent a way of generalizing from a given set of data, and all these theories could fit the data equally well. The major implication of the underdetermination or nonuniqueness of generalizations from particulars of experience is that experience alone is not sufficient to account for our knowledge.

The Normative and Social Basis for Knowledge. The ambiguity of perception and the empirical underdetermination of theories have implied a number of things to philosophers of science. The 18th century philosopher Immanuel Kant argued that the senses are not alone responsible for what we know. The knower himself contributes *a priori* forms by which experience is to be organized and represented (Kant, 1781/ 1965). Implicit in Kant's argument is that there might be other forms by which to represent experience than those we use. Wittgenstein (1953) regarded the ambiguity of experience as an arena in which social norms regulate the way communities of individuals represent what is experienced. The implication is that social norms regulate a priori the individual's perception in ways that reduce ambiguity (Mulaik, 1993a). Because specific forms of experience have to be taught, communicated, justified, and maintained in language, he regarded *grammar*, the broad

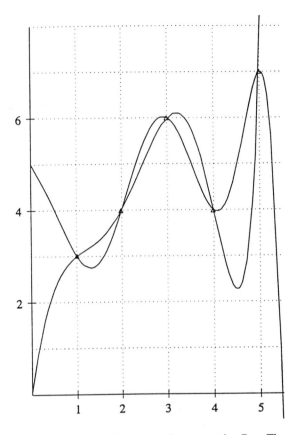

Figure 7.1. More Than One Curve May Be Constructed to Pass Through a Given Set of Points

range of social norms governing the use of language, as imposing a priori structures and constraints on the way we experience and communicate our experiences. The acquisition and justification of knowledge is thus regarded as a social process.

That knowledge is acquired and justified in a social context is another major achievement of postpositivistic science. From the introspective meditations of Descartes in the 17th century through Leibniz, Locke, Hume, and Mill, down to the logical positivists, like A. J. Ayer of the 20th century, the acquisition and justification of knowledge was seen as a personal activity the individual conducted privately. Jason (1989) characterizes this as the solipsistic concept of knowledge and contrasts it with the social concept of knowledge.

Dialogue and Dialectic. Jason (1989) regards one of the major impediments that the solipsistic concept of knowledge had on philosophical understanding was the idea that reasoning is inferential rather than dialectical (i.e., dialogue). Inference for the solipsist is regarded as a timeless activity. One lays out all of one's assertions before oneself and then proceeds to see what assertions can be deduced from the others. The inferential process drives the knower to seek premises for knowledge in incorrigible foundations such as self-evident truths or self-evident experiences. The goal is absolute truth and certainty. Dialectic, on the other hand, is an activity that is memory bound and proceeds through time between two parties, who may or may not be distinct persons (Jason, 1989). Dialectic can take place between different individuals, between the individual and nature (in asking questions of nature), and within the individual, with himself as the other party. The logic of dialectic, however, is acquired from the ethics of social dialogue and is projected inward when the individual learns to carry on a conversation with himself, or outward when treating the world of nature metaphorically, as if it is another person in being able to provide answers in response to questions. Dialectic also does not demand absolute certainty, only reasonable certainty. Pollock's (1986) defeasible reasoning, which we have already considered, does not demand absolute certainty and is a form of dialectical reasoning.

Jason (1989) argues that dialectic is the logic of discovery as well as of justification. Jason's point is to counter Popper's (1959) assertion that there is no logic to discovery in science. Popper regarded our ways of initially seeking to formulate hypotheses and theories as irrational, a subject for psychology, perhaps, but not philosophy or logic. Logic, the inferential variety, enters the picture only when we seek to justify theories and hypotheses from experience. For Jason (1989), the dialectic of science provides us with a broader logic that guides not only our processes of discovery but our processes of justifying knowledge as well. Scientists have many rational frameworks for seeking new knowledge. Descartes (1637/1901) argued one should start by analyzing a problem into its elemental, component parts. Then, one should reverse the process and seek rules of synthesis, by which the components may be combined again into the phenomenon that was to be understood. This strategy has guided many scientists to the present day. Descartes's method of analysis and synthesis is dialectic, in that it does not take place all at once. As the researcher proceeds with the method, she and/or her research community continually ask probing questions about whether she has found the elementary components, and then whether she has properly combined them to reproduce the phenomenon to be understood. Bacon (1620/1858) and Mill (1874) put forth a method of eliminative induction: To determine the underlying causes of something, consider a number of potential, hypothetical causes that are supported by being present in the phenomenon to be understood. Then, eliminate from further consideration those causes that are still present when the phenomenon itself is absent. Or eliminate from further consideration those causes that do not covary with the variation in the phenomenon. This again involves a dialectical series of questions about each of the potential causes (Jason, 1989).

No Private Rules. Wittgenstein (1953) undermined the solipsistic foundations of logical positivism as well as traditional rationalism and empiricism when he argued that there is no such thing as a private language, or as following a rule in a logically private manner. The phenomenalist who thinks he can make up a private rule to use a sign to stand for a certain private sensation is mistaken. There is no way the private individual can distinguish between seeming to be right in applying the rule and being right (Schulte, 1992). For that matter, the individual cannot distinguish between making up the rule as he goes along and using the same rule (Mulaik, 1993b). The essentially private individual has no independent way to make these kinds of distinctions, but being able to make these kinds of distinctions is essential to the use of rules in social situations. In our dialogues with other persons, others can provide independent confirmation or disconfirmation of our properly using a rule, or that we are using the same rule.

Objectivity Based on the Metaphor of Consciousness. Central to science are the concepts of subjectivity and objectivity. Mulaik (1991) drew upon the writings of Kant and Gaston Bachelard (Tiles, 1984) to describe the role the concept of an object and objectivity play in science. Mulaik held that,

> The object of knowledge is not some noumenal thing in itself which we know independently of experience, but rather is a concept which synthe-

sizes appearances in (possibly) many different sensory modes and from
many points of view in such a way that one can state the rule how each
mode and point of view reveals the object in a different and even possibly
distorted but characteristic way. (p. 96)

More recently, Mulaik (in press) described how, central to the metaphors of consciousness, the subject-object relationship is a metaphor,
derived from a bodily image schema of proprioception and its intimate
relationship with object perception. In perception, we distinguish invariants resulting from our bodily actions (proprioception) from those
invariants we ascribe to "external" objects, which synthesize diverse
views of them, so that as our bodies and heads move, we can adjust for
such movements' varying effects on our perceptions of objects.

This account of the relationship of subject to object, given as the
relationship between appearances, physical objects, and varying observational acts of the bodily subject, is itself but a metaphor for other
forms of the subject-object distinction. The self comes to "know" itself
(by reflection and through the reported observations of others) by those
acts it commonly performs in varying circumstances and their consequences. It must know how things it does or the tools it uses to observe
an object will characteristically distort what is observed, and be able to
factor out the effects of its own actions to assess the independent
existence of what it regards as an object. But what is subject and what
is object is not an absolute determination but a dynamic, changing one,
shaped and developed through social dialogue and interaction with the
world within communities of individuals. What may be objective today
may reveal a subjective aspect tomorrow, and frequently it will take one
who breaks with the constraints of an outmoded community view of
objectivity and emphasizes her own subjectivity to be able to forge a
new concept of subjectivity and objectivity for the community (Mulaik,
1991, 1993b, 1994; Tiles, 1984).

Relevance to Structural Equation Modeling

We hold that structural equation models as mathematical models
represent objective states of affairs. There is, we assert, a language for
representing objective states of affairs, the language of objects (Mulaik,
1993b, 1994). Thus mathematical models will be constrained to represent within them the grammatical features of the object language, if they

are to represent objective states of affairs. In the language of objects, we speak about objects bearing properties, of how the properties of objects cause or determine other properties of the same or other objects. Formally speaking, objects are subjects, and their properties are predicates. Whereas early 20th century logicians tended to regard properties as logically independent of other properties, it was early on recognized that, in our natural languages, properties come grouped together in families, and only one property from a family is ever assigned to an object at any one time (Wittgenstein, 1975). Thus families of properties can be represented by variables, and the assignment of a specific value to a variable in mathematics can represent the assignment of a specific property to a given object (Mulaik, 1986, 1987).

Next, we assert that causality is the relation to represent dependencies between the properties of objects in the object language. But because properties of objects are logically grouped together as the values of variables, causality takes the form of a functional relationship between variables (James, Mulaik, & Brett, 1982). Philosophers have been puzzled by how to implement causal relations in nondeterministic contexts. Simon (1977) suggested in a passing remark the way a functional relation concept of causality could be implemented in a probabilistic context. Influenced by Simon's remark, Mulaik (1986) realized that Rasch's (1960) item response model could be seen as a probabilistic causal model, in which item difficulty and subject ability jointly determine a specific probability distribution on the response variable. Varying ability or varying item difficulty varies the probability distribution of outcomes on the response variable. Thus, Mulaik (1986) concluded, in general, a probabilistic causal relation could be represented by a functional relationship between an independent variable whose values are the domain of the relation and a set of conditional probability distributions that is the range of the relation, all defined on the dependent variable. This placed probabilistic causality in the realm of Markov processes, that is, processes involving sequences of random variables, in which any particular variable is stochastically dependent only on the variable immediately preceding it, and none preceding that.

Mulaik (1986, 1993b) deduced further that if a variable x is a probabilistic cause of other variables $y_1, \ldots, y_n$, and these are observed in the absence of other causes of them, or conditional on other causes of them, at a given value x_i of the causal variable x, then a local (conditional) independence holds; that is,

$$f(y_1, \ldots, y_n \mid x_i) = f(y_1 \mid x_i) f(y_2 \mid x_i) \ldots f(y_n \mid x_i). \qquad (7.1)$$

The local or conditional independence assumption is fundamental in numerous probabilistic models (Anderson, 1959; Lazarsfeld, 1958; Lord & Novick, 1968). More recently, a generalized variant of it has been cited as the "Causal Markov condition" by Spirtes, Glymour, and Scheines (1993). It corresponds to the assumption in structural equation modeling of the independence of the disturbance variables, given all prior relevant causes of a dependent variable (Mulaik, 1986). In other words, once the exogenous causes of the system have been set to fixed values, observed values of the dependent variables vary independently over repeated observations. This condition is the analog of the condition in deterministic models of causation, which state that fixing the exogenous causes results in no change in the dependent variable once effects have stabilized.

A FACETED DEFINITION OF THE CAUSAL RELATION

Drawing upon developments of the theory of causality in James et al. (1982), Mulaik (1987) used Guttman's method of "facet analysis" (Gratch, 1973; Levy & Guttman, 1981; Shye, 1978) to analyze the concept of causality into its component concepts or "facets," then used those facets to develop a faceted definition of causality: "Causality concerns the *objective* (conception) of the manner by which the *variable* (properties) of an (object) at a specified (point) in *space* and *time determine unidirectionally* by a (functional relation) the *variable* (probabilistic, nonprobabilistic) (properties) of an (object) at a *later* (point) in *space* and *time* within a *closed, self-contained system* of *interacting* (objects), defined in connection with a specific set of *fixed background* (conditions)" (Mulaik, 1987, p. 25).

In the above definition, words in italics represent constant features of the definition for all applications of the concept. Words in parentheses stand for variables or, if more than one word is contained in parentheses, the values of variables, to indicate where the definition has freedom to be applied in numerous ways. Aside from specifying the functional relation nature of the causal relation between variables in space and time, this definition also contains or implies epistemological criteria that must be reasonably met to establish that the objective conception of some causal relation applies to some empirical situation.

BACKGROUND CONDITIONS

James et al. (1982) argued that to be objective causal models, structural equation models must reasonably satisfy a number of conditions. Mulaik (1987) believed these conditions arise from applying the functional relation concept of causality to empirical situations. Bollen (1989b) has cited a similar set of conditions. Drawing upon James et al. (1982) and Mulaik (1987), we briefly reformulate them here, adding a few conditions for thoroughness.

A Formal Statement of the Structural Equation Model as a Model of Objective States of Affairs. Objectivity first requires an explicit rule by which evidence is to be evaluated. Objective states of affairs are to be expressed in object language, that is, in terms of objects, their properties, and the causal (functional) relations between them.

Disconfirmability of the Model. To be objective, models must be disconfirmable. Just-identified models cannot be disconfirmed by tests of lack of fit because they will always perfectly reproduce the data. But just-identified models are never unique. This does not mean that there is no place for just-identified models in hypothesis testing, because they can be used as alternative models against which more constrained models are compared in tests of fit. Once a just-identified model is specified, a more constrained, disconfirmable model may be constructed from it by introducing overidentifying constraints into the model. Introducing overidentified constraints results in fewer parameters to estimate than data points available from which to estimate them. Thus estimates of parameters can be inconsistent if estimable by different aspects of the data, and this will indicate inappropriateness of the constraints. The residual data, representing the difference between the data and the reproduced data based upon the model, contains the evidence for disconfirming the model, because it is not based upon that aspect of the data used by the researcher to determine parameter estimates, which happens to be the reproduced data. The degrees of freedom of the model represent the number of dimensions in which the data are free to differ from the reproduced model and thus are a measure of the disconfirmability of the model (Mulaik, 1990).

In linear models with latent variables, at least four indicators should be introduced for each latent variable to provide for tests of the hypothesis that, among the indicators of the latent variable, there is only one common factor. The use of four or more indicators of a given latent construct using different methods of measurement establishes not only criteria for but the independence of the construct from the researcher's methods of measuring it (Mulaik, 1994). For a given set of data, models with excellent fit and more degrees of freedom are to be preferred, because such models are subjected to more conditions of disconfirmability. For models of a given hypothesis tested by different sets of data, the model to be preferred is the excellent fitting one with more degrees of freedom (Carlson & Mulaik, 1993; James et al., 1982; Mulaik, 1986, 1987, 1990; Mulaik, James, Van Alstine, Bennett, Lind, & Stillwell, 1989).

Relevant Objects. Causal relations are functional relations between the properties (either probabilistic or nonprobabilistic) of objects, and the objects in question should be explicitly identified by identifying their fixed properties (Mulaik, 1987). This practice is normally fulfilled in psychological studies by describing the attributes of the subjects chosen and by specifying the criteria for their inclusion in the study. This requirement is closely involved with a requirement for closure, because the subjects selected for study should not vary on variables related to the dependent variables of the study, unless these variables are explicitly represented in the model. Objects chosen for study should also be causally homogeneous, so that the relations among their variable attributes are accounted for by the same causal relations.

Coupling or Mediating Mechanisms. When formulating causal hypotheses, one should specify the mechanisms or media by which causal influences are transmitted to their effects. To allow for an unambiguous interpretation of negative evidence for the effect, one must show that the mechanisms or media coupling the causes to the effects are intact and uninterrupted, so that if the cause is present, the effect should also appear.

Closure and Self-Containment. The functional relation concept of the causal relation requires that for each value of the independent variable, there corresponds only one value (or one probability distribution) of the dependent variable. If a model of an experimental situation fails to represent the presence in the situation of other relevant causes of the dependent variable, then for a given value of the independent variable, there may occur more than one value (or probability distribution) of the dependent variable, and a functional relation will then not exist between the independent and dependent variable in the setting studied. This can lead to biased and misleading results. Closure is achieved in a number of ways: (a) inclusion in the model of all distinct relevant causes in the situation; (b) isolation (Bollen, 1989b), that is, shielding off the chosen independent and dependent variables from the effects of extraneous variables; (c) holding constant extraneous variables; and (d) randomization to make exogenous variables independent of other relevant causes in the system (cf. Carlson & Mulaik, 1993). Methods (b) and (c) may yield misleading results if exogenous variables interact nonlinearly with extraneous variables.

Causal Direction. A given causal model will specify which variables are independent variables, which are not, and which endogenous variables are causes of other endogenous variables by fixing causal directions between variables within a model. It is quite possible to fit models with different directions of causation to the same correlational data, and even achieve comparable fit (Lee & Hershberger, 1990; MacCallum, Wegener, Uchino, & Fabrigar, 1993; Stelzl, 1991). Specifying causal direction will be difficult and even problematic when cross-sectional data involving variables measured essentially at the same time are studied, less of a problem when selected causes clearly precede effects in time.

Stability. Causes do not always produce their effects instantly. This creates a problem of when to measure the effect in order to model the causal relationship. The reasonable solution is to measure the effect when it has achieved equilibrium in not changing further (Heise, 1975). This often requires preliminary studies to determine when effects achieve equilibrium. In some models, especially nonrecursive ones and those with random shocks, equilibrium may be impossible (Dwyer, 1983, Ch. 11).

Probabilistic Conditions. Part of any probabilistic causal model is the assumptions made about the probability distributions for the variables studied, and the concern is with the reasonableness of these assumptions in representing the reality of the situation. For example, the assumption of multivariate normality is frequently made and must be considered a part of the formal statement of a model (see Chapter 4). The reasonableness of this assumption may be challenged, and it is challenged frequently with polychotomous data. The issue then may be the extent to which assuming multivariate normality allows for a reasonable approximation to the actual state of affairs.

Linearity. Linear structural equation models assume linearity or additivity of effects. The researcher must assess the reasonableness of this assumption, if only as a first approximation. Many phenomena may not be accurately represented by linear models.

Defeasible Reasoning About Assumptions. Whether the scientific community will accept a given structural equation model as satisfying the background conditions we have described will depend upon defeasible reasoning from evidence in support of each condition. We stress the use of defeasible reasoning to counter what we feel is an unreasonable skepticism directed against the use of structural equation models. Usually the skeptical critic (e.g., Freedman, 1987) begins with a discussion of a particular application of structural equation modeling and then shows how the researcher who made the application failed to meet the assumptions of the model. Frequently, an important relevant cause was overlooked or not considered by the researcher, and the critic points this out as evidence defeating the acceptance of the researcher's model. Or linearity was assumed when general experience with the phenomenon in question suggests a nonlinear model is more appropriate. Such criticisms are legitimate criticisms of that application. But the critic does not stop there. The critic then goes on to observe that, all too frequently, many researchers do not make an effort to evaluate the assumptions of their models when testing structural equation models against their data. Again, this may be a legitimate criticism, but one that is easily dealt with by researchers making such efforts. So, to clinch his case, the critic argues for a universal defect involving all applications of structural equation modeling to a particular field X: He argues that unlike in the physical sciences, there is in field X "no reliable methodology in place for identifying the crucial variables or discovering the functional form of their relationships" (Freedman, 1987, p. 120), where X may be econometrics, sociology, psychology, or biology. The persuasiveness of this argument depends on the degree to which you believe there are, or always have been, methodologies in place in the physical sciences for this purpose, and so the physical sciences have been able to progress at a uniform, smooth rate in developing and testing their models. But that, the critic asserts, is not to be expected in a social science like field X. Hence, because to apply structural equation modeling requires meeting certain difficult-to-assess assumptions in field X, its usefulness is dubious in that field. Against such criticisms one might argue that anyone who knows the history of the various physical sciences, especially chemistry, knows that these fields initially had difficulties in identifying the crucial variables and discovering the functional forms of relationships, but this did not deter the formulation, testing, and criticism of models. The presumption of such criticisms is that, because we generally know abstractly what the general formal requirements are for applying a causal model to experience, we should be able to tell in any application of such models whether *all* these assumptions are satisfied and, if we cannot, we should not use the model. But that is not the way we reason with experience. We approach experience dialectically, that is, with imperfect knowledge about our assumptions, and gather evidence for or against our models gradually over time, while debating among ourselves as we go along as to whether we have or have not properly met our assumptions. To defeat our models, we demand positive empirical evidence of lack of fit, or of the inappropriateness of our background assumptions, and regard purely skeptical doubts as irrelevant. Our reasoning is to defeasible conclusions rather than to absolute certainties like those given in mathematics.

Evaluating Structural Equation Models With Nested Sequences of Models. In testing a model, it is important to do so in a way that allows the researcher to isolate where lack of fit arises within a model. James et al. (1982) recommended using the following nested sequence of models for this purpose:

1. *The measurement model.* This is a confirmatory factor analysis model that treats the latent variables of the structural equation model as common factors with no constraints on the correlations among the factors. This model tests the measurement assumptions, relating the indicators of the structural equation model to the latent variables. If this model does not obtain satisfactory fit, there is no point in proceeding to test the structural model until proper measurement of the latent variables is achieved.

When a measurement model fails to fit, the researcher has a number of options: (a) Use modification indexes to identify fixed parameters that may be freed to achieve improved fit. This should be done cautiously and accompanied with explicit reasons justifying why freeing

the parameter produces a meaningful result (see Chapter 2). This may
be done most innocently when freeing up zero pattern loadings. It is far
more dangerous to free zero covariances among disturbance variables
without independent evidence for the causes of such covariances, because this violates the condition of local independence. (b) Perform an
exploratory common factor analysis of the indicator variables to determine if additional latent variables are required. Reformulate the measurement model in a way that reflects how many degrees of freedom
were lost in performing the less constrained exploratory analysis. (c) If
these procedures fail to get reasonable fit for a measurement model, the
researcher is urged to construct new indicators, obtain new data, and
perform new confirmatory analyses until adequate fit is obtained.

2. *The structural equation model.* This is the model one sought to
study in the first place. It differs from the measurement model in
introducing additional constraints on the relations among the latent
variables. One wants this model to fit. If it does not, one can again
consider freeing up the structural coefficients, but only of those relating
latent variables to other latent variables. Remember, you lose one
degree of freedom for each parameter freed, implying that one less
condition will be tested in the ultimate model. There is no guarantee
that this process will produce a realistic model.

3. *The uncorrelated factors model.* This is a confirmatory factor
analysis model, just like the measurement model, but with the latent
variables constrained to be uncorrelated. This provides a simultaneous
test that the parameters corresponding to free structural parameters
relating latent variables to other latent variables are all zero. One wants
to reject this model. The aim is to establish that what one has regarded
as free parameters are also nonzero parameters. Remember that freeing
a parameter does not imply that it is nonzero. Alternatively, one can
perform tests individually on each of the free structural parameters,
using the standard errors of the parameter estimates given in the estimation process. If the uncorrelated factors model fits, it means there
are no causal relations among the latent variables, and you are allowed
to go on to test the next model.

4. *The null model or uncorrelated variables model.* This model is
estimated primarily to provide goodness-of-fit indexes, based upon the
lack of fit of this model as a baseline of "worst fit" (see Chapter 5). If
the uncorrelated factor model was accepted, this allows one to test
whether there is any relationship between the indicators and the common factors. Again, one hopes to reject this model. The difference in

lack of fit between this model and a saturated model that fits the data perfectly represents relations among the variables not accounted for by the uncorrelated variables model, which must be accounted for by some less constrained model.

Conclusion

Reasoning about structural equation models takes place within the framework of general philosophical assumptions. We briefly considered several philosophical frameworks such as logical empiricism, Popper's falsificationism, and several recent epistemologies that stress the dialectic nature of reasoning with experience. We favor the more recent epistemologies and provide arguments against these other positions because they are often the basis for criticisms and misunderstandings of the use of structural equation modeling. We also argued that causal models involve more specific assumptions about the nature of causal relations. Causal relations concern the varying properties of objects, and norms of the language of objects for the representation of properties group the properties into sets of mutually exclusive properties known as variables. In a deterministic world, causal relations thus take the form of functional relations between variables, but in a probabilistic world, they take the form of functional relations, in which independent variables determine probability distributions by which values of dependent variables occur. The grammar of the language of objects and the functional relationship form of causal relations together imply certain general conditions, known as background assumptions, that must be met when formulating and testing a causal model. Reasoning about causal models involves, in turn, reasoning about whether these background assumptions are met; however, we remind researchers that our reasoning about how the formal properties of our causal models are satisfied in experience proceeds dialectically through time or defeasibly, rather than axiomatically and deductively. We also described a nested sequence of models to consider when evaluating a given structural equation model, so that one can determine whether measurement assumptions are met before testing theories about relationships among latent constructs dependent on satisfying those assumptions, as well as isolate where lack of fit arises in structural equation models.

8 One Application of Structural Equation Modeling From Two Perspectives

Exploring the EQS and LISREL Strategies

BARBARA M. BYRNE

This past decade has seen rapid growth in the application of structural equation modeling (SEM) to data representing a wide array of disciplines. (For reviews of applications and papers related to medical and marketing research, e.g., see Bentler & Stein, 1992, and Bagozzi, 1991, respectively.) Keeping pace with this research activity has been the ongoing development and improvement of related statistical software packages. Although there are now several computer programs designed for the analysis of structural equation models (e.g., CALIS, SAS Institute, 1991; COSAN, McDonald, 1978; EZPATH, Steiger, 1989; LISCOMP, Muthén, 1988), two stand apart from the rest in terms of their popularity and widespread use. I refer, of course, to the EQS (Bentler, 1992a) and LISREL (Jöreskog & Sörbom, 1993b, 1993c) programs.

Although EQS and LISREL both address the same issues related to SEM, they do so in sometimes subtle, albeit sometimes blatantly different, ways. The purpose of this chapter is to demonstrate a few of the dual approaches to the analysis of covariance structures as they relate to the same model and based on the same data. More specifically, using both the EQS (version 4) and LISREL 8 (including PRELIS 2) programs, I illustrate how to (a) test for the validity of a second-order factor analytic model separately for each of two groups; (b) given findings of inadequate fit, conduct post-hoc model-fitting to pinpoint sources of misfit, followed by respecification and reestimation of the model; and (c) test for its invariance across the groups. Additionally, given the known kurtotic nature of the present data, I also describe the two conceptually different approaches taken by EQS and LISREL in addressing such nonnormality. Because space limitations necessarily preclude elaboration of basic principles and procedures associated with both SEM and the two statistical packages, readers are referred to Byrne (1989, 1994) for a nonmathematical approach to understanding these processes.

The Data

Data to be used in this chapter are adapted from a study by Byrne, Baron, and Campbell (1993) and comprise scores on the Beck Depression Inventory (BDI; Beck, Ward, Mendelson, Mock, & Erbaugh, 1961) for 730 adolescents (grades 9-12) attending the same high school in Ottawa, Canada. Listwise deletion of data that were missing completely at random (Muthén, Kaplan, & Hollis, 1987) resulted in a final sample size of 658 (males, $n = 337$; females, $n = 321$).

The BDI is a 21-item scale that measures symptoms related to cognitive, behavioral, affective, and somatic components of depression. Although originally designed for use by trained interviewers, it is now most typically used as a self-report measure (Beck, Steer, & Garbin, 1988). For each four-point Likert-scaled item, respondents select the statement that most accurately describes their own feelings; higher scores represent a more severe level of reported depression.

The study providing the basis for our work here is one of a series conducted by Byrne and Baron (1993, 1994; Byrne, Baron, & Campbell, 1993, 1994; Byrne, Baron, Larsson, & Melin, 1993a, 1993b) in validating a higher-order factor structure of the BDI for nonclinical adolescents. Their research has demonstrated strong support for a second-order structure consisting of one higher-order general factor of depression and three lower-order factors that they labeled Negative Attitude, Performance Difficulty, and Somatic Elements. In the present chapter, we examine this structure as it applies to males and females. Let us turn now to a more detailed view of the model under study.

The Hypothesized Model

The postulated model of BDI factorial structure is portrayed in Figure 8.1 (pp. 142-143) in terms of both EQS and LISREL notation. It represents a typical covariance structure model and can therefore be decomposed into two submodels—a structural model and a measurement model (see Chapter 1). The *structural model* defines the pattern of relations among the unobserved factors and is typically identified in schematic diagrams by the presence of interrelated ellipses, each of which represents a hypothetical construct (or factor). Turning to Figure 8.1, we see a hierarchical ordering of ellipses such that if the page were turned sideways, the "Depression" ellipse would be on top, with the three smaller ellipses beneath it. Let us now review this diagram in terms of both EQS and LISREL lexicon.

Figure 8.1 can be interpreted as representing one second-order factor (Depression: F4; ξ_1), and three first-order factors (Negative Attitude: F1; η_1; Performance Difficulty: F2; η_2; Somatic Elements: F3; η_3). The single-headed arrows leading from the higher-order factor to each of the lower-order factors (F1,F4; F2,F4; F3,F4; γ_{11}, γ_{22}, γ_{33}) are regression paths that indicate the prediction of Negative Attitude, Performance Difficulty, and Somatic Elements from a global Depression factor; they represent the second-order factor loadings. Finally, the angled arrow leading to each first-order factor (D1, D2, D3; ζ_1, ζ_2, ζ_3) represents residual error in the prediction of the Negative Attitude, Performance Difficulty, and Somatic Elements factors from the higher-order factor of Depression.

The *measurement model* defines relations between observed variables and unobserved hypothetical constructs. In other words, it provides the link between item scores on an assessment instrument and the underlying factors they were designed to measure. The measurement model, then, specifies the pattern by which each item loads onto a particular factor. This submodel can be identified by the presence of rectangles, each of which represents an observed score. Turning to Figure 8.1 again, we see that each rectangle represents an observed score for one BDI item. The single-headed arrows leading from each first-order factor to the rectangles (V1-V21; λ_{11}-$\lambda_{21,3}$) are regression paths that link each of the factors to their respective set of observed scores; these coefficients (V,Fs; λs) represent the first-order factor loadings. For example, Figure 8.1 postulates that items 16, 18, 19, and 21 load onto the Somatic Elements factor. Finally, the single-headed arrow pointing to each rectangle (E1-E21; ε_1-ε_{21}) represents observed measurement error associated with the item variables.

One important omission in Figure 8.1 is the presence of double-headed arrows among the first-order factors thereby indicating their intercorrelation. This is because in second-order factor analysis, all covariation among the first-order factors is explained by the second-order factor.

Expressed more formally, the CFA model portrayed in Figure 8.1 hypothesized a priori that (a) responses to the BDI could be explained by three first-order factors and one second-order factor of General Depression, (b) each item would have a nonzero loading on the first-order factor it was designed to measure and zero loadings on the other two first-order factors, (c) error terms associated with each item would be uncorrelated, and (d) covariation among the three first-order factors would be explained fully by their regression onto the second-order factor.

Assessment of Model Fit

The focal point in analyzing structural equation models is the extent to which the hypothesized model "fits" or, in other words, adequately describes the sample data (see Chapter 5). This assessment entails a number of criteria, some of which bear on the fit of the model as a whole and others on the fit of individual parameters. Traditionally, overall model fit has been based on the χ^2 statistic; however, given the known sensitivity of χ^2 to variations of sample size, numerous alternative indexes of fit have been proposed and evaluated (for reviews, see Gerbing & Anderson, 1993; Marsh, Balla, & McDonald, 1988; Tanaka, 1993; Chapter 5, this volume). Certain of these criteria, commonly referred to as "subjective," "practical," or "ad hoc" indexes of fit, are now commonly reported as adjuncts to the χ^2 statistic. I turn now to a review of these as they relate to each of the two programs. (Although both programs yield statistics related to the residual matrix, these are not included here.)

EQS ANALYSES

EQS provides several goodness-of-fit indexes that address statistical and practical fit, as well as model parsimony. First, it yields a χ^2 statistic

EQS

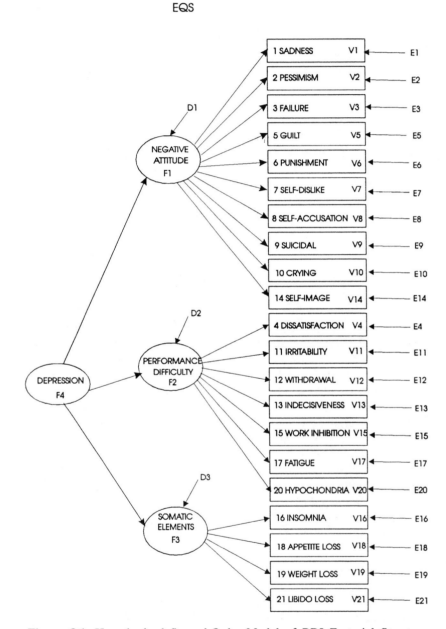

Figure 8.1. Hypothesized Second-Order Model of BDI Factorial Structure Expressed in Both EQS and LISREL Notation

LISREL

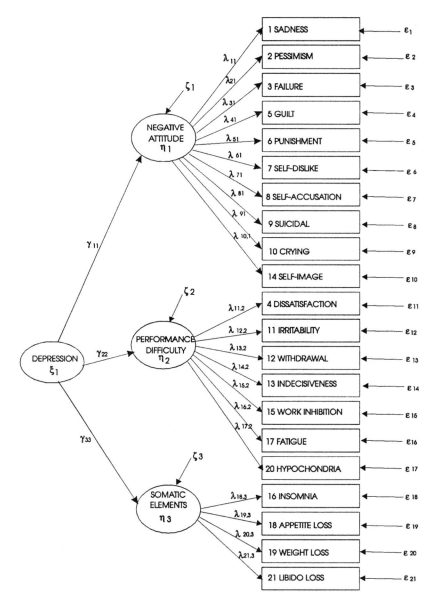

Figure 8.1. Continued

for both the hypothesized and independence models; the latter argues for complete independence of all variables (in this case, items) in the model. EQS also provides an optional statistic called the SCALED χ^2 statistic (Satorra & Bentler, 1988a, 1988b). This statistic incorporates a scaling correction for the χ^2 statistic when distributional assumptions are violated.

Practical indexes of fit include the normed and nonnormed fit indexes (NFI, NNFI; Bentler & Bonett, 1980) and the comparative fit index (CFI; Bentler, 1990), a revised version of the NFI that overcomes the underestimation of fit in small samples (i.e., given a correct model and small sample, the NFI may not reach 1.0, Bentler, 1992a). Although these three indexes of fit are provided in the EQS output, Bentler (1992b) recommends the CFI to be the index of choice. Values for both the NFI and CFI range from 0 to 1 and are derived from the comparison of a hypothesized model with the independence model; each provides a measure of complete covariation in the data, with a value greater than .90 indicating an acceptable fit to the data (cf. Chapter 5). The NNFI was originally designed to improve the NFI's performance near 1. However, because NNFI values can extend beyond the 0-1 range, evaluation of fit is not as readily discernible as it is with the standardized indexes.

Finally, to address concerns of parsimony related to model fit, EQS provides for the evaluation of both the independent and the hypothesized models based on Akaike's (1987) information criterion (AIC) and Bozdogan's (1987) consistent version of the AIC (CAIC); these criteria take goodness of fit as well as number of estimated parameters into account.

LISREL ANALYSES

Versions of the program up to and including LISREL 7 included as standard output three indexes of model fit—the χ^2 statistic for the hypothesized model, the goodness-of-fit index (GFI); an index of the relative amount of variance and covariance jointly explained by the model; and the adjusted GFI (AGFI), which takes into account the number of degrees of freedom in the model (see Chapter 5). In the most recent version (LISREL 8), however, the amount of model-fit information provided in the standard output has been increased dramatically to include all the goodness-of-fit measures that have been addressed in the literature (Jöreskog & Sörbom, 1993b); in total, 32 evaluation criteria are reported. In this chapter, assessment of model fit for the EQS example, as it relates to single-sample analyses, is based on the SCALED χ^2 statistic and CFI*, an analog of the CFI that is computed from SCALED χ^2 instead of χ^2 values (the SCALED χ^2 is not yet available for multigroup analyses); the LISREL example is based on the χ^2 statistic and the CFI.

Preliminary Analyses

These analyses are an essential prerequisite to SEM for several reasons. First, it is important to know if there are missing data and, if so, the reason why they are missing. Given a sufficiently large sample size and data that are missing completely at random (Muthén et al., 1987), listwise deletion is usually recommended when working with SEM. Second, one critically important assumption of SEM is that the data are multivariately normal. The extent to which they are not bears on the validity of findings. Although it is unlikely that the maximum likelihood estimates would be affected, nonnormality could lead to downwardly biased standard errors that would result in an inflated number of statistically significant parameters (Muthén & Kaplan, 1985; Chapter 4, this volume). Finally, cases exhibiting extreme values of multivariate kurtosis can serve to deteriorate model fit. It is therefore important to identify and delete these outliers from the analyses.

Let us now examine sample statistics related to the present data; as noted earlier, the data are complete for both sexes.

EXAMINATION OF SAMPLE STATISTICS

EQS Analyses. When raw score data are used as input, EQS automatically provides univariate as well as several multivariate sample statistics; further insight can be obtained through descriptive analyses and the many graphical features now available in the new Windows version (Bentler & Wu, 1993) of the program. The *univariate* statistics represent the mean, standard deviation, skewness, and kurtosis. As expected from previous work in this area (Byrne & Baron, 1993, 1994; Byrne, Baron, & Campbell, 1993, 1994; Byrne et al., 1993a, 1993b), several BDI items were found to be severely kurtotic; values ranged from 0.19 to 39.40 (M = 4.93) for males and from 0.15 to 10.43 (M = 1.92) for females.

The *multivariate* statistics reported by EQS represent variants of Mardia's (1970) coefficients of multivariate kurtosis; two reported values bear on normal theory and two on elliptical theory. For adolescent males, the normalized estimate of Mardia's coefficient was 68.51, whereas for adolescent females, it was 39.49; both are distributed in very large samples from a multivariate normal population as a normal variate so that large positive values, as shown here, indicate significance.

At this time, EQS is unique in its ability to identify multivariate outliers. The program automatically prints out the five cases contributing most to Mardia's multivariate kurtosis coefficient. Identification of an outlier is based on the estimate presented for one case relative to those for the other four cases; there is no absolute value upon which to make this judgment, and it is possible that none of the five cases is actually an outlier; this was the case here for both adolescent males and adolescent females.

LISREL Analyses. Preliminary analyses for LISREL are performed via its companion package, PRELIS. As with EQS, the input of raw data that represent continuous variables allows for the reporting of univariate statistics representing the mean, standard deviation, skewness, and kurtosis. The standard output for ordinal variables, of course, differs substantially from the output for continuous variables. Although the present data are technically of ordinal measurement, they are treated as if they were continuous for purposes of consistency with the EQS analyses as well as those of the original study. (Although EQS/Windows provides for the analysis of categorical variables, the current version of the program requires a limit of 20 variables.)

In addition to reporting the minimum and maximum frequency values (information that is also presented in bar chart form), PRELIS 2 also provides for single tests of zero skewness and kurtosis, as well as for an omnibus test of these two moments in combination; the single skewness and kurtosis tests are reported as z-statistics, and the omnibus test as a χ^2 statistic.

For all continuous variables jointly, PRELIS 2 similarly tests for multivariate normality. (For an extensive discussion of these tests, see Bollen, 1989b.) Tests for multivariate normality related to the present data revealed the following statistics for skewness (males, z = 84.56; females, z = 61.36), kurtosis (males, z = 35.99; females, z = 25.42), and for third and fourth moments considered jointly (males, $\chi^2[2, N = 337]$ = 8445.74; females, $\chi^2[2, N = 321]$ = 4410.81).

TREATMENT OF NONNORMALITY

An important assumption underlying SEM is that the data are multivariate normal. Violation of this assumption can seriously invalidate statistical hypothesis-testing such that the normal theory test statistic may not reflect an adequate evaluation of the model under study (Browne, 1982, 1984a; Hu, Bentler, & Kano, 1992; Chapter 4, this volume). One approach to resolution of the problem has been the development and use of asymptotic (large-sample) distribution-free (ADF) methods for which normality assumptions are not required (Browne, 1982, 1984a). (For an extensive discussion of other solutions to the problem, see Bollen, 1989b.) This is the approach embraced by LISREL in dealing with data that are nonnormal. The strategy involves a two-step process. First, using PRELIS, the researcher recasts the data into asymptotic matrix form. LISREL analyses are then based on this matrix using weighted least squares (WLS) estimation. Nonetheless, Jöreskog and Sörbom (1988) note that the question of whether or not this approach is superior to one that uses maximum likelihood (ML) or general least squares (GLS) estimation is still open to conjecture; furthermore, the question of how nonnormal the data must be before this process is implemented has not yet been resolved.

One major limitation associated with this treatment of nonnormality has been its excessively demanding sample size requirement. As a consequence of a major change in the storage and computation of asymptotic covariance matrices using PRELIS 2, however, the sample size restriction is now somewhat less stringent. Nevertheless, users are still cautioned that the minimum sample sizes specified by the program (for a covariance matrix, $k(k + 1)/2$, where k equals the number of variables) offer no guarantee of good estimates of the asymptotic covariance matrix (Jöreskog & Sörbom, 1993c).

Recently, however, Bentler and associates (Chou, Bentler, & Satorra, 1991; Hu et al., 1992) argued that it may be more appropriate to correct the test statistic rather than use a different mode of estimation. As such, Satorra and Bentler (1988a, 1988b) developed the SCALED χ^2 statistic, which incorporates a scaling correction for the χ^2 statistic when distributional assumptions are violated; its computation takes into account the model, the estimation method, and the sample kurtosis values. From a Monte Carlo study of six test statistics under seven distributional conditions, Hu et al. (1992) reported the SCALED χ^2 to be the most reliable. This is the approach taken by the EQS program in the treatment of nonnormal data. In contrast to LISREL, then, EQS uses an estimation method that assumes the data are multivariate normal but bases evaluation of model fit on a test statistic that has been corrected to take nonnormality into account.

Testing the Hypothesized Model
of BDI Structure

A summary of selected fit indexes for both the EQS and LISREL analyses is presented in Table 8.1. Results are reported both for analyses that took the nonnormality of the data into account and for those based on normal theory estimation (i.e., data were considered to be normally distributed). ML estimation was used for all analyses except those based on nonnormal data using LISREL 8; the latter were based on ADF estimation as recommended by Jöreskog and Sörbom (1988). Not unexpectedly (see Hu et al., 1992; Jöreskog & Sörbom, 1988), the LISREL model-fitting results based on ADF estimation are somewhat at odds with the findings based on ML estimation. Although the basic pattern is similar, the χ^2 (as a measure of badness of fit) and CFI (as a measure of goodness of fit) values are excessively high. One possible explanation of the latter may lie with the enormous χ^2 value for the highly misspecified independence model; this of course, would lead to an inflated CFI value. Interpretation of findings, then, are therefore limited to the ML estimates and are based on the SCALED χ^2 and CFI* for EQS, and on the χ^2 and CFI for LISREL.

As indicated by the CFI* (EQS) and CFI (LISREL) values reported in Table 8.1, goodness of fit for the initially hypothesized model of BDI structure was exceptionally good for males; it was somewhat less so for females. However, before turning to the problematic fit for adolescent females, let us first complete our evaluation of the hypothesized model for adolescent males by assessing the fit of individual parameters in the model. For both EQS and LISREL, there are two aspects of concern here: (a) the appropriateness of the estimates and (b) their statistical significance. Any differences between the two programs are noted later in the discussion of these criteria.

TABLE 8.1 Summary of Goodness-of-Fit Statistics for Adolescent Males and Females

Model	df	Nonnormality Taken Into Account				Nonnormality Not Taken Into Account			
		EQS[a]		LISREL[b]		EQS[a]		LISREL[a]	
		SCALED χ^2	CFI*	χ^2	CFI	χ^2	CFI	χ^2	CFI
Males									
0 Null[c]	210	906.13		NA		NA		NA	
1 Hypothesized	187[d]	224.62	.95	465.66	.98	306.50	.92	306.49	.91
Females									
0 Null	210	1136.75		NA		NA		NA	
1 Hypothesized	187[d]	266.66	.91	667.11	.95	340.16	.88	340.16	.88
2 Model 1 with covariance between items 20 and 21	186	NA	NA	663.63	.95	NA	NA	316.80	.90
3 Model 2 with item 20 cross-loaded on F1	185	235.33	.95	650.57	.95	296.07	.92	296.07	.92
4 Model with item 20 loaded on F1 instead of F2	186	236.52	.95	650.82	.95	297.69	.92	297.69	.92

NOTE: F1 = Factor 1 (Negative Attitude); F2 = Factor 2 (Performance Difficulty)
NA = Not Applicable.
a. Based on maximum likelihood estimation.
b. Based on the large-sample asymptotic matrix with weighted least squares estimation.
c. Required for calculation of CFI*.
d. Disturbance terms associated with F2 and F3 constrained equal for purposes of statistical identification.

149

FEASIBILITY OF PARAMETER ESTIMATES

The first step in assessing the fit of individual parameters is to determine the plausibility of their estimated values. Any estimates falling outside the admissible range signal that either the model is wrong or the input matrix lacks sufficient information. Examples of parameters exhibiting unreasonable estimates are (a) correlations greater than 1.0, (b) standard errors that are abnormally large or small (a standard error approaching zero usually results from the linear dependence of the related parameter with some other parameter in the model; such a circumstance renders testing for the statistical significance of the estimate impossible), and (c) negative variances. Whereas LISREL permits these estimates to be printed, EQS prevents their estimation by constraining the value of the offending parameter to zero; the message "PARAMETER XX,XX CONSTRAINED AT LOWER BOUND" will appear on the output.

STATISTICAL SIGNIFICANCE OF PARAMETER ESTIMATES

The test statistic here represents the parameter estimate divided by its standard error; as such, it operates as a z-statistic in testing that the estimate is statistically different from zero. Based on an α level of .05, then, the test statistic needs to be greater than 1.96 in absolute value before the hypothesis (that the estimate equals 0) can be rejected. LISREL 7 and its predecessors referred to these values as "T-values." The output for LISREL 8, however, is consistent with that of EQS in reporting these test statistics, and their standard errors, immediately under each parameter estimate. One additional difference between the two programs is that if the EQS user requests robust statistics (i.e., SCALED χ^2), the output will report two sets of test statistics and standard errors—one for the original and one for the corrected χ^2 statistics.

For purposes of comparison across programs and estimation processes, EQS and LISREL estimates are presented in Table 8.2. In consideration of space, however, only the first-order factor loading estimates are reported, and only as they pertain to adolescent males. With respect to the previous point, note that although the ML estimate (under normal theory) for item 19 was significant, it was not so when multivariate kurtosis was taken into account by the robust statistics reported by the EQS program.

TABLE 8.2 Summary of EQS and LISREL First-Order Factor Loading Estimates for Adolescent Males

| | Nonnormality Taken Into Account | | | | | | Nonnormality Not Taken Into Account | | | | | |
| | EQS[a] | | | LISREL[b] | | | EQS[a] | | | LISREL[a] | | |
BDI Item	F1	F2	F3	F1	F2	F3	F1	F2	F3	F1	F2	F3
1	1.00			1.00			1.00			1.00		
2	1.08			0.90			1.08			1.08		
	(.14)			(.06)			(.12)			(.12)		
3	1.10			0.82			1.10			1.10		
	(.18)			(.06)			(.12)			(.12)		
5	0.87			0.76			0.87			0.87		
	(.15)			(.05)			(.10)			(.10)		
6	1.06			1.04			1.06			1.06		
	(.02)			(.09)			(.15)			(.15)		
7	1.16			1.00			1.16			1.16		
	(.13)			(.05)			(.12)			(.12)		
8	1.30			1.10			1.30			1.30		
	(.18)			(.07)			(.14)			(.14)		
9	0.79			0.72			0.79			0.79		
	(.16)			(.06)			(.10)			(.10)		
10	0.71			0.87			0.71			0.71		
	(.15)			(.10)			(.18)			(.18)		
14	0.90			0.72			0.90			0.90		
	(.18)			(.07)			(.12)			(.12)		
4		1.00			1.00			1.00			1.00	
11		0.61			1.07			0.61			0.61	
		(.14)			(.15)			(.14)			(.14)	
12		0.67			0.87			0.67			0.67	
		(.12)			(.08)			(.09)			(.09)	
13		1.01			1.50			1.01			1.01	
		(.12)			(.12)			(.13)			(.13)	
15		0.82			1.10			0.82			0.82	
		(.10)			(.11)			(.11)			(.11)	
17		0.80			0.92			0.80			0.80	
		(.10)			(.09)			(.11)			(.11)	
20		0.67			0.80			0.67			0.67	
		(.12)			(.08)			(.10)			(.10)	
16			1.00			1.00			1.00			1.00
18			1.13			0.46			1.13			1.13
			(.27)			(.06)			(.26)			(.26)
19			0.28[c]			0.16			0.28			0.28
			(.15)			(.03)			(.12)			(.12)
21			0.58			0.12			0.58			0.58
			(.29)			(.01)			(.14)			(.14)

NOTE: F1 = Factor 1 (Negative Attitude); F2 = Factor 2 (Performance Difficulty); F3 = Factor 3 (Somatic Elements). Standard errors in parentheses.
a. Based on maximum likelihood estimation.
b. Based on the large-sample asymptotic matrix with weighted least squares estimation.
c. Not significant.

Post-Hoc Model-Fitting
to Establish Baseline Models

When a hypothesized model is tested and the fit found to be inadequate, it is customary to proceed with post-hoc model-fitting to identify
misspecified parameters in the model. If multigroup equivalence is of
interest, it is particularly important that a baseline model be established
for each group separately before testing for their invariance across
groups. This model represents one that is most parsimonious as well as
statistically best fitting and substantively most meaningful. Identification of misspecified parameters differs substantially between the EQS
and LISREL programs. Whereas EQS takes a multivariate approach
based on the Lagrange multiplier test (LM test), the LISREL approach
is univariate and is based upon the modification index (MI). Nonetheless, the objective of both tests is to determine if a model that better
represents the data would result with certain parameters specified as
free, rather than fixed, in subsequent runs.

Before putting these techniques into practice, however, one vitally
important caveat needs to be stressed with respect to use of both the
LM test and MIs in the respecification of models. It bears on two
factors: (a) that both techniques are based solely on statistical criteria
and (b) that virtually any fixed parameter (constrained either to zero or
to some nonzero value) is eligible for testing. Thus it is critical that the
researcher pay close heed to the substantive theory before relaxing
constraints as may be suggested by both the LM test and MI statistic;
model respecification in which certain parameters have been set free
must be substantiated by sound theoretical rationale (MacCallum, 1986;
Chapter 2, this volume).

Let us now return to the problematic fit of BDI structure for adolescent females and examine these differential post-hoc model-fitting
procedures within the context of the two statistical packages.

EQS ANALYSES

Examination of the multivariate LM χ^2 values related to the initially
hypothesized model (Model 1) for females revealed substantial improvement in model fit to be gained from the additional specification
of an error covariance between items 21 and 20, LM $\chi^2(1, N = 321) =$
22.59 and the cross-loading (the loading of a single item on more than

one factor) of item 20 on the higher-order factor of Depression, LM $\chi^2(2, N = 321) = 15.81$ (i.e., item 20 loaded on F4 as well as on F2). Because the loading of item 20 onto the Depression factor would lead to a psychometrically ambiguous specification, the model was reparameterized as a first-order CFA model in order to assess possible misspecification at the lower structural level. Estimation of this model replicated the misspecification of both the error covariance and item 20; the latter was shown to cross-load on Factor 1. Thus the hypothesized model (Model 1) for females was respecified to include these two additional parameters and then reestimated. That we were able to reparameterize the model by respecifying multiple parameters in a single run represents a major difference from the LISREL program, in which only one parameter can be respecified at a time. As a consequence, this respecified model represents Model 3 in Table 8.1, because Model 2 is redundant with the EQS analyses.

To assess the extent to which each newly specified model exhibits an improvement over its predecessor, we examine the difference in χ^2 ($\Delta\chi^2$) between the two nested models. This differential is itself χ^2 distributed, with degrees of freedom equal to the difference in degrees of freedom, and can thus be tested statistically; a significant $\Delta\chi^2$ indicates a substantial improvement in model fit. As is evident in Table 8.1, the inclusion of these two parameters in the model yielded a statistically significant and substantial improvement in model fit, ΔSCALED $\chi^2(2, N = 321) = 31.33$, ΔCFI* = .04. Closer scrutiny of the parameter estimates, however, revealed the original loading of item 20 on Factor 1 to be nonsignificant. In the interest of parsimony, then, the model was respecified with this parameter deleted. Because Model 4 was deemed to be substantively reasonable (see Byrne et al., 1993, for an extended explanation) and exhibited an excellent fit to the data, it was considered the most plausible in representing the data for adolescent females.

LISREL ANALYSES

Consistent with the EQS analyses, the LISREL results based on ML estimation also yielded a better-fitting model for males than for females, as indicated by CFI value less than .90 for females (Table 8.1). A review of the MIs revealed two parameters to be potentially worthy of estimation. The more prominent fixed parameter (MI = 22.60) represented the error covariance between items 21 and 20; the other (MI =

17.04) represented the cross-loading of item 20 onto the Negative Attitude factor. As shown in Table 8.1, three separate models (Models 2-4) were subsequently specified and estimated.

A review of results related to these models reveals each to yield a highly significant improvement in model fit over its predecessor. As with the EQS analyses, for statistical, psychometric, and theoretical reasons, Model 4 was considered to be the most plausible in representing BDI data for adolescent females.

Testing for Invariance Across Gender

Having determined the baseline model for each sex, analyses proceeded next to test for their factorial equivalence across males and females. At first blush, except for the differential loading pattern of item 20 and the specification of an error covariance for females, one might be quick to conclude that the BDI was factorially equivalent across gender. Such a conclusion would be premature, however, because a similarly specified model in no way guarantees the equivalence of item measurements and underlying theoretical structure; related hypotheses must be tested statistically in a simultaneous analysis of data from both groups. I turn now to these analyses as they are addressed separately within the EQS and LISREL programs.

EQS ANALYSES

Because we already know, prior to testing for cross-group invariance, that item 20 is apparently perceived differently by adolescent males and females, the factor loading for this item was not constrained equal across gender; the error covariance is also unique to females and is free to take on any value. Such specification addresses the issue of partial measurement invariance in the testing of equivalence across multiple samples (see Byrne, Shavelson, & Muthén, 1989).

In EQS, we can test for the invariance of both the first- and second-order factor loadings simultaneously. This approach is made possible in two important ways. First, it employs the multivariate LM test in the evaluation of equality constraints and, second, it makes the detection of misspecified constraints easy by providing probability values associated with the LM χ^2 statistic for each. A review of these statistics revealed four constraints to be untenable. Probability values less than

.05 were associated with items 8, 10, 12, and 18, thereby arguing for their nonequivalence across adolescent males and females.

LISREL ANALYSES

Testing for invariance based on LISREL involved the testing of three increasingly restrictive hypotheses, each nested within the one preceding; these related to the equivalency of (a) number of underlying factors, (b) first-order factor loadings, and (c) second-order factor loadings. (For an elaboration of this procedure, see Byrne, 1989.)

Analyses involved specifying a model in which certain parameters were constrained equal across gender, then comparing that model with a less restrictive one in which the same parameters were free to take on any value. As with model-fitting, the $\Delta\chi^2$ between competing models provided a basis for determining the tenability of the hypothesized equality constraints; a significant $\Delta\chi^2$ indicating noninvariance (i.e., nonequivalence). Turning to the summary of LISREL analyses shown in Table 8.3, we see that the first invariance model (Model 1) tested for the equivalence of an underlying three-factor structure (irrespective of factor loading pattern) across males and females. This initial specification simply tests for adequacy of model fit in a simultaneous analysis of multigroup data and provides the criterion against which the two subsequent invariance models are compared; given a CFI value of .92, multigroup model fit was considered to be reasonably good. A second model was then specified in which the pattern of lower-order factor loadings was constrained equal across the two groups. (Note that item 20 was not constrained equal across groups.) Comparison of this model (Model 2) with Model 1 yielded a statistically significant difference in model fit ($p < .01$), thereby substantiating rejection of the hypothesis that item measurements were equivalent across males and females.

Given findings of some gender specificity related to the lower-order factors, the next task was to identify the BDI items contributing to this noninvariance. This was accomplished by first testing separately for the invariance of each BDI subscale (i.e., all items composing each subscale were tested as a group). Given significant findings for any one of these three tests, analyses proceeded next in testing for the invariance of each item within each subscale. Finally, constraining all first-order loadings known to be group-invariant, analyses then focus on the second-order factor loadings. Because of limitations of space, results related to these nested series of tests are simply summarized, as shown

TABLE 8.3 Summary of LISREL Tests for Invariance Across Gender

Model	χ^2	df	CFI	Model Comparison	$\Delta\chi^2$	Δdf
1 Baseline multigroup model	604.18	373	.92	—	—	—
2 All first-order loadings invariant[a]	641.25	390	.91	2 vs. 1	37.07**	17
3 Item loadings for F1 invariant	626.88	382	.91	3 vs. 1	22.70**	9
4 Item loadings for F2 invariant	610.91	378	.91	4 vs. 1	6.73	5
5 Item loadings for F3 invariant	611.87	376	.91	5 vs. 1	7.69	3
6 All first-order loadings invariant[b] except items 8 and 20	632.70	389	.91	6 vs. 1	28.52*	16
7 All first-order loadings invariant except items 8, 19, and 20	627.85	388	.91	7 vs. 1	23.67	15
8 Model 7 with all second-order loadings invariant	636.01	391	.91	8 vs. 7	8.16*	3
9 Model 7 with second-order loadings for F1 and F2 invariant[b]	628.41	390	.91	9 vs. 7	0.56	2

NOTE: F1 = Factor 1 (Negative Attitude); F2 = Factor 2 (Performance Difficulty); F3 = Factor 3 (Somatic Elements); CFI = Comparative Fit Index; $\Delta\chi^2$ = difference in χ^2 values; Δdf = difference in degrees of freedom.
a. Item 20 was not constrained equal across gender.
b. Equality constraints were imposed separately for each item loading.
*$p < .05$, **$p < .01$.

in Table 8.3. Readers who may wish a more detailed description of this model-testing procedure are referred to Byrne (1989, 1994; Byrne et al., 1989).

Summary

Working from a common database and hypothesized model, this chapter has provided an example of the EQS and LISREL strategies in testing for an invariant second-order factor structure across groups. Along the way, similarities and differences between the two programs were noted with respect to (a) approach to and information derived from preliminary analyses of the data, (b) treatment of data that violate the assumption of multivariate normality, (c) assessment of overall model fit, (d) identification of parameter misspecification, (e) post-hoc model-fitting, and (f) tests for multigroup invariance.

Although, substantively, results based on ML estimation were consistent across the two programs, those bearing on the equality of BDI measurement and structure across groups differed with respect to two parameters—one first-order and one second-order loading. The discrepancy in these findings is undoubtedly a consequence of the univariate versus multivariate approach to the identification of misspecified equality constraints taken by LISREL and EQS, respectively. Of most concern is the inconsistent finding related to the second-order loading of F3 on F4. One explanation likely lies in the highly correlated structure among the first-order factors for both males (mean $r = .78$) and females (mean $r = .76$), which would not be taken into account in the univariate test for invariance.

EQS and LISREL model fit statistics related to analyses that took the nonnormality of the data into account were widely discrepant. Whereas the EQS approach in correcting the χ^2 statistic yielded results that were reasonable, the χ^2 statistic and CFI value produced by LISREL, based on the ADF estimator, were unreasonably high. These findings support those reported by Hu et al. (1992), who found that when sample size is small ($N = 250$ or less), the capability of the ADF statistic in correctly assessing model fit is extremely poor; typically, models that are in fact true are rejected far too frequently. Their Monte Carlo study revealed that only when sample size approximates 5000 cases does the ADF statistic perform as a χ^2 variate. Given that most practical applications of SEM involve substantially smaller sample sizes, the SCALED χ^2 statistic produced by EQS appears to be the more useful measure of model fit when the data are in violation of the normality assumption.

Although this comparison of the EQS and LISREL programs has highlighted only a few of their differential approaches to SEM application, it is hoped that the issues addressed here will be helpful to readers who may be relatively unfamiliar with the two programs and/or the methodological procedures presented.

9 Writing About Structural Equation Models

RICK H. HOYLE

ABIGAIL T. PANTER

The increasing complexity of decision making about structural equation models and comprehensiveness of computer software for estimating them has created a significant burden for researchers in the social and behavioral sciences. Researchers who choose to address substantive research questions using the structural equation modeling (SEM) approach are faced with the task of sifting through the large amount of output routinely generated by SEM software and deciding how to present information in a way that permits a reasoned evaluation and understanding of their analysis, yet does not overwhelm or confuse readers. Our goal in this chapter is to provide a set of general recommendations that promote effective and complete communication of results from SEM analyses. The requirements of particular journals and disciplines as well as theoretical and technical developments in the SEM field may necessitate adjustments to some of our recommendations, but, on the whole, our recommendations should be acceptable for most forms of communication in most social and behavioral science disciplines.

Describing the Conceptual and Statistical Models

The typical application of SEM is to a system of relations, collectively referred to as a model. A model can include relations among measured variables and latent variables (i.e., factors, constructs) as well as nondirectional and directional (direct and indirect) relations (see Chapter 1). Given the potential complexity of structural equation models, a clear description of the model is critical. Indeed, it provides the foundation on which the remainder of the communication rests. The model typically is presented at two levels: conceptual and statistical. In a well-crafted communication, the presentations are complementary and nonredundant.

THE CONCEPTUAL MODEL

The conceptual model specifies the relations among concepts that are operationalized in the empirical study. A diagram can provide an effective means of presenting the full system of relations in a unified and integrated manner and represents a direct translation of theoretical predictions (Tanaka, Panter, Winborne, & Huba, 1990). In presentations at the conceptual level, we recommend against presenting a full path diagram with all indicators, measurement errors, and loadings depicted, as it may be better suited for presenting the statistical model and results. Rather, we recommend that the model be first introduced conceptually using a diagram that refers to constructs and their interrelations using familiar terminology from the substantive literature.

In such a diagram the concepts are clearly labeled according to the substantive theories in which they are embedded, and understanding of the diagram requires no familiarity with notation rules for path diagrams. If the model is integrative rather than representative of a single theory, the diagram might further be embellished by labeling the paths between concepts with the names of the theoretical perspective or theorist whose work underlies the predicted relation. Alternatively, multiple panels may be presented showing the conceptual diagram and highlighting predictions made by competing theories.

Each diagram should be accompanied by written explanation and justification in text for each proposed relation or path, as well as each lack of relation or path. The written description of the model can either culminate in the presentation of the diagram (e.g., "The set of relations we have described is displayed in Figure x.") or the diagram can serve as a starting point for describing the model (e.g., "The model we are proposing is displayed in Figure x."). In either case, the diagram should include no relations that are not explained and fully justified in the text of the communication and should omit no relations that are proposed or implied in the text. Moreover, the provision of a theoretical rationale for the absence of relations among constructs is as vital as the rationale for predicted relations among constructs.

THE STATISTICAL MODEL

The precise statistical model that will be tested cannot be deduced from the presentation of the conceptual model. As such, each construct represented in the conceptual model must be operationalized, and the model must be translated into the statistical manifestation that has been or is to be tested. A path diagram can be an effective means of communicating structural equation models at the statistical level and, in some cases, can help clarify thinking about testing hypotheses within a particular theoretical framework (Tanaka et al., 1990). MacCallum (Chapter 2) describes and illustrates the use and notation of path diagrams (see also Figures 8.1, 10.1, 11.1, 12.1, 12.2, 13.1, and 13.2 in this volume).

Ideally, the path diagram, although more detailed, is a direct extension of the conceptual model. A reader should be able to ascertain precisely the statistical model to be tested from the number of observed indicators, latent variables, and the presence and absence of paths depicted in the diagram. Furthermore, the diagram should clearly indicate the location of all fixed and free parameters in the model (Chapter 2). It is particularly useful if the written description of the diagram points out the number and types (e.g., factor loadings, error variances) of free parameters and derives the number of degrees of freedom on which the χ^2 test will be based (see Chapter 2). Care in labeling constructs and variables in the diagram will simplify presentation of parameter estimates in a table or in the text.

There is no clear consensus about where the description of the statistical model should be placed in a manuscript. One possible placement for this description would be in a separate section just after the presentation of the conceptual model. Such a positioning may be desirable because it emphasizes the direct translation of the conceptual hypotheses into hypotheses based on specific operationalizations of variables in the study. Alternatively, the description of the statistical model could be placed in a separate section in the Methods portion of the manuscript. That location might be advantageous because it would directly follow the detailed description (including psychometric properties) of the measures that give rise to the observed variables in the model. A third option is to place the description of the statistical model at the beginning of the section in which the results are presented. A virtue of that positioning is that it would provide a clear context for evaluating the results of the data analyses. We see no consistent advantage of one placement over the other; individual styles, disciplines, and research studies will determine where in the manuscript the statistical model is presented. The important point is that a detailed presentation of the statistical model appears in a separate section in the manuscript.

Details About the Data

Not unlike more traditional approaches to data analysis, the validity of the SEM approach rests on first meeting assumptions regarding the data that are analyzed. Indeed, because questions remain in the technical literature about the behavior of particular methods of estimation and assessments of fit under certain conditions, a presentation of basic descriptive information about the data on which an SEM analysis is based is essential. Such information is of two sorts: the matrix to be analyzed and distributions of the individual variables on which the matrix is based.

MATRIX TO BE ANALYZED

Estimation of structural equation models should always be based on covariance, not correlation, matrices (Cudeck, 1989). Although there was a time when it was reasonable to estimate from a correlation matrix in order to obtain standardized parameter estimates, this is not the case at present in light of the well-documented liabilities of employing correlation matrices as data under particular model constraints and the ability of SEM software to provide standardized estimates when covariances are used as input. Of course, covariances are not as informative as correlations for communicating the pattern of bivariate relations among measured variables. Thus we recommend presenting a correlation matrix accompanied by standard deviations of the variables, thereby permitting the interested reader to recover the covariance matrix (major SEM software packages will recover the covariance matrix when provided a correlation matrix and standard deviations). In reporting these data, rounding to three rather than the customary two decimal places will ensure that additional data analyses take full advantage of the precision offered by SEM computer programs.

Barring nonnegotiable page limitations, the covariance matrix or correlation matrix and standard deviations should be included in the body of the manuscript or in an appendix. Inclusion of the covariance/correlation matrix offers two appealing benefits. First, it provides the opportunity for other researchers to fit their own alternative models— models that either were not considered or not formally proposed in the published report. Second, these data show the relations among variables in the most rudimentary fashion, permitting curious (and suspicious) readers to see the simple bivariate relations that underlie the models that were estimated.

When the data to be analyzed are ordered categorical data, not interval-level data, a sample covariance matrix is no longer appropriate for SEM analyses and may in some cases lead to incorrect statistical inference (e.g., Huba & Harlow, 1987; Muthén, 1993). In such cases, which often arise when analyzing item-level information (e.g., true-false or yes-no response formats), the data may be preprocessed so that a tetrachoric (for dichotomous data) or polychoric (for ordered-categorical variables) matrix is estimated and analyzed. Software such as PRELIS (Jöreskog & Sörbom, 1993c) followed by LISREL (Jöreskog & Sörbom, 1993b) and LISCOMP (Muthén, 1984, 1988) can easily handle dichotomous, ordered categorical data, and mixtures of such data, although sample size requirements for estimating latent correlations become especially large and sometimes beyond the practical constraints of data collection. When additional assumptions are made about the measurement level of the raw data in the model, such assumptions should be explicitly reported in the manuscript, so that readers readily see that estimation methods for noncontinuous variables were employed.

DISTRIBUTIONS

Information should be provided about the distributions of individual variables and the multivariate distribution of the variables in the model(s) to be estimated. Typically, that information can be presented in summary form in the body of a manuscript, although certain applications that necessitate greater detail may call for adding such information to the table that includes the covariance or correlation matrix (e.g., additional columns for skewness and kurtosis parameters). Two pieces of information are of particular import and, therefore, we recommend that authors routinely present them at least in summary form in reports of SEM analyses. The validity of normal theory estimators such as maximum likelihood and generalized least squares does not hold under excessive kurtosis (Browne, 1984a; Hu, Bentler, & Kano, 1992; Chapter 4, this volume). Descriptive information about univariate kurtosis is provided by PRELIS (Jöreskog & Sörbom, 1993c), EQS (Bentler, 1989; when raw data are used as input), and CALIS (SAS Institute, 1991) and should be consulted, summarized, and interpreted. In addition, information about multivariate normality should be presented (and interpreted) in the form of Mardia's (1970) coefficient (also provided by PRELIS, EQS, and CALIS). Significant departure from normality should prompt corrective measures (see Chapter 4) that will affect presentation of fit indexes and parameter estimates later in the manuscript.

Describing the Results

Interpretation and evaluation of SEM results requires knowledge of the method used to obtain parameter estimates and the criteria by which the overall model and individual estimates will be evaluated. A complete presentation of results necessitates complete disclosure of parameter estimates and fit statistics, as well as a clear rationale for modification and comparison of models. Following is a set of recommendations for providing an informative and complete account of the results of an SEM analysis.

ESTIMATION AND FIT CRITERIA

It is increasingly apparent that not all estimation methods and fit indexes lead to the same inferential outcome when evaluating structural equation models (e.g., Hu et al., 1992; Chapters 3 and 5, this volume). As such, an informed evaluation of the results of an SEM analysis requires knowledge of the estimation method used to produce the estimates reported in the manuscript and the fit criteria used to evaluate the model and the estimates.

Method of Estimation. The standard method of estimating free parameters in structural equation models is to employ maximum likelihood (ML). A growing body of research indicates that ML performs reasonably well under a variety of less-than-optimal analytic conditions (e.g., small sample size, excessive kurtosis). Because ML is so widely available and is the most widely researched estimator among those otherwise available (e.g, ordinary least squares, generalized least squares, asymptotic distribution-free), we recommend that authors routinely report results from ML estimation. If characteristics of the data raise question as to the appropriateness of ML, then the results of alternative estimation procedures might be reported in summary form if they contradict ML results or in a footnote if they corroborate them. In light of recently published analyses (Hu et al., 1992; Chapter 5, this volume), we recommend against asymptotic distribution-free estimation in favor of distribution-based adjustments to results of ML estimation (Satorra & Bentler, 1988a, 1988b, 1994).

Fit Criteria. Consistent with recommendations by Tanaka (1993), we suggest that authors provide an inferential context within which indexes of overall fit are to be presented and interpreted prior to reporting results of SEM analyses. A suitable context includes at least three pieces of information: (a) Authors should state which omnibus fit indexes will be reported along with justification for choosing those indexes based on characteristics of the study and information from the most recent literature on the indexes chosen. (b) Authors should provide a clear conceptual definition of each index to be reported. Incremental fit indexes often are interpreted as indicators of percentage of variance accounted for—a transfer of multiple-regression logic that is incorrect. The type-2 and type-3 indexes we recommend below carry somewhat different interpretations despite the fact that the range of values they take on are similar. (c) The "critical value" of each index that will indicate acceptable fit should be specified prior to reporting and interpreting observed values of the indexes. As Hu and Bentler (Chapter 5, this volume) note, with the exception of χ^2, the sampling distributions of overall indexes of fit are unknown. Therefore, for most omnibus fit indexes, critical values in the standard sense are not defined. Bentler and Bonett (1980) proposed a value of .90 for normed indexes that are not parsimony adjusted as a reasonable minimum for model acceptance; that value is used widely among social and behavioral researchers. Hu and Bentler report emerging evidence that .90 might not always be a reasonable cutoff for all adjunct fit indexes under all modeling circumstances. At present, however, there exists no empirical or reasoned basis for choosing particular alternative cutoff values. Thus, .90 stands as the agreed-upon cutoff for overall fit indexes. As such, the choice of an alternative cutoff value, particularly a lower one, should be justified in the manuscript.

INDICATORS OF OVERALL FIT

Typically, initial evaluation of a structural equation model concerns omnibus fit. The performance of omnibus fit indexes has been a particularly active area of SEM research and development and regularly produces updated evaluations of a growing number of indexes. The recommendations we provide below are well-reasoned given the current state of the literature; however, that literature changes frequently and should be consulted when choosing and justifying the use of particular indexes of fit.

The meaning of the term "fit," as it applies to evaluating structural equation models, is not entirely straightforward (Tanaka, 1993). At the most general level, references to and evaluations of the fit of a structural equation model can refer to one of two characteristics of the model:

1. *Absolute fit* concerns the degree to which the covariances implied by the fixed and free parameters specified in the model match the observed covariances from which free parameters in the model were estimated (see Chapter 1). Indexes of absolute fit typically gauge "badness of fit"; optimal fit is indicated by a value of zero, and increasing values indicate greater departure of the implied covariance matrix from the observed covariance matrix.

2. *Incremental fit* concerns the degree to which the model in question is superior to an alternative model, usually one that specifies no covariances among variables (i.e., the "null" or independence model), in reproducing the observed covariances. Indexes of incremental fit typically gauge "goodness of fit"; larger values indicate greater improvement of the model in question over an alternative model in reproducing the observed covariances.

At present there is little consensus concerning the best index of overall fit for evaluating structural equation models. Thus most investigators who have evaluated and compared extant indexes encourage reporting multiple indexes of overall fit (Bollen, 1989b; Marsh, Balla, & McDonald, 1988; Tanaka, 1993; Chapter 5, this volume). We concur, yet we do not recommend that researchers, for completeness sake, report a long list of fit indexes such as those routinely provided in SEM computer output.

In Table 9.1 we describe some recommended indexes of overall fit for evaluating structural equation models. We have divided the indexes

TABLE 9.1 Currently Recommended Indexes of Overall Model Fit

Index	Reference	Description and Comments
Stand-Alone/Absolute Indexes		
χ^2; SCALED χ^2	Bollen (1989b, pp. 263-269) Satorra & Bentler (1994)	Statistical test of the lack of fit resulting from over-identifying restrictions placed on a model. Contrary to common belief, the χ^2 evaluates the fixed rather than the free parameters in a structural equation model.
Goodness-of-fit index (GFI)	Jöreskog & Sörbom (1981) Tanaka & Huba (1985, 1989)	Indexes the relative amount of the observed variances and covariances accounted for by a model. Analogous to R^2 commonly used to summarize results of multiple regression analyses.
Type-1 Indexes		
Not recommended.		
Type-2 Indexes		
Tucker-Lewis index (TLI)/Nonnormed fit index (NNFI)	Bentler & Bonett (1980) Tucker & Lewis (1973)	Compares the lack of fit of a target model to the lack of fit of a baseline model, usually the independence model. Value estimates the relative improvement per degree of freedom of the target model over a baseline model. Not recommended for very small samples (< 150), particularly with GLS estimation.
Incremental fit index (IFI)	Bollen (1989a)	Same interpretation as TLI/ NNFI. Less variable than TLI/ NNFI in small samples and more consistent across estimators than TLI/NNFI.

continued

TABLE 9.1 Continued

Index	Reference	Description and Comments
Type-3 Indexes		
Comparative fit index (CFI)	Bentler (1989, 1990)	Indexes the relative reduction in lack of fit as estimated by the noncentral χ^2 of a target model versus a baseline model. CFI is an adaptation of FI/RNI forced to vary between 0 and 1. It overcomes liabilities of the popular and intuitive but problematic normed fit index by replacing the central with the noncentral χ^2.
Fit index (FI)/ Relative noncentrality index (RNI)	Bentler (1989, 1990) McDonald & Marsh (1990)	Equivalent to CFI. Differs only in that FI/RNI is not truncated at 0 and 1, extremes it can exceed because of sampling error or overfitting.

NOTE: Typology of incremental fit indexes is based on Hu and Bentler's (Chapter 5, this volume) typology.

into the categories described by Hu and Bentler in Chapter 5 of this volume. From among the stand-alone or absolute fit indexes, we recommend χ^2. Despite the numerous ambiguities associated with interpreting χ^2 according to the traditional dichotomous decision rule, the value of the statistic itself holds the most promise for the development of an index of fit for which the sampling distribution is known. It also forms the basis for nested model comparisons. Reports of χ^2 should be accompanied by degrees of freedom, sample size, and *p*-value (see example format later in this chapter). When the distributions of the observed variables depart from normality, Satorra and Bentler's (1988a, 1988b, 1994) adjustment, referred to as SCALED χ^2, should be reported along with the unadjusted χ^2 (for more detail on this adjustment, see Chapter 5, this volume).

In addition to χ^2, researchers may wish to report the value of the goodness-of-fit index (GFI; Jöreskog & Sörbom, 1981) as an index of absolute fit. Although GFI (Equation 5.8, this volume) is moderately associated with sample size (Marsh et al., 1988), it carries an intuitive interpretation because it is analogous to the familiar R^2-value often reported alongside F-values associated with multiple regression models (Tanaka, 1993; Tanaka & Huba, 1985, 1989). If overfitting (i.e., an excessive number of free parameters) is a potential problem, either the shrinkage adjustment proposed by Jöreskog and Sörbom (1981) or the parsimony correction described by Mulaik, James, Van Alstine, Bennett, Lind, and Stillwell (1989) might be reported along with GFI (for a classification of these indexes, see Tanaka, 1993).

In terms of incremental fit indexes, we recommend that researchers report at least two, one each from the type-2 and type-3 indexes described by Hu and Bentler (Chapter 5, this volume). (In agreement with Hu and Bentler, we recommend against reporting the normed fit index and Bollen's, 1986, type-1 index.) From among the type-2 indexes, we recommend either Tucker and Lewis's (1973) index (TLI), also called the nonnormed fit index (NNFI; Bentler & Bonett, 1980), or Bollen's (1989a) incremental fit index (IFI; referred to as "BL89" in Chapter 5). TLI/NNFI (Equation 5.3, this volume) performs well when ML estimation is used but is significantly downwardly biased when based on generalized least squares (GLS) estimation and the relatively small sample sizes (< 1000) characteristic of social and behavioral research (Hu & Bentler, 1993). IFI (Equation 5.4, this volume) performs consistently across ML and GLS and, therefore, is to be preferred over TLI/NNFI when estimates are obtained using the GLS method.

From among the type-3 indexes, we recommend Bentler's (1989, 1990) fit index (FI; referred to as BFI in Chapter 5, this volume), which is the same as McDonald and Marsh's (1990) relative noncentrality index (RNI), and the comparative fit index (CFI; Bentler, 1989, 1990). As noted by Hu and Bentler (Chapter 5, this volume), the FI and RNI (Equation 5.6, this volume) are identical to CFI (Equation 5.7, this volume) when their values fall between 0 and 1; unlike FI and RNI, values of CFI cannot fall outside the 0-1 range. Thus CFI is somewhat preferable because its values fall within the familiar "normed" range. Overfitting and sampling error can lead to values of FI/RNI greater than 1.

Formats for presenting statistical results vary somewhat across disciplines. Using the format prescribed by the American Psychological Association's style manual (APA, 1994, p. 247), overall fit information for a structural equation model can be written, for example, $\chi^2(48, N = 500) = 303.80, p < .001$, TLI = .86, CFI = .90. Although other styles of presentation may be required by other disciplines, we recommend presentation of all the information included in the example.

An additional issue regarding omnibus fit indexes concerns comparisons between competing models. In general, we recommend against the relatively common practice of making decisions between different models based on comparisons of incremental fit indexes. As a rule, comparison of absolute fit indexes is reasonable, although such comparisons must account for model complexity. Thus χ^2-difference tests between nested models (i.e., all of one model's free parameters are a subset of a second model's free parameters), which index χ^2-change relative to difference in number of free parameters between two models, and parsimony-adjusted absolute indexes, which control for number of free parameters in competing models, are to be preferred.

PARAMETER ESTIMATES

Full information about parameter estimates should be reported and accompanied in the text of the manuscript by a full explanation of the information reported. We offer the following recommendations regarding presentation of the parameter estimates:

1. The plausibility of parameter estimates, particularly variances, should be established in text. Heywood cases (negative error variances) and out-of-range covariances (standardized estimates greater than 1) indicate problems with estimation or model specification and raise questions about the validity of the remaining estimates in the model.

2. All parameter estimates, including error variances and variances of latent variables, should be reported. Estimates can be tied to particular paths as part of a diagram (see Figures 13.1 and 13.2, this volume) or can be given in a table (see Tables 8.2, 10.3, and 11.2, this volume). A virtue of presentation of parameter estimates in a diagram is that the location of specific estimates in the model is clear. One drawback to that method of presentation, however, is that a diagram that includes many variables, constructs, and paths can become indecipherable when parameter estimates are added to it. One means of avoiding such clutter is to present parameter estimates for the measurement model in one diagram or set of diagrams, then, in a second diagram or set of diagrams (one that omits indicators of latent variables) present only estimates relevant to the structural model. The virtue of presentation in a table is that multiple estimates of each parameter (e.g., ML, GLS; see Table 8.2, this volume) can be presented along with standard errors, critical ratios, and p-values. One drawback to presenting parameter estimates

in a tabular format is that, apart from using Greek letters and subscripts to denote parameters (the use of LISREL notation is a strategy we do not recommend), labeling parameters in a manner that makes clear their place in the model can be difficult and can require an extra layer of processing by the reader. The Bentler-Weeks (1980) "double-label" notation (e.g., F1,F1 for the variance of factor 1) is more straightforward than LISREL notation (i.e., subscripted Greek letters); however, we prefer even more straightforward labels that make reference to the variables and constructs with which each estimate is associated. For example, following our recommendation, the row in a table that includes information about the estimate of the variance of the latent variable self-esteem would refer to "Self-Esteem" rather than "ξ_1" (LISREL) or "F1" (Bentler-Weeks).

3. Either standard errors of estimates, critical ratios (i.e., estimate/ standard error) for estimates, or notation that indicates p-values associated with estimates (e.g., $*p < .05$, $**p < .01$, etc.) should be presented. The last option is least preferred because it discloses the least about the parameter estimates. When unstandardized estimates are presented, then either standard errors or critical ratios should be provided. The provision of standard errors or critical ratios (from which standard errors can be recovered if unstandardized estimates are given) carries two additional benefits over the "rs and stars" approach (Chaplin, 1994). First, atypically high or low standard errors can signal estimation problems or instability in a model. Second, standard errors can be used by readers to construct tests of differences of estimates from values other than 0.

4. Estimates fixed at nonzero values (e.g., one factor loading per latent variable to fix the metric of the latent variables) were neither estimated nor tested and should be clearly indicated as such.

5. As with the presentation of information about overall fit, information about parameter estimates should be presented within an interpretational context. The critical value of the test statistic (usually ±1.96) should be noted explicitly prior to presentation and interpretation of estimates. Figures and tables should indicate clearly whether unstandardized or standardized estimates are presented. In either case, readers should be given a conceptual definition of the kind of estimate being provided (see Chapter 1).

ALTERNATIVE MODELS

Rarely does an SEM analysis involve estimating a single model (Jöreskog, 1974). Indeed, the strategic choice of alternatives to the target model can strengthen support for it. Alternative models emerge at one of two points in an SEM analysis. Either the researcher specified a priori alternative models to be compared with the target model (the deductive approach) or the estimation process revealed misspecification in the target model that led to post-hoc modifications of it (the inductive approach). In either case, the report must provide details concerning estimation of alternative models, particularly when the alternatives are based on consultation of empirical modification indexes. Such information typically appears in a separate section within the Results section, clearly labeled (e.g., "Alternative Models," "Model Respecification") so as to differentiate fit information and parameter estimates associated with alternative models (particularly empirically derived models) from similar information about the target model.

A Priori. The strongest SEM analysis proposes a target model based on careful consultation of relevant theory and prior research and then compares that model with one or more previously specified competing models indicated by other theoretical positions, contradictions in the research literature, or parsimony. Jöreskog (1993) refers to that approach as the *alternative models* approach. When possible, alternative models should be specified prior to estimation of the target model so that nested comparisons can be made between each alternative model and the target model. For instance, multifactor measurement models might be compared to the more parsimonious (i.e., fewer free parameters) single-factor model. The statistical criteria for choosing one model over the other should be clearly specified and χ^2-difference tests ($\Delta\chi^2$, Δdf) should be conducted when the target and alternative models are nested. As a rule, the comparison of adjunct fit indexes such as those described above, particularly the incremental fit indexes, should be avoided. When a number of alternative models are compared to the target model, a single table that details omnibus fit indexes for the various alternatives along with results of model comparisons (e.g., Table 8.1, this volume) can provide the reader with a comprehensive view of the data-analytic strategy and results.

Post-Hoc Modifications. A less desirable yet more common approach to model comparison—the *model generating* approach (Jöreskog, 1993)—involves respecification of a target model based on misspecification revealed after initial estimation and examination of the target model (MacCallum, Roznowski, & Necowitz, 1992). The most significant implication of respecifying a target model in successive iterations based on post-hoc criteria is the potential for capitalizing on the idiosyncracies of the particular sample on which the covariance matrix is based. The potential is particularly great in small samples (MacCallum et al., 1992; Tanaka, 1987), with which the likelihood of finding a replicable model is quite low.

Two types of post-hoc modifications are particularly problematic: (a) correlated errors of measurement (note that some models, for instance, longitudinal models with latent variables, include correlated errors of measurement that are specified a priori) and (b) nonstandard, or specific, effects (see Hoyle & Smith, 1994). Errors of measurement, which typically are assumed to be independent, frequently are freed to covary in order to improve the fit of measurement models. Rarely are plausible explanations offered for covariances among error terms. Indeed, covariances among error terms identified by empirical modification methods frequently are implausible and, therefore, unjustifiable. Similarly, nonstandard effects—those that involve the covariance between an error of measurement and another substantive variable in the model—often are discovered post hoc and are, therefore, unlikely to replicate.

As a rule, we recommend against post-hoc modifications unless there exists an unusually clear and compelling substantive reason why such modifications are reasonable. MacCallum et al. (1992) provide some evidence that post-hoc modifications are likely to replicate when sample size is at least 800; however, the luxury of a sample that large in social and behavioral research is rare. Post-hoc modifications of models estimated for samples of the more typical size (100 to 400) should not be taken seriously unless they are replicated in an independent sample. Finally, we urge researchers to consider the plausibility of post-hoc modifications, avoiding those that make no sense given the constructs and the model and offering clear, compelling explanations for those retained.

We believe it is particularly important that authors distinguish between results based on estimation of theory based models that were specified prior to analysis of the data and results based on post-hoc modifications of a priori models. On occasion, presentations of SEM results report a mixture of predicted and "discovered" paths without distinguishing between the two (Biddle & Marlin, 1987). A straightforward means of distinguishing between predicted and discovered findings in reports of SEM results is to relegate presentation of the latter to a separate, clearly labeled section in the Results section of the manuscript. If the eventual model was derived through multiple, sequential modifications of an a priori model, then authors should describe the history of the development of the final model from the a priori model (Biddle & Marlin, 1987).

Equivalent Models. A frequently ignored class of alternative models consists of models that are statistically equivalent to the target model (Lee & Hershberger, 1990). Because equivalent models comprise the same variables and are no more or less parsimonious than the target model, they cannot be ruled out as alternatives to the target model (Breckler, 1990; MacCallum, Wegener, Uchino, & Fabrigar, 1993). In agreement with MacCallum et al. (1993), we recommend that authors routinely derive and report, either in a separate section of the Results section or as a component of interpretation of the results in the Discussion section, equivalent models in order to facilitate understanding of what can and cannot be inferred from their results.

ADDITIONAL INFORMATION ABOUT MODEL FIT

In addition to the essential information described above, two additional pieces of information bring clarity to the task of evaluating the overall fit of a structural equation model and, therefore, merit consideration for inclusion in reports of SEM analyses. Recent progress in the area of power analysis of structural equation models (e.g., Saris & Satorra, 1993; Chapter 6, this volume) has made the task more straightforward and the process more understandable for applied researchers. Moreover, simulation research (MacCallum et al., 1992) has revealed the unreliability of post-hoc model modification in small samples typical of social and behavioral research (see also Breckler, 1990). Thus information about statistical power and replicability of structural equation models is desirable and likely to become commonplace in reports about SEM analyses in the near future.

Statistical Power. It is not uncommon for researchers who estimate models from large-sample data to discredit the χ^2 test as too powerful and, therefore, likely to reject models that account for their data reasonably well. That claim should be weighed carefully for at least two reasons: (a) few studies in the social and behavioral sciences can boast samples of sufficient size to qualify as large and (b) the statistical power of a structural equation model is as much a function of characteristics of the model as size of the sample (Saris & Satorra, 1993; Chapter 6, this volume). An irony of the χ^2 test of overall fit is that low statistical power can lead to a nonsignificant χ^2 value and failure to reject a model that does not adequately fit the data from which it was estimated. Thus, when power is low (< .60) and χ^2 is nonsignificant or when power is high and χ^2 is significant, the question of whether a model adequately reflects a set of observed relations remains unanswered. In order to strengthen the basis on which inferences are made about structural equation models, we recommend a consideration of statistical power in reports of structural equation models.

Cross-Validation. A recent analysis by MacCallum et al. (1992) revealed that post-hoc model modifications based on empirical criteria are unlikely to replicate in samples smaller than 800. Because post-hoc modification is quite common in applications of SEM (Breckler, 1990), the likelihood of unreliable associations appearing in SEM analyses is high. One means of increasing confidence in the replicability of a model, particularly one that has been "discovered" through modification of an a priori model, is to either cross-validate the final model or estimate the likelihood of cross-validation from the data on which the final model is based. Cudeck and Browne (1983) described a two-sample cross-validation index based on the value of the fitting function (see Chapters 1 and 3), and Browne and Cudeck (1989) proposed a single-sample index that approximates the value of the two-sample index. We recommend that authors report one of these indexes after a series of modifications have identified a model unanticipated on the basis of a priori theory or reasoning.

Interpretation

Perhaps the strongest criticisms (e.g., Freedman, 1987) and cautions (e.g., Cliff, 1983) regarding the SEM approach have targeted the interpretation of findings from SEM analysis. Early references to SEM used the term "causal modeling" and at least implied that the SEM approach could reveal causal relations in nonexperimental data. The conditions for establishing causality (e.g., Holland, 1986) are no different when data are analyzed using SEM than when they are analyzed using correlation, multiple regression, or analysis of variance. Independent variables must be isolated, association must be demonstrated, and directionality must be established (Hoyle & Smith, 1994). The directionality criterion has created the most confusion among readers and, too often, users of the SEM approach.

The literature on equivalent models (e.g., Lee & Hershberger, 1990; MacCallum et al., 1993) provides the most compelling demonstration of the inability of SEM to establish directionality. In many models, switching the direction of the association between two variables changes neither the overall fit of the model nor the parameter estimate of the association between the variables. In the end, directionality is established either by logic (e.g., ethnicity cannot be caused by income), manipulation of the putative cause, or strong theoretical arguments.

So, how are the results of SEM analyses to be interpreted? In most instances, the associations in a structural equation model are necessary but not sufficient evidence of causal relations. In other words, one might argue that a particular model is consistent with a set of causal hypotheses, although the data on which the model is based might be equally consistent with other causal hypotheses. In the end, associations in structural equation models are interpreted no differently from associations in traditional statistical models. If the research methods and design that generated the data favor a causal inference, then such an inference can be made. Otherwise, the appropriate inference is that variables are reliably associated in the context of the model but the exact nature of the association cannot be demonstrated.

Additional limitations regarding the interpretation of SEM results might also be included in the written discussion and interpretation of them. If the sample size is small, the liabilities associated with small sample estimation and inferences should be discussed. If the distributions of the variables are nonnormal, then the limitations imposed by nonnormality should be noted. In particular, if the final model was obtained through a series of empirically determined modifications, it should be described as tentative until replicated.

Conclusions

The typical application of SEM is to a sometimes complex system of relations among measured and latent variables. The result can be an overwhelming amount of technical information regarding estimation, fit, and parameter estimates. Although the conscientious researcher will attend to all of that information during the course of analyzing and elucidating the data, he or she must distill it, sometimes radically, for presentation in manuscript form. In this chapter we have proposed a set of recommendations for describing and reporting results of SEM analyses. In some instances, our goal has been to provide advice on narrowing a list of options (e.g., estimators, fit indexes); in other instances we have proposed desirable formats for presenting information in text, diagrams, and tables and have proposed reporting information that, at present, is not routinely included in reports of SEM results. As we noted earlier, the SEM approach is the subject of a large amount of research and development; theory, software, and recommended strategy are updated regularly. Thus the recommendations we provide, particularly those that concern estimation and fit, must be considered in light of recent advances in the application of SEM. As such, our final and perhaps most important recommendation is that authors keep abreast of the latest developments in SEM as they evaluate, describe, and interpret results of their own applications of SEM.

10 Latent Variable Models of Multitrait-Multimethod Data

HERBERT W. MARSH

DAVID GRAYSON

Campbell and Fiske (1959) argued that construct validation requires both convergent and discriminant validity. They proposed the multitrait-multimethod (MTMM) design, which apparently is the most widely used paradigm for assessing construct validity. In this design two or more traits are each measured with two or more methods. Traits are attributes such as multiple abilities, attitudes, behaviors, or personality characteristics, whereas methods refer broadly to multiple test forms, methods of assessment, raters, or occasions. In the Campbell-Fiske approach an evaluation of an MTMM matrix is used to infer convergent validity, discriminant validity, and method effects. Convergent validity refers to true score or common factor trait variance; it is inferred from large, statistically significant correlations among different measures of the same trait. Discriminant validity refers to the distinctiveness of the different traits; it is inferred when correlations among different traits are less than the convergent validities and reliabilities. Method effect refers to the influence of a particular method that inflates a correlation among the different traits measured with the same method; it is inferred when correlations among traits measured by the same method exceed correlations among the same traits measured by different methods. Construct validity is supported when convergent validity and discriminant validity are high and method effects are negligible. Here we briefly summarize the original Campbell and Fiske (1959) guidelines used to inspect an MTMM correlation matrix and subsequent latent variable models that employ structural equation modeling.

Important problems with the Campbell-Fiske guidelines are well known (e.g., Marsh, 1988, 1989; Schmitt & Stults, 1986) and have led to many alternative analytic approaches. Considerable attention was given to confirmatory factor analysis (CFA) approaches (Jöreskog, 1974; Marsh, 1988, 1989; Widaman, 1985); however, researchers have noted an apparently inherent instability in the general CFA model, leading Kenny and Kashy (1992) to conclude that even after 30 years of widespread use, we still do not know how to analyze MTMM data adequately. Partly in response to this problem, researchers have proposed alternative approaches that are more likely to result in proper solutions, including the correlated uniqueness model (Kenny, 1976; Kenny & Kashy, 1992; Marsh, 1988, 1989) and the composite direct product model (CDP; Browne, 1984b, 1989; also see Bagozzi & Yi, 1992; Cudeck, 1988) considered here.

The Campbell and Fiske (1959) Approach

For present purposes we will consider data described by Marsh (1988, 1989), who examined the relations between three academic self-concept traits (T1 = Math, T2 = Verbal, and T3 = General School) measured by three different instruments (M1, M2, M3). The nine scores representing all combinations of the three traits and three methods were based on multi-item scales, and the three instruments had strong psychometric properties. Consistent with theory and considerable prior research, it was found that the math and verbal self-concepts were nearly uncorrelated with each other and were substantially correlated with school self-concept (satisfying the Campbell-Fiske recommendation to include two traits "which are postulated to be independent of each other," p. 104). This MTMM matrix (Table 10.1) is divided into triangular submatrices of correlations among different traits assessed with the same method (heterotrait-monomethods; HTMM), square submatrices of relations among measures assessed with different methods (heterotrait-heteromethods; HTHM), and relations among the same traits assessed with different methods (convergent validities). Campbell and Fiske proposed four guidelines that we apply to this MTMM matrix.

1. Convergent validities are substantial. All nine convergent validities are statistically significant, varying between .54 and .87 (mean r = .70), thus providing strong support for this guideline.

TABLE 10.1   An MTMM Correlation Matrix With Three Traits and Three Methods

Method 1									
T1M1	(.89)[a]								
T2M1	.384	(.79)							
T3M1	.441	.002	(.92)						
Method 2									
T1M2	.622	.368	.353	(.84)					
T2M2	.438	.703	.008	.441	(.89)				
T3M2	.465	.069	.871	.424	.136	(.95)			
Method 3									
T1M3	.678	.331	.478	.550	.380	.513	(.87)		
T2M3	.458	.541	.057	.381	.658	.096	.584	(.90)	
T3M3	.414	.027	.825	.372	.029	.810	.592	.135	(.94)

NOTE: T1 = general school self-concept, T2 = verbal self-concept, T3 = math self-concept; M1, M2, and M3 are three different self-report instruments.
a. Values in parentheses are coefficient alpha estimates of reliability.

2. Convergent validities are higher than HTHM correlations. Because convergent validities (mean $r = .70$) are higher than the HTHM correlations (mean $r = .31$) in all 36 comparisons, there is good support for this guideline of discriminant validity.

3. Convergent validities are higher than HTMM correlations. Because the convergent validities (mean $r = .70$) are higher than the HTMM correlations (mean $r = .35$) for 33 of 36 comparisons, there is reasonable support for this criterion of discriminant validity. All three failures involve M3, for which correlations among the traits (mean $r = .44$) are higher than for M1 ($r = .28$) or M2 ($r = .33$).

4. The pattern of correlations among different traits is similar for different methods. All correlations between T2 and T3 are consistently small (mean $r = .06$) whereas T1 is substantially correlated with both T2 (mean $r = .42$) and T3 (mean $r = .45$), thus providing support for this guideline.

Campbell and Fiske (1959) further noted that a clear violation of discriminant validity occurred "where within a monomethod block, the heterotrait values are as high as the reliabilities" (p. 84). They also stated that "the presence of method variance is indicated by the difference in level of correlation between parallel values of the monomethod block and the heteromethod block, assuming comparable reliabilities among the tests" (p. 85). Marsh and Grayson (in press) proposed additional guidelines based on these suggestions.

Campbell and Fiske (1959) were aware of most of the limitations in their approach, specifically stating that their guidelines should be viewed as "common-sense desideratum" (p. 83). Their intent was to provide a systematic, *formative evaluation* of MTMM data at the level of the individual trait-method unit, qualified by the recognized limitations of their approach, not to provide a *summative evaluation* or global summaries of convergent validity, discriminant validity, and method effects. More generally, Campbell and Fiske had a heuristic intention to encourage researchers to consider the concepts of convergent validity, discriminant validity, and method effects; in this intention they were remarkably successful. Unfortunately, this formative, heuristic aspect that was the very essence of the Campbell-Fiske approach seems to have been lost in the quest to develop ever more mathematically sophisticated approaches to MTMM data. Thus one of our intentions is to evaluate latent-variable approaches critically in relation to this formative goal—assessing construct validity at the level of the individual trait-method combination and providing diagnostic information on how to improve the measures.

The Confirmatory Factor Analysis (CFA) Approach

MTMM matrices, like other correlation matrices, can be factor-analyzed to make inferences about the possible underlying dimensions. Factors defined by different measures of the same trait suggest trait effects, whereas factors defined by measures assessed with the same method suggest method effects. With CFA the researcher can define models that posit a priori trait and method factors and can test the ability of such models to fit the data. The CFA approach to MTMM data is the most widely applied alternative to the Campbell-Fiske guidelines. Furthermore, the subsequently popularized CFA representation of MTMM data was apparently a basis of the guidelines proposed by Campbell and Fiske (1959; also see Campbell & O'Connell, 1967; Kenny & Kashy, 1992). Kenny and Kashy (1992) are even more emphatic, stating that "this [general CFA] model is particularly attractive in that its structure directly corresponds to Campbell and Fiske's original conceptualization of the MTMM matrix" (p. 165).

In the general MTMM model adapted from Jöreskog (1974; also see Marsh, 1988, 1989; Widaman, 1985) (a) there are at least three traits (T = 3) and three methods (M = 3), (b) T × M measured variables are used to infer T + M a priori factors, (c) each measured variable loads on one trait factor and one method factor but is constrained so as not to load on any other factors, (d) correlations among trait factors and among method factors are freely estimated but correlations between trait and method factors are fixed to be zero, and (e) the uniqueness of each scale is freely estimated but assumed to be uncorrelated with the uniquenesses of other scales. This general model, which we refer to as the CFA model with correlated traits and correlated methods (CFA-CTCM), is presented (Figure 10.1) for a 4T × 4M design. As has been noted elsewhere (e.g., Kumar & Dillon, 1992, p. 54), the lack of correlation between trait and method factors is an assumption that may be unrealistic in some situations. The constraint seems to be routinely applied to avoid technical estimation problems and to facilitate decomposition of variance into trait and method effects, not because of the substantive likelihood or empirical reasonableness. This potential limitation of the CFA approach is common to all the latent variables models considered in this chapter.

An advantage of this general CFA-CTCM model is the apparently unambiguous interpretation of convergent validity, discriminant validity, and method effects: large trait factor loadings indicate support for convergent validity, large method factor loadings indicate the existence of method effects, and large trait correlations—particularly those approaching 1.0—indicate a lack of discriminant validity. Also, in standardized form, the squared trait factor loading, the squared method factor loading, and the error component sum to 1.0 and can be interpreted as components of variance for each item. It is important to emphasize that these effects are not the same as the convergent, discriminant, and method effects inferred from the Campbell-Fiske approach. Consistent with Kenny and Kashy's (1992) assertion, our interpretation of Campbell and Fiske (1959) suggests that their original guidelines were implicitly based on a latent trait model like the CFA models. From this perspective, the operationalizations of convergent validity, discriminant validity, and method effects in the CFA approach apparently better reflect Campbell and Fiske's (1959) original intentions than do their own guidelines.

Widaman (1985) proposed a taxonomy of models that systematically vary different characteristics of the trait and method factors; the taxon-

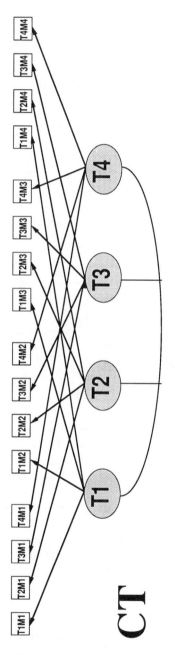

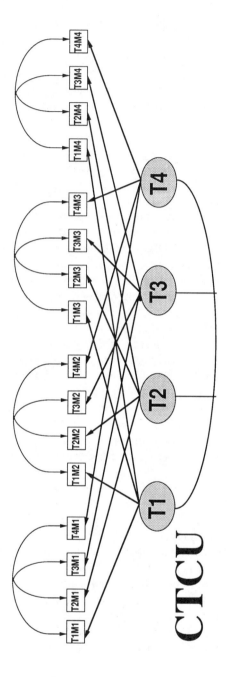

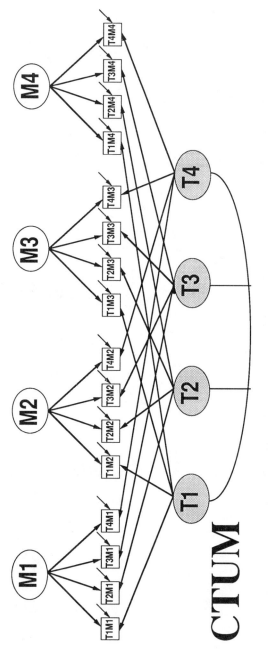

Figure 10.1. Four Confirmatory Factor Analysis (CFA) Models for a Design With Four Traits (T) and Four Methods (M)

NOTE: Each of the T × M = 16 measured variables (T1M1, T2M1, . . . , T4M4) is represented by a single measured variable (the boxes) and the latent trait factors (T1, . . . , T4) and latent method factors (M1, . . . , M4) are represented as ovals. CT = correlated trait model. CTCU = correlated trait/correlated uniqueness model. CTCM = correlated trait/correlated method model.

184

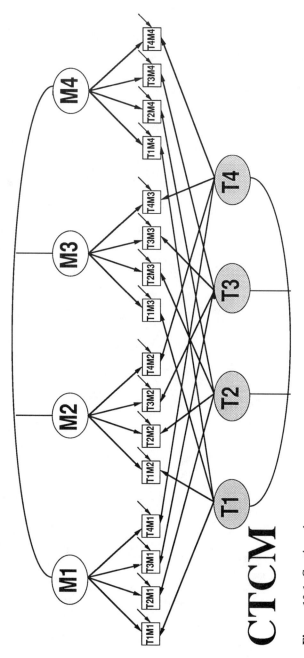

CTCM

Figure 10.1. Continued

omy was expanded by Marsh (1988, 1989). This taxonomy is designed to be appropriate for all MTMM studies, to provide a general framework for making inferences about the effects of trait and method factors, and to objectify the complicated task of formulating models and representing the MTMM data. Whereas detailed consideration of the taxonomy is beyond the scope of the present investigation (see Marsh, 1989), four models (Figure 10.1) are considered that we recommend as the minimum set of models for all CFA-MTMM studies.

The trait-only model (CFA-CT; Figure 10.1) posits trait factors but no method effects, whereas the remaining models posit trait factors in combination with different representations of method effects. Hence, the trait-only model is nested under the other CFA models so that the comparison of its fit with the fit of the other CFA models provides an indication of the size of method effects. Implicit in this operationalization of method effects is Jöreskog's (1971) contention that "method effects are what is left over after all trait factors have been eliminated" (p. 128; also see Marsh, 1989). The model with correlated trait factors but uncorrelated method factors (CFA-CTUM; Figure 10.1) differs from the CFA-CTCM model only in that correlations among the method factors are constrained to be zero. Hence the comparison of the CFA-CTCM and CFA-CTUM models provides a test of whether method factors are correlated.

In the correlated uniqueness model (CFA-CTCU; Figure 10.1), method effects are inferred from correlated uniquenesses among measured variables based on the same method instead of method factors (see Kenny, 1976; Kenny & Kashy, 1992; Marsh, 1989; Marsh & Bailey, 1991). Like the CFA-CTUM model, the CFA-CTCU model assumes that effects associated with one method are uncorrelated with those associated with different methods. The CFA-CTCU model differs from the CFA-CTCM and CFA-CTUM models in that the latter two models implicitly assume that the method effects associated with a given method can be explained by a single latent method factor (hereafter referred to as the assumption of unidimensionality of method effects), whereas the correlated uniqueness model does not. This important distinction is testable when $T > 3$. When $T = 3$ the CFA-CTUM and the CFA-CTCU models are formally equivalent (i.e., the number of estimated parameters and goodness of fit are the same, and parameter estimates from one can be transformed into the other).

The juxtaposition of the CFA-CTUM, CFA-CTCM, and CFA-CTCU models is important. The comparison of the CFA-CTUM and CFA-

CTCU models tests the unidimensionality of method effects (i.e., whether the method effects associated with each method form a single latent method factor), whereas the comparison of the CFA-CTUM and CFA-CTCM models tests whether effects associated with different methods are correlated. In general, the CFA-CTCU and CFA-CTCM are not nested, so their comparison is more complicated. For example, if both the CFA-CTCM and CFA-CTCU models fit the data substantially better than the CFA-CTUM, all three models may be wrong: The CFA-CTUM may be wrong because it assumes that the effects associated with each method are unidimensional and unrelated to the effects associated with other methods; the CFA-CTCM may be wrong because it assumes that the effects associated with each method are unidimensional; and the CFA-CTCU may be wrong because it assumes that the effects associated with each method are unrelated to the effects associated with other methods.

From a practical perspective, the most important distinction between the CFA-CTCM, the CFA-CTUM, and the CFA-CTCU models is that the CFA-CTCM model typically results in improper solutions, the CFA-CTUM model often results in an improper solution, and the CFA-CTCU almost always results in proper solutions (Kenny & Kashy, 1992; Marsh, 1989; Marsh & Bailey, 1991). For example, Marsh and Bailey (1991), using 435 MTMM matrices based on real and simulated data, showed that the CFA-CTCM model typically resulted in improper solutions (77% of the time) whereas the CFA-CTCU model nearly always (98% of the time) resulted in proper solutions. Improper solutions for the CFA-CTUM and particularly the CFA-CTCM models were more likely when the MTMM design was small (i.e., 3T × 3M vs. 5T × 5M), when the sample size was small, and when the assumption of unidimensional method effects was violated. From this practical perspective, the complications in comparing the CFA-CTCM, CFA-CTUM, and CFA-CTCU models may be of limited relevance because in many applications only the CFA-CTCU model results in a proper solution.

In conclusion, some recommendations can be offered about the design of CFA-MTMM studies. The typical MTMM study is a 3T × 3M design with a sample size of about 125. This design is apparently not adequate for the appropriate application of the CFA approach and may account for some of the problems typically encountered. The minimum sample size should be at least 250 and probably much larger given the apparent instability of CFA-MTMM solutions. It may be unrealistic to estimate six latent factors from only nine measured variables. The

Marsh and Bailey (1991) study suggests that more stable solutions can be obtained when the number of traits and methods increased at least up to the 7T × 4M and 6T × 6M designs that they considered. Also, the differentiation of models in Figure 10.1 requires T > 3. For these reasons we recommend a minimum of 4 traits and 3 methods, although it would be preferable to have even more traits and methods. If these minimal recommendations of T = 4, M = 3, and $N > 250$ cannot be achieved, the CFA approach may not be appropriate and should be interpreted cautiously.

Direct Product Models

The CFA approach to MTMM data discussed above assumes that trait and method factors contribute additively to the MTMM correlations, but Campbell and O'Connell (1967) suggested that the MTMM data sometimes show a multiplicative structure. They noted that MTMM matrices based on observed data (CORR) may have a structure consistent with intertrait correlations being attenuated by a multiplicative constant (smaller in magnitude than unity) when different methods are used. Swain (1975) proposed a direct product (DP) model that posits this type of structure for the observed covariance matrix but is easily reformulated to apply to the observed correlation matrix (see Browne, 1984b, section 4):

$$\text{CORR} = \begin{pmatrix} R_{11} & R_{12} & R_{13} \\ R_{21} & R_{22} & R_{23} \\ R_{31} & R_{32} & R_{33} \end{pmatrix} = \begin{pmatrix} R & S_{12}R & S_{13}R \\ S_{21}R & R & S_{23}R \\ S_{31}R & S_{32}R & R \end{pmatrix} = \begin{pmatrix} 1 & S_{12} & S_{13} \\ S_{21} & 1 & S_{23} \\ S_{31} & S_{32} & 1 \end{pmatrix} \times R = S \times R,$$

$$(10.1)$$

where "×" represents the direct product, and S and R have the same structure as correlation matrices, although they need not be interpreted in this way (see below). The typical element S_{ij} (= S_{ji}) of S represents the attenuation of trait-intercorrelations associated with different methods, i and j. The elements in S and R may or may not have an immediate interpretation in terms of method and trait factors (see distinction 2 below). Swain's DP model is more restrictive than the multiplicative model implied by Campbell and O'Connell (e.g., the DP model assumes HTMM correlations, R, are constant across methods). In subsequent discussion we use the multiplicative observed data to refer to data that conform to Swain's DP model.

The particular strength of this DP model is that when the data conform to the model, the model provides a mathematically elegant, summative test of the Campbell-Fiske criteria discussed previously (see Bagozzi & Yi, 1990; Cudeck, 1988, pp. 133-137; and Kumar & Dillon, 1992, for good expository accounts of this relation between parameters and criteria). Under certain conditions, the observed correlation matrix, $CORR = S \times R$, will satisfy all four of the Campbell-Fiske criteria. Criterion 1 is met if the S_{ij} terms are "large"; criteria 2 and 4 are ensured because R has the structure of a correlation matrix; criterion 3 is met whenever all the off-diagonal elements of S are larger than the off-diagonal elements of R.

Browne (1984b) extended this model to what is referred to as the composite direct product (CDP) model. In terms of the observed correlation matrix (see Goffin & Jackson, 1992), the CDP model may be written as

$$CORR = Z(CORR_c + E)Z = Z(S_c \times R_c + E)Z, \qquad (10.2)$$

where Z and E are diagonal and the direct product $S_c \times R_c$ can now be viewed as applying to the common factor scores underlying the $T \times M$ observed measures and disattenuated of "error" with correlation matrix $CORR_c$. That is, R_c and S_c play the same role with the common factor scores and $CORR_c$ in Browne's CDP model as R and S played in Swain's (1975) DP model in relation to the observed scores and $CORR$, these latter being the locus of Campbell and O'Connell's (1967) comments. The parameters in Z are designed primarily to absorb scaling changes in going from a covariance matrix to common factor correlation matrix and are typically of little interpretive interest. The E values reflect measurement error. Browne (1990) subsequently developed the MUTMUM statistical package used in the present investigation to estimate parameters for the CDP models.

At this stage, it is appropriate to emphasize several distinctions that may serve to avoid confusion in subsequent discussion of this new and frequently ill-understood area.

1. *"Additive" versus "Multiplicative" observed data.* We can anticipate multiplicativity of the above sort in relation to the observed MTMM matrix CORR. We also can contemplate observed data in which

additivity replaces multiplicativity (i.e., $S_{ij} + R$ replaces $S_{ij}R$, while still allowing CORR to be a correlation matrix). Whether the data conform to either of these patterns is entirely an empirical question. Additive data in this sense are not much discussed in the literature, and we may expect data in actual applications, particularly "formative" ones, not to conform to either of these types. However, if the data are multiplicative then the parameters in R and S provide an elegant and succinct way of describing how such data relate to the Campbell-Fiske (1959) criteria. Conversely, if the data do not have such a multiplicative structure and such a DP model is fit, then criteria 2 and 4 are forced on the data and the parameters relate to criteria 1 and 3 in some "summative" or aggregated manner that may be misleading (e.g., the model forces monomethod blocks to be identical).

2. *"Additive" versus "Multiplicative" score models.* Suppose y_{ir} is the score (omitting the subject subscript) observed with trait i and method r. Then y_{ir} may empirically have arisen from an additive combination of trait and method factors: $y_{ir} = a + t_i + m_r + e$, where a and e represent constant intercept and error-score components, respectively. This is the view underlying the CFA approach and much psychometric thinking in, say, the usual interpretations of correlation coefficients. Alternatively, y_{ir} may have arisen from the multiplication of trait and method factor scores that are themselves of empirical interest: $y_{ir} = a + \tau_i \mu_r$. If these latter multiplicative components are independent, then such a multiplicative-score model will yield multiplicative data like that discussed by Campbell and O'Connell (1967). In this case Swain's (1975) DP model will be appropriate and parameter matrices R and S will have direct empirical interpretations in terms of correlations among trait factors or correlations among method factors that combine multiplicatively to produce the data. However, such multiplicative data may also arise from an additive score model (see Kumar & Dillon, 1992). In this case, the DP model will fit, but R and S should not be interpreted directly as trait and method factor score intercorrelations; they are no more than elegant mathematical parameters that enable succinct summarization of the (additive) Campbell-Fiske (1959) criteria, and even they may be misleading when the data are not actually multiplicative. Similarly, the parameters in R_c and S_c will have empirical interpretations if the common factor scores have arisen from multiplication of trait and method factors (but will have only heuristic value when the common factor scores have arisen additively). So the "user" must decide whether a multiplicative or an additive score model is substan-

tively and theoretically appropriate, as this profoundly affects the interpretation of the DP (or CDP) parameters, even when the observed (or
common factor) data may be unambiguously multiplicative in the sense
of distinction 1 above. We join Kumar and Dillon (1992, see particularly pp. 58-59) in warning that entertaining multiplicative score models may have a substantial impact on much of what is psychometrically
taken for granted.

3. *Multiplicative/additive observed data versus multiplicative/addi-
tive score models.* These issues are potentially even more confusing
when one examines the relations between data and models. Swain's
(1975) DP model can produce only multiplicative observed data; however, both the general CFA model and the CDP model can produce
observed data that are multiplicative or additive. One situation in which
the CDP model must produce multiplicative data is when it specializes
to the DP model (i.e., when $Z = I$ and $E = 0$). Furthermore, the same
data are predicted by both the CDP and the CFA models under some
specific conditions (see Browne, 1989).

In summary, these distinctions serve to emphasize that CFA and CDP
models can sometimes both fit the same data, whether or not the data
are "multiplicative." So the CDP parameters should be interpreted as
either parameters that may aid in the "summative" evaluation of the
Campbell-Fiske (1959) criteria if we entertain an additive-score model
or as trait factor and method factor intercorrelations if we entertain a
multiplicative-score model—and in this case the Campbell-Fiske criteria may no longer by psychometrically appropriate. The choice between
additive and multiplicative score models, however, must be made external to the analysis and based on substantive and theoretical grounds.
We strongly emphasize that if a multiplicative score model is assumed,
the concepts of convergent and divergent validity need psychometric
rethinking (see Kumar & Dillon, 1992).

Application of the CFA and CDP Approaches

Initially we focus on the ability of the CFA and CDP models to fit
the data in Table 10.1. The evaluation of fit in structural equation modeling
has recently received considerable attention and a detailed discussion
of the issues is beyond the scope of this chapter (see Bentler, 1990;
Cudeck & Henly, 1991; Marsh, Balla, & McDonald, 1988; McDonald

& Marsh, 1990; and Chapter 5, this volume, for general discussions; and Marsh, 1989, for a discussion in relation to MTMM data). Although there are no well-established guidelines for what minimal conditions constitute an adequate fit, a general approach is to (a) establish that the solution is "proper" by establishing that the model is identified, the iterative estimation procedure converges, parameter estimates are within the range of permissible values, and the size of the standard error of each parameter estimate is reasonable; (b) examine the parameter estimates in relation to the substantive, a priori model and common sense; and (c) evaluate the χ^2 and subjective indexes of fit for the model and compare these to values obtained from alternative models.

PROPER SOLUTIONS

For both the CFA and CDP models, solutions are proper if the model is identified and if the estimated parameters fall within their permissible range. For models considered here a proper solution requires that all matrices of parameter estimates are positive definite. Thus, for example, in the CFA models there are no negative or zero variance estimates, and in the CDP models the matrices of scaling components and error components contain no negative or zero values. For the MTMM matrix considered here (Table 10.1), the CFA-CT and CFA-CTCU resulted in proper solutions whereas the CFA-CTUM and CFA-CTCM did not. Although the analysis of a single data set provides no basis for generalization, this pattern is typical of the CFA approach to MTMM data (see Marsh & Bailey, 1991).

The CDP model resulted in an improper solution and so we considered the slightly more restrictive version of the CDP model (see CDP-KE in Table 10.2) in which errors are constrained to have a direct product structure (see Browne, 1984b, 1990), a model that did result in a proper solution. In published studies the CDP typically results in proper solutions, so our improper solution for one data set may be atypical. We, however, used a somewhat more conservative definition of what constitutes a proper solution in that we judged a solution to be improper if it had "boundary conditions" (e.g., residual variance estimates of 0.0 or correlations of 1.0). This is consistent with our earlier criterion that all parameter estimation matrices must be positive definite. This is an important concern for CDP solutions based on Browne's (1990) MUTMUM statistical package, because it invokes many inequality constraints that require parameter estimates to fall within their

TABLE 10.2 Goodness of Fit of Alternative MTMM Models

Model	Proper	χ^2	df	TLI	RNI
CFA-CT	Yes	452	24	.877	.918
CFA-CTUM	No	65	15	.977	.990
CFA-CTCM	No	28	12	.991	.997
CFA-CTCU	Yes	65	15	.977	.990
CDP	No	150	21	.958	.975
CDP-KE	Yes	232	25	.943	.961

NOTE: TLI = Tucker-Lewis Index, RNI = Relative noncentrality index. See Figure 10.1 for a description of the CFA models. The null model used to compute the TLI and RNI posited that the nine measured variables represented nine uncorrelated factors ($\chi^2 = 5310$, df = 36).

permissible range (e.g., nonnegative variance estimates) so that boundary conditions typically reflect what would have been out-of-range parameter estimates (e.g., negative residual variances) if no constraints were imposed. Fortunately, however, the program specifically identifies all boundary conditions so the users can use appropriate caution in making interpretations.

More generally, whenever the CFA or CDP models result in improper solutions, it may be possible to impose further constraints on the models that will result in proper solutions as demonstrated with the two CDP models considered here (for a more detailed discussion of alternative, more highly constrained CDP models see Bagozzi & Yi, 1992; Browne, 1984b, 1990). For the CFA models, Marsh, Byrne, and Craven (1993) demonstrated how constraining parameters to be equal across multiple groups or constraining parameters to be equal within a single group can result in proper solutions when less constrained models result in improper solutions.

GOODNESS OF FIT

Here we evaluated goodness of fit in terms of the χ^2 that can be used to compute values for most other indexes, the relative noncentrality index (RNI; McDonald & Marsh, 1990; also see Bentler, 1990), and the Tucker-Lewis index (TLI; Tucker & Lewis, 1973; also see Marsh et al., 1988; McDonald & Marsh, 1990). Both the TLI and RNI indexes scale goodness of fit along a scale that, except for sampling fluctuations, varies between 0 and 1. Values greater than .9 are typically interpreted as indicating an acceptable fit, although it may be more useful to compare the values of alternative models. The TLI and RNI differ in that the TLI contains a penalty function based on the number of estimated parameters whereas the RNI does not. For all the models considered here the RNI and, except for the CFA-CT model (TLI = .877), the TLI are greater than .90. Although the best fit is for the CFA-CTCM model (TLI = .991), this model resulted in an improper solution. The next best fit was for the CFA-CTCU model (TLI = .977) and this solution was proper. Although the fit of the CFA-CT model was clearly poorer, even this parsimonious model that posited no method effects resulted in a marginal fit (at least in relation to the ".90 guideline"), suggesting that the method effects are not large. For the CDP models, the more highly constrained CDP solution with a direct product error structure does not fit the data as well as the unconstrained CDP model, even though the CDP solution is improper (Table 10.2).

The comparison of the fit indexes for the various CFA models (Table 10.2) is facilitated by the nested relations among the models. The CFA-CT model is nested under the other CFA models considered here so that comparisons with the other models provide an indication of the size of the method effects. Table 10.2 shows that the fit of the CFA-CT model is significantly poorer than those of the other CFA models, indicating the existence of method effects. Although the comparisons vary somewhat depending on which models are compared, the inferred method effects are not large.

The comparison of the CFA-CTUM and CFA-CTCU models provides a test of the unidimensionality of method effects associated with each method. When T = 3, as is the present situation, the CFA-CTUM and the CFA-CTCU models are equivalent although the CFA-CTUM solution may be improper if the three correlated uniquenesses in the CFA-CTCU model cannot be represented as a single latent factor. Thus inspection of Table 10.2 indicates that the CFA-CTCU solution is proper even though the CFA-CTUM solution is improper.

The comparison of the CFA-CTUM and CFA-CTCM models provides a test of whether the method effects associated with different methods are correlated. Table 10.2 shows that the fit of the CFA-CTCM is better than that of the CFA-CTUM model, suggesting that effects associated with different methods may be correlated. These results must, however, be viewed cautiously because both the CFA-CTCM and CFA-CTUM solutions are improper.

In general the CFA-CTCM and CFA-CTCU models are not nested, so it is possible for either model to fit the data better; however, when

T = 3, the models are equivalent, and so it follows that both the CFA-CTCU and CFA-CTUM models are nested under the CFA-CTCM model. Table 10.2 indicates that whereas the CFA-CTCM fit is marginally better than the CFA-CTCU fit, interpretations must be made cautiously because the CFA-CTCM solution is improper.

The examination of goodness of fit (proper solutions and the fit indexes) supports the CFA-CTCU model. There are, however, some relevant qualifications to these conclusions. Several different models provided apparently acceptable fits in that the solutions were proper and both the TLI and RNI were larger than .90. Because the CFA-CTCU model is considerably less parsimonious—uses more estimated parameters to fit the same data—it may be premature to claim that it fits the data better. Also, because the CFA and CDP models are so different, it is important to evaluate the usefulness of alternative models in terms of interpretations of the parameter estimates in relation to providing information about convergent validity, discriminant validity, and method effects, and to providing a formative evaluation of each trait-method unit.

INTERPRETATION OF PARAMETER ESTIMATES

Standardized CFA Parameter Estimates. For all the CFA models, large and statistically significant trait factor loadings provide an indication of convergent validity, whereas large trait factor correlations—particularly those approaching 1.0—suggest a lack of discriminant validity. Method effects are inferred from large and statistically significant method factor loadings in the CFA-CTCM and CFA-CTUM models, and from large and statistically significant correlated uniquenesses (among different variables assessed by the same method) in the CFA-CTCU model. In the CFA-CTCU solution (Table 10.3) the trait factor loadings are consistently very large, the trait factor correlations are small or moderate, and the correlated uniquenesses are small to moderate. As predicted, correlations between T2 and T3 are small whereas other trait correlations are larger. It is also evident that method effects are smaller for M1 than for M2 and particularly M3, whereas trait effects are smaller for M3. These results provide strong support for the construct validity of interpretations of these data.

CDP Parameter Estimates. We fit the CDP model with errors posited to be structured as direct products (see Browne, 1984b, 1990;

TABLE 10.3 Parameter Estimates for the Best-Fitting Models

	Trait Factor	Uniqueness	SMC	Uniqueness Correlations		
			CFA-CTCU Model			
T1M1	.852	.275	.724	1.000		
T2M1	.775	.394	.604	−.100	1.000	
T3M1	.942	.113	.887	−.010	−.116	1.000
T1M2	.707	.498	.501	1.000		
T2M2	.865	.224	.770	.145	1.000	
T3M2	.931	.142	.859	.130	.495	1.000
T1M3	.766	.381	.606	1.000		
T2M3	.758	.450	.561	.538	1.000	
T3M3	.849	.241	.750	.455	.213	1.000

Trait Correlations

T1	1.000		
T2	.605	1.000	
T3	.606	.046	1.000

CDP Model Direct Product Error Structure

Trait Correlations				Method Correlations			
T1	1.000			M1	1.000		
T2	.695	1.000		M2	.964	1.000	
T3	.616	.164	1.000	M3	.849	.838	1.000

Squared Multiple Correlations

T1M1	T2M1	T3M1	T1M2	T2M2	T3M2	T1M3	T2M3	T3M3
.640	.698	.901	.645	.707	.904	.857	.886	.968

NOTE: Each measured variable is a trait-method unit. T1M1, for example, is Trait 1 measured by Method 1. The squared multiple correlations (SMC) are an estimate of the communality for each measured variable.

Cudeck 1988) as a pragmatic alternative to the CDP model, because the CDP model resulted in an improper solution (Table 10.3). Critical parameters in the CDP solution, with or without additional constraints on the error structure, are those in the R_c and S_c matrices previously discussed. In light of earlier distinctions there are two ways of interpreting these results in relation to the P_c (disattenuated) matrix. If we assume that the data arose additively, we can apply the Campbell-Fiske guidelines in a summative sense. In this case, as noted earlier, large values in the off-diagonal of the S_c matrix are interpreted as support for convergent validity. Support for discriminant validity is inferred when the off-diagonal values in S_c are all larger than the off-diagonal values in R_c. In the present application, S_c parameter estimates are consistently very large and consistently larger than the parameter estimates in R_c. The estimated parameters, however, should not be directly interpreted as correlations among underlying additive trait and method factors, and so their formative value is limited.

If we assume that the common factor scores arose multiplicatively, then we are justified in interpreting the R_c parameters as trait correlations and the S_c parameters as method correlations; however, such a multiplicative relation would undermine much of the intuitive appeal of the Campbell-Fiske guidelines that are based on an additive logic (and, more generally, classical approaches to psychometrics; see Kumar & Dillon, 1992).

Summary and Implications

Different approaches to the analysis of MTMM data are described here. Even though all the approaches use a similar terminology (convergent validity, discriminant validity, and method effects), they employ different operationalizations of these terms and so are not equivalent. This has led to considerable confusion in MTMM research. For this reason it is useful to summarize strengths and weakness of the different approaches and to offer recommendations for their use.

The Campbell-Fiske (1959) approach continues to be the best known and most widely applied of the approaches. Despite important limitations such as a reliance on measured variables instead of latent constructs, this approach continues to be a potentially useful and heuristic approach to the formative evaluation of MTMM data. We recommend a systematic application of the expanded set of Campbell-Fiske guidelines to provide a preliminary inspection of the MTMM data prior to the application of more sophisticated approaches. The guidelines should not, however, be the sole basis for evaluating MTMM data.

The widely known terminology used in the Campbell-Fiske (1959) approach has provided an important starting point for other approaches; however, the terms convergent validity, discriminant validity, and method effects were not adequately defined in the Campbell-Fiske approach and so there is ambiguity in how they are operationalized in the alternative approaches. As asserted by Kenny and Kashy (1992), it appears that Campbell and Fiske (1959) implicitly based their original guidelines on a general CFA model. In the CFA-CTCM model it is clear that convergent validity, discriminant validity, and method effects are a function of the sizes of trait factor loadings, trait factor correlations, and method factor loadings, respectively. Because of this apparently unambiguous interpretation of these features based on the CFA-CTCM model, we recommend that this model should be used as a touchstone for defining terminology in MTMM studies and for evaluating new models or different approaches.

The CFA approach is the most widely used latent variable approach for the evaluation of MTMM data. A major limitation of this approach has been its reliance on the CFA-CTCM model that typically results in improper or unstable solutions. A growing body of research (e.g., Kenny & Kashy, 1992; Marsh, 1989; Marsh & Bailey, 1991) indicates that the problem of improper and unstable solutions is largely overcome through the application of the CFA-CTCU model. We recommend that at least the subset of CFA models considered here should be applied in all MTMM studies, but that the major emphasis should be placed on only those models that result in proper solutions. The preferred model within this set will depend on which models result in proper solutions and the ability of the alternative models to fit the data, but the CFA-CTCU model appears to be the strongest model in the CFA approach.

Although the direct product models have not been applied as widely as the CFA models, published findings reviewed earlier suggest that the CDP model typically results in proper solutions and provides an apparently good fit to MTMM data. Consistent with Browne's (1984b) claim, the CDP model may provide evidence about the Campbell-Fiske guidelines and about convergent and discriminant validity as embodied in these guidelines. Whereas the CDP model is extremely parsimonious, this may be at the expense of considerable formative information that was the original focus of the MTMM design. Although this inevitable compromise between parsimony and detail is both a strength and a weakness of the CDP approach, researchers need to be aware of this consideration when applying the CDP model. Indeed, we contend that DP and CDP models are of limited use to researchers who want to focus on the trait and method components associated with a particular trait-method combination, on the formative evaluation of their measures, and on the improvement of measurement instruments as originally advocated by Campbell and Fiske (1959).

Beyond the scope of this chapter is a discussion of a variety of new directions in MTMM analyses. Most MTMM studies using Campbell-

Fiske guidelines, CFA models, or CDP models begin with single indicators of each trait/method combination even though each trait/method combination is often based on multiple indicators (e.g., the individual items composing a scale). There are, however, important advantages in incorporating the multiple indicators into models like those considered here (see Marsh, 1993; Marsh & Hocevar, 1988). Although MTMM studies typically consider data from only one group, Marsh et al. (1993) demonstrated pragmatic and substantive benefits in testing the invariance of solutions across multiple groups. There may also be advantages in testing invariance constraints within a single group for CFA (Marsh et al., 1993) or direct-product (Bagozzi & Yi, 1992) models. MTMM studies typically focus on a "within-construct" component of construct validation, but Marsh (1988) and Marsh et al. (1993) demonstrated how external validity criteria can be incorporated into CFA-MTMM models.

In conclusion, this chapter has an important message for applied researchers who wish to use the MTMM paradigm. MTMM data have an inherently complicated structure that will not be fully described in all cases by any of the models or approaches typically considered. There is, apparently, no "right" way to analyze MTMM data that works in all situations. Instead, we recommend that researchers consider several alternative approaches to evaluating MTMM data—an initial inspection of the MTMM matrix using the Campbell-Fiske guidelines followed by fitting at least the subset of CFA models recommended by Marsh and Grayson (in press) and the CDP model. The Campbell-Fiske guidelines should be used primarily for formative purposes, the CDP model seems most appropriate for summative evaluations of the extent to which the MTMM data fulfill the Campbell-Fiske guidelines, and the CFA models apparently serve both summative and formative purposes. It is, however, important that researchers understand the strengths and weaknesses of the different approaches. For each of the different latent-variable approaches, researchers should evaluate results in relation to technical considerations such as convergence to proper solutions and goodness of fit, but they should also place more emphasis on substantive interpretations and theoretical considerations. Despite the inherent complexity of MTMM data, we feel confident that the combination of common sense, a stronger theoretical emphasis on the design of MTMM studies, a better quality of measurement at the level of trait-method units, an appropriate arsenal of analytical tools such as recommended here, and a growing understanding of these analytic tools will allow researchers to use the MTMM paradigm effectively.

11 Sex-Race Differences in Social Support and Depression in Older Low-Income Adults

JANE A. SCOTT-LENNOX

RICHARD D. LENNOX

Biomedical research, after years of using a universal (young, white male) model, has been forced to recognize the important influences of sex, race, age, and other characteristics on disease processes and treatment outcomes. Social science has long recognized sex, race, and their interaction as fundamental stratifying attributes in American society. They help define social roles and responsibilities, resources, socialization, and experiences a person has throughout life. Lifelong exposure to health hazards, economic disadvantage, and limited access to health care place female and black American rural elders at greater risk of physical disability, multiple chronic illnesses, and poverty (Crystal & Shea, 1990). Chronic stresses such as these increase the risk of depressive symptoms, which, in turn, reduce the effectiveness of medical treatments and discourage interaction with others, thereby perpetuating

AUTHORS' NOTE: We would like to thank Jane E. Morrow, E. Michael Bohlig, Lore K. Wright, Deborah L. Gold, Rick Hoyle, and an anonymous reviewer for helpful comments on earlier drafts of this chapter, and Dr. Harold L. Cook for the use of the data analyzed here.

The research was supported by NIH Multipurpose Arthritis Center Grant AM-30701 to the University of North Carolina at Chapel Hill, by the Numerical Science Core of the UNC Thurstone Multipurpose Arthritis Center, and by a National Institute of Aging Post-Doctoral Research Training Fellowship grant to the Center for the Study of Aging and Human Development at Duke University Medical Center.

the chronic stress cycle (Blazer, 1982). Despite these disadvantages, or perhaps because of them, high levels of informal social support—the care and help received from family members and friends—often are observed among populations at the most risk of chronic stress (Mercier & Powers, 1984).

As its label implies, social support theory generally assumes the universal utility of social relationships: If available and needed, supportive relationships with other people should help protect an individual from stress and its consequences. Hence, high levels of available support among disadvantaged groups would be expected to reduce their experience of stress and prevent distress. However, supportive relationships are embedded in social networks consisting of bivalenced ties— social relationships that contribute to stress in people's lives, even though they are supportive on other dimensions. The amount of support needed, the size of the network available to provide it, and even the characteristics of supporters all contribute to the adequacy of a social support network and to the extent of dependence on bivalenced networks.

Studies that find that the types and amounts of support available vary depending on a person's sex and/or race do not violate this basic assumption of the universal utility of support (e.g., Chatters, Taylor, & Jackson, 1985; Palinkas, Wingard, & Barrett-Connor, 1990; Scott & Roberto, 1985). However, studies also have found that the same social support resources differ in their ability to reduce or prevent distress for men and women (Dean, Kolody, & Wood, 1990; Haines & Hurlbert, 1992), for blacks and whites (Krause, 1989; Quevillon & Trennery, 1983; Vaux, 1985), or for men and women of the same race (Husaini et al., 1991). The source of supportive relationships and the extent to which the support source affects the proportion of bivalenced ties in the social network are important qualifiers to gender differences (Leffler, Krannick, & Gillespie, 1986), and perhaps race differences, in the benefits of social support.

In one of the most intriguing studies of gender differences in social support, Haines and Hurlbert (1992) found that three dimensions of support network range (density, diversity, and size) differentially affect exposure to stress for men and women, access to social support, and level of distress. Because their analyses were based on data from a population survey that could not fully control for major life stress associated with poverty or chronic illness, the complex relationships among support, stress, and depression implied by chronic stress theories are only partially explicated by these results. In addition, their analyses did not explore moderating effects of race or of sex-race interactions suggested by Husaini et al. (1990, 1991) and others.

Universal Versus Group-Specific Models of Support and Depression

The coincidence of high levels of social resources on one hand and high exposure to chronic stressors on the other, when combined with the many stratifying effects of sex and race, raises the following question: Given comparable levels of chronic stress and similar life circumstances, are the same social support resources equally available and valuable for reducing psychological distress, regardless of moderating effects of sex, race, or their interaction (sex-race)? Empirically, the most precise answer to this question lies in results of multigroup structural equation modeling (MSEM), wherein dimensions of support are used to predict depression for sex-race subgroups. When the theory underlying the model indicates that a mediating relationship among predictors of outcomes may vary by population subgroups, MSEM is preferable to multiple linear regression path-analytic models.

MSEM is uniquely suited for exploring this question because of its ability to test a theoretical model for its applicability to different groups simultaneously. MSEM models do not require cumbersome interaction terms and nested models to estimate hypothesized group differences in path-analytic model coefficients or model fit. A single χ^2 goodness-of-fit statistic evaluates a set of complex models—one for each group. To validate the usual assumption that groups are equivalent, groups can be required to have identical estimates for all parameters (a "fully constrained" or universal model). Differences among groups can be evaluated for their appropriateness by "freeing" some parameters (allowing one or more groups to vary uniquely), "fixing" (setting parameters to zero), and/or "constraining" (requiring two or more groups to have equal parameters) any or all parameters for different groups. MSEM analyses often begin by estimating a fully constrained model (equivalent to a full sample regression model), then relaxing constraints to allow for group-specific differences in particular parameters based on theory or inductive evidence (e.g., Lagrange multiplier tests for impact of freeing one or more constraints on model fit).

In deference to the substantial literature on social support and depression in older adults (for reviews, see Blazer, 1982; George, 1989), our study focuses on two dimensions of social networks that are likely to impact the mental health of older adults undergoing chronic stress. The first and most powerful social support dimension is a person's perception of the adequacy of her or his support network. Because evaluation of the adequacy of support resources is a function of resources *desired*, *available*, and *used* (Krause, 1989), satisfaction with support is a psychological experience in its own right and thus is closely associated with depressive symptoms and other measures of mental health. In contrast, quantitative or structural aspects of a person's social support network help determine whether a person is satisfied with her or his support, and only indirectly contribute to depressive illness. From the path-analytic perspective, this places satisfaction with support as a mediator in the linear relationship between support network characteristics and depression (Lin, 1986).

Based on Haines and Hurlbert (1992), three measures of network range are expected to predict satisfaction with support: network size, network density, and sex composition of network. People with larger social networks (size) are assumed to have, on average, access to more social resources overall, and thus a greater probability of having access to appropriate and desired social support. If so, network size should be an important predictor of satisfaction with available support and of mental health. Social resources also are more likely to be rallied to the person's support if the members of the network know one another well (high network density). Finally, differential gender roles that occupy today's social environment may translate into the provision of different types and amounts of social support. All other things equal, this would suggest that people whose networks contain both men and women are more likely to have access to a wider range of support than are those whose networks consist only of same-sex network members. When considering self-reported mental health, however, these structural features of social networks are likely to be useful only if people perceive them to be adequate and desirable. Therefore, objective components of network size, network density, and sex homophily are expected to affect self-reported mental health only as mediated through perceived adequacy of social support.

This theoretical model is illustrated in the path diagram in Figure 11.1, wherein three intercorrelated network structure components (size, density, and sex homophily) determine perceived support adequacy, which in turn predicts an individual's level of depressive symptoms. The three network structure variables do not directly influence depres-

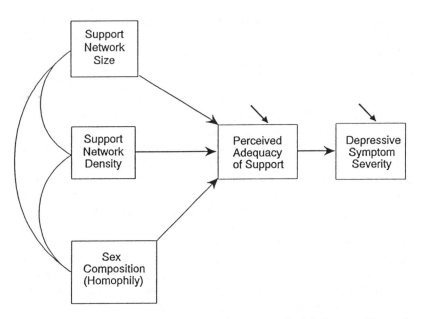

Figure 11.1. A Model of the Relationship Among Social Support Network Structure, Perceived Adequacy of Social Support, and Depressive Symptoms

sion in this model. Of course, all things are not equal, particularly when considering the various socioeconomic roles and resources allocated by gender and race. For this reason, we suspect that the adequacy of this model, or at least specific parameters in it, is likely to differ for men and women of different races.

TESTING THE EMPIRICAL MODEL

Three multigroup structural equation models are evaluated to test the theorized mediating effect of satisfaction with support, illustrated in Figure 11.1, as well as the moderating effects of sex and race. Comparison of the goodness-of-fit indexes for the models allows us to evaluate the appropriateness of each model.

For each group, depressive symptom severity is the ultimate dependent variable. It is predicted by perceived adequacy of social support, which mediates the effect of network size, density, and sex homophily. Residual variances in the dependent variables (depressive symptom severity and perceived adequacy of social support) not explained by the model are estimated as well. Network size, density, and sex homophily are free to correlate. Because all effects of support networks are expected to be mediated through perceived adequacy of support, their direct effects on depression are assumed to be zero, except in the final model, where the appropriateness of this assumption is formally tested.

The first model tested is a "universal" model that constrains all sex-race subgroups to have equal parameter estimates. It is comparable to a traditional path analysis for the full sample. Sex and race differences in the utility of support resources detected in past studies are assumed to be artifacts of the higher incidence of disadvantage experienced by some groups compared to others. Presumably, neither sex nor race is responsible for observed differences in depression but, rather, the higher incidence of disability, poverty, illness, and levels of support available that covary with sex and race is responsible. Once income, disability levels, and rural residence are controlled (as was done through the sampling frame in these data), the universal model hypothesizes (a) no significant group differences in parameter estimates and (b) equivalent model fit for all groups.

The second, "group-sensitive," model estimated acknowledges that sex-race subgroups may have distinct relationships among support and depression, despite the general applicability of the theoretical model. Its theoretical basis arises from Haines and Hurlbert (1992) and other studies that have found that sex or race stratify the utility of support resources for promoting psychological well-being. Extending these single modifier studies, our model assumes that the interaction of sex and race may predict different relationships in the theoretical model of depression and support. To identify significant group-specific differences, Lagrange multiplier (LM) tests of equality constraints across samples estimated in the universal model were examined. Equality constraints were removed only if they dramatically improved model fit. A change in χ^2 of 5.0 or more points per degree of freedom (i.e., $p <$ .01) was considered significant, rather than the usual 3.84 (when df = 1) or less.

Finally, in addition to freeing the parameters identified in the group-sensitive model, a third "direct-effect" model tested the assumption that most of the effects of support structure on depressive symptoms are mediated through satisfaction with support.

Method

SAMPLE

Assessing the effects of informal support among economically disadvantaged Americans precludes the use of patients who present themselves for treatment. Barriers to treatment associated with race, age, and economic disadvantage create a selection bias that would adversely affect the validity of the study. Therefore, we used data from a survey designed specifically to sample multiply disadvantaged rural elders who had arthritis (Cook et al., 1986). To participate in the study, a person had to (a) reside in a rural region of a predominantly rural Southern county, (b) have an annual household income at or below 185% of the federally established poverty level, and (c) believe he or she had arthritis. Because there were no rheumatology clinics in the county, and because low-income rural residents are less likely to use specialty medical care, subjects were recruited from lists of names referred by local general practice physicians, social service and county extension agents, enrolled study participants, and indigenous lay interviewers. Telephone screening and scheduling excluded the poorest candidates, whose homes had no telephone. Of those that could be contacted, roughly equal numbers of black and white Americans of each sex were used to test for the interaction of sex and race.

Demographics. Of the 219 subjects interviewed, 214 had complete data on all variables. Normal age distributions associated with arthritis generated a predominantly older sample with more than two thirds of the subjects age 60 or older (range = 32 to 88 years); however, mean age did not differ significantly across subgroups, $F(3, 210) = 1.59, p =$ ns. Years of education, $F(3, 210) = 5.04, p < .01$; percent married, $F(3, 210) = 12.38, p > .01$; percent widowed, $F(3, 210) = 19.54, p > .01$; household size, $F(3, 210) = 4.44, p > .01$; and proportion living alone, $F(3, 210) = 5.77, p > .01$, varied by sex, race, or their interaction. Women of both races completed more years of formal education than did black males and were more likely to live alone, with almost half (48%) of the white females living alone. Equally as many black males as white females were currently married, but black males reported substantially larger average household size than white females (2.4 vs. 1.2, respectively). Black females were dramatically more likely to be widowed than any other group, but many black widowed women still lived with others.

Health Status. Sex-race subgroups had comparable levels of functional limitations, pain severity, and years with arthritis, but white respondents reported more doctor diagnosed chronic illnesses, $F(3, 210) = 5.75$, $p < .01$, possibly a reflection of greater lifetime use of medical services than a true difference in health status across races. Epidemiologic studies would not have anticipated differences in type of arthritis observed in this sample (Cunningham & Kelsey, 1984). In particular, the overrepresentation of white males with rheumatoid arthritis (37.9%, compared with 20.4% for white females, 13.2% for black males, and 16.7% for black females) indicates a marked difference in health status among groups. Absence of differences in levels of functional disability or pain severity notwithstanding, there may be psychological or social consequences of having rheumatoid arthritis versus other type of arthritis that may have contributed to differences observed here.

PROCEDURE

In-home, 1.5- to 2-hour structured interviews conducted by sex- and race-matched interviewers provided self-report information on subjects' health status, functional limitations, social networks, and depressive symptoms, and authorization for rheumatologists to examine subjects' health records. For subjects whose medical records did not report the results of a standard rheumatological examination, arthritis diagnosis and physician assessment of functional limitations were obtained during examinations conducted by licensed rheumatologists associated with the project. Although 12.5% of the respondents were not examined by a rheumatologist, arthritis diagnosis was confirmed in 95% of all subjects who underwent a diagnostic examination, suggesting a high correspondence between self- and physician-diagnosis of arthritis in this sample.

MEASURES

Depressive Symptoms. The dependent variable, depressive symptom severity, was operationalized as the number and severity of self-reported depressive symptoms experienced during the two weeks preceding the interview using items from the Center for Epidemiological Studies Depression Scale (Radloff, 1977). The summary score used here is based on a total of the 16 negatively worded symptoms to avoid educational confounding of positively worded symptoms reported by Lin (1989). Each item has a possible range of 0 to 3 (0 = *not at all* to 3 = *5 or more days in the last two weeks*); hence, the summary score had a possible range from 0 to 48; 43 was the highest reported score in these data. Internal consistency of the unit-weighted CESD16 scale was high (coefficient alpha = .90).

Perceived Adequacy of Social Support (PASS). How satisfied a person was with her or his network was operationalized as the sum of responses to questions adapted from the Instrumental-Expressive Support Scale (Ensel & Woelfel, 1986) and from measures developed by Strogatz (Strogatz & James, 1986) to detect desire for more support. Scores for how often a respondent was bothered by not having a close companion, not seeing enough of people he or she feels close to, not having enough close friends, and not having someone who shows love and affection (with values ranging from 1 = *all the time* to 5 = *never*) were added to scores for whether the respondent wished she or he knew more people to talk with, to have a "good time" with, to depend on for help with chores or errands, and to rely on for help with arthritis-related problems (coded 1 = *wish I knew more people* to 5 = *already know enough people*). The unit-weighted sum of these eight items appeared to be internally consistent (coefficient alpha = .80) and resulted in the Perceived Adequacy of Support Scale (PASS), which ranged from extremely dissatisfied (coded as 8) to completely satisfied (coded as 40) with the quality and quantity of a subject's social support network.

Measures of Social Support Networks. To identify who subjects considered to be members of their social networks, the survey included two network "name generator" questions: one identifying all the people close to the respondent (a) who had (or would have) helped during a hard time or emergency and (b) with whom the respondent discussed important matters. *Network size* was operationalized as a count of all names elicited in response to the two network name generators (observed range = 0 to 13). *Network density* and *sex homophily* measured the structure and sex composition of a respondent's network. Density, based on "core" networks (the first five names mentioned in response to either question; Marsden, 1987), is a measure of how close the respondent believes network members are to each other. It is the mean of tie-level (member 1's relationship to member 2 and so on) variables that were coded 0 if the network members were strangers to one another, 1 if they were very close, and .5 if they were neither close nor strangers (range: 0 = *completely disconnected* to 1 = *completely connected*). Sex homophily, the proportion of the respondents' total support network members that were the same sex as the respondent, was created by coding each network member as same sex (1) or opposite sex (0) of respondent, the sum of which was then divided by total network size (range: 0 = *all opposite sex* or *no network* to 1 = *all same sex*).

STATISTICAL ANALYSES

Mean Comparisons. Group differences in access to support were evaluated as mean differences in each of the support measures across subgroups. Having controlled for socioeconomic and health status variations usually argued to determine mean psychological well-being and social support, mean support levels across sex-race subgroups were compared using analysis of variance.

Multigroup Structural Equation Models. Covariance matrices of the variables for each group were analyzed using EQS (Bentler, 1992a). In the first model, all parameters were constrained to be equal for all groups.

Results

SEX-RACE DIFFERENCES IN ACCESS TO SUPPORT

Table 11.1 presents means, standard deviations, and Pearson product moment correlations for each study variable by sex-race subgroup.

Depressive Symptoms (CESD16). Considering the multiple chronic disadvantages that study respondents were experiencing, it is not surprising that subgroups reported uniformly high levels of depressive symptoms, $F(3, 210) = 1.24$, $p > .29$. Indeed, means for all subgroups exceeded national averages for the 20-item standard scale, which average below 10 out of 60 possible points (Radloff, 1977). However, they

TABLE 11.1 Variable Means and Correlations by Sex-Race Subgroup

Variable	Mean	SD	CESD16	PASS	Size	Density
White Males						
CESD16	11.9	8.4				
PASS	33.9	5.9	−0.26			
Size	2.9	2.0	−0.01	0.01		
Density	0.8	0.4	0.04	−0.15	0.36	
Homophily	0.3	0.3	0.02	−0.00	0.37	0.52
White Females						
CESD16	15.4	10.2				
PASS	30.7	8.3	−0.43			
Size	3.2	1.5	−0.01	0.12		
Density	0.8	0.3	0.17	0.19	0.39	
Homophily	0.5	0.3	0.24	−0.31	0.29	0.30
Black Males						
CESD16	14.9	12.9				
PASS	30.2	8.1	−0.25			
Size	3.8	2.3	−0.11	0.06		
Density	0.8	0.3	−0.11	0.07	0.45	
Homophily	0.4	0.3	0.04	−0.07	0.37	0.02
Black Females						
CESD16	13.7	9.8				
PASS	31.4	7.4	−0.42			
Size	4.2	2.3	0.32	−0.02		
Density	0.8	0.4	0.06	0.04	0.45	
Homophily	0.6	0.3	0.03	0.34	0.32	0.32

NOTE: CESD16 = 16-item Center for Epidemiological Studies Depression Scale; PASS = Perceived Adequacy of Social Support Scale.

were comparable to means reported in samples of disabled adults (Turner & Wood, 1985).

Satisfaction With Support (PASS). Most subjects were satisfied with the number of supporters in their social networks and felt the support they had was adequate. White males reported higher levels of satisfaction with their support networks, on average, but only marginal subgroup differences in means were observed, $F(3, 210) = 2.62, p = .052$.

Structure of Support Networks. For all sex-race subgroups except white males, average network size was greater than the 3.01 ties reported in the national probability survey (1985 General Social Survey; GSS) that used a similar name generator (Marsden, 1987). Bonferroni tests found the most significant differences between groups were those between the large networks of black females and small networks of white males, $F(3, 210) = 4.46$, $p < .005$. Networks reported here generally were more dense than those observed in national samples (Marsden, 1987), presumably because of the combined effect of rural residence, poverty, and advanced age, which have each been argued to constrain the range of social networks (Linn, Husaini, Whitten-Stovall, & Broomes, 1989). There were no sex-race differences in mean density, $F(3, 210) = .25$, $p > .86$. A comparison of sex-race subgroup means revealed dramatic differences in sex composition of networks, with same-sex ties more common for women, especially black women, $F(3, 210) = 11.47$, $p < .001$.

THE UNIVERSAL MSEM MODEL

Derivations of Degrees of Freedom. The universal model estimated the theoretical model depicted in Figure 11.1, assuming that sex-race groups would not differ in parameter estimates or model fit. The universal structural equation model is based on four covariance matrices, each with five measured variables, for a total across the samples of 20 variances and 40 covariances (df = 60). For all three models, variances are free to differ by group for all variables. In the universal model, 27 parameters were estimated for all four groups simultaneously: three coefficients for the covariances among the exogenous variables, another three for the direct effects of network variables on perceived social support, one for direct effects of perceived social support on depression, plus the 20 variances (five variables × four groups). Thus the χ^2 for the universal model is based on 33 degrees of freedom (60 possible parameters minus 27 estimated parameters). The group-specific model consumes an additional 5 degrees of freedom to estimate differences implied by LM tests (df = 28). Finally, the model evaluating the appropriateness of the mediation model uses another 12 degrees of freedom (df = 16).

Table 11.2 presents standardized coefficients and goodness-of-fit tests estimated in the fully constrained universal model and in the group-sensitive multisample structural equation models tested here.

TABLE 11.2 Standardized Coefficients for Two Models of Social Network Characteristics (Size, Density, and Sex Homophily), Perceived Adequacy of Social Support (PASS), and Depressive Symptom Severity (CESD16)

Parameters	Universal Model Estimates				Group-Sensitive Model Estimates			
	White Males	White Females	Black Males	Black Females	White Males	White Females	Black Males	Black Females
CESD16-PASS	−.33*	−.39*	−.29*	−.38*	−.32*	−.39*	−.30*	−.38*
PASS-Size	.03	.02	.03	.03	.04	.02	.03	.03
PASS-Density	.00	.00	.00	.00	−.11	.33*	−.07	−.08
PASS-Homophily	−.00	−.00	−.00	−.00	.04	−.44*	−.07	.36*
Size-Density	.39*	.47*	.37*	.37*	.40*	.48*	.41*	.38*
Size-Homophily	.37*	.41*	.26*	.27*	.38*	.42*	.30*	.27*
Density-Homophily	.36*	.33*	.29*	.31*	.45*	.41*	−.04	.37*
CESD16 Equation Error	.94	.92	.95	.93	.95	.92	.95	.93
PASS Equation Error	1.00	1.00	1.00	1.00	1.00	.90	1.00	.94

Goodness-of-Fit Indexes

Model chi-square	$\chi^2 = 51.94$, df = 33, $p = .02$	$\chi^2 = 24.60$, df = 28, $p = .66$
Nonnormed fit index	.79	1.04
Comparative fit index	.83	1.00

Asterisks indicate parameters that are different from 0 at the .05 level of statistical significance. Group differences in standardized parameter estimates reflect group-specific differences in variances for the variable.

Not surprisingly, the fully constrained model produced a less than desirable fit to the observed data. The nonnormed fit index (= .79) was unimpressive, as was the comparative fit index (= .83). From an inferential perspective, the fit between the observed and modeled covariance matrix was reasonably good, $\chi^2(33, N = 214) = 51.94$, $p = .02$, although it was statistically significant at less than the .05 level, which indicates the fit may be improved by freeing some of the equality constraints.

THE GROUP-SENSITIVE MODEL

LM tests indicated that the removal of five equality constraints would significantly improve the fit of the model. The LM tests indicated that releasing the requirement that network density and sex homophily be associated at the same level for the white and black males would improve the fit of the model, $\Delta\chi^2(1, N = 214) = 8.06$, $p = .005$. Evidence of this inequality is reflected in the correlations between sex homophily and network density (see Table 11.1) for these two groups. The r for density-homophily was .51 for white males but only .02 for black males; correlations for women of both races were nearly identical, although somewhat lower than for white males. These differences suggest that the tendency for dense networks to comprise members of the same sex does not hold for black males but does for all other subgroups, particularly white males.

Allowing group-specific estimates for the relationship between sex homophily and perceived social support also should significantly improve the fit of the model. Specifically, men of both races appeared to be more similar in the effects of sex ratio on satisfaction with support than were women; however, white and black women had opposite relationships between satisfaction with support and the sex composition of their networks. This is reflected in the correlation (Table 11.1) between PASS and sex homophily; for white women, the correlation is substantial and negative ($r = -.31$), whereas black women have a strong positive association between same-sex networks and satisfaction with support ($r = .34$). The LM test indicated that allowing groups to have unique estimates of the degree of association between sex homophily and satisfaction would reduce the χ^2 by at least 10.66 (df = 3, $p < .005$).

Finally, race and sex also interacted to predict the relationship between network density and perceived social support. Dense networks were associated with low perceived social support in the white male sample but with high perceived social support among white females; however, network density was not a strong predictor of satisfaction with support for either black men or women in this sample. LM test results indicated that releasing the constraint that white females be equal to other groups would reduce the χ^2 by 5.46 (df = 1, $p = .019$).

The appropriateness of the implied group-specific model was confirmed by the expected impact both on parameter estimates and on model fit. The following constraints were removed to capture significant group-specific differences in the universal model:

1. White females were allowed a unique parameter estimate for the relationship between network density and perceived support adequacy (1 df).
2. All groups were allowed unique estimates for the association between sex composition of support networks and satisfaction with support (3 df).
3. Black males were allowed a unique parameter estimate for the association of density and sex composition (1 df).

The goodness-of-fit indexes for the group-specific model support the removal of these equality constraints. All three indexes indicate that the group-specific model provides an excellent fit to the observed data with little significant covariance left to be explained. Removing these five equality constraints significantly improved overall model fit, $\Delta\chi^2(5, N = 214) = 27.34$, $p < .001$—a significantly better fit between the observed and modeled covariance matrices for all subgroups. The value of the nonnormed fit index fell outside its usual range because of sampling fluctuation as a result of the small sample on which the analyses are based. The comparative fit index, which is more reliable in smaller samples, indicates an excellent fit of these data with the group-specific model.

From the perspective of the fit indexes, the group-specific model in which the effects of three network variables are mediated through perceived social support is consistent with the data. Satisfaction with support was a strong predictor of lower levels of depressive symptoms for all four groups. However, network characteristics predicted satis-faction only for women. This is reflected in individual parameter esti-mates as well as in larger R^2 for the equation predicting satisfaction.

Relationships Among Network Characteristics. Correlations among the three network variables were positive and significant, with the exception of network density and sex homophily in the black male sample ($r = -.04$). The contrast among the groups on this specific relationship was most striking when black males were compared to white males ($r = .45$).

Network Characteristics as Predictors of Satisfaction With Support. Direct effects of network variables on perceived adequacy of social support were more distinctive than were relationships among network characteristics. None of the parameter estimates of the direct effects of structure on satisfaction for males of either race was significantly different from zero. In contrast, dense networks and networks with opposite sex network members predicted satisfaction with support in the white female sample. The relationship between sex-composition of network and satisfaction was reversed in the black female sample; female-dominated networks were associated with greater satisfaction with support for black women.

Satisfaction With Support and Depressive Symptom Severity. Perceived social support predicted depression for all groups, although the estimate of this relationship varied by almost .10.

DIRECT EFFECTS OF NETWORKS ON DEPRESSIVE SYMPTOMS

To evaluate the assumption that direct effects of support structure on depressive symptoms are unimportant, a final model was tested (parameters not reported). This direct-plus-mediated-effect model freed each group to have unique estimates of the direct effects of network structure variables on depressive symptoms beyond those captured by the mediating effects through perceived adequacy of support. Twelve new parameters were tested for their ability to improve the fit to the observed data.

Out of the twelve new parameters, z-tests indicated that only two were statistically different from zero. For white females, there was a positive relationship between network density and depression that was significant ($b = .27$, $z = 1.98$, $p < .05$), whereas for black females the direct relationship between network size and depression was statistically different from zero ($b = .34$, $z = 2.34$, $p < .05$). For white women, the more dense their social network, the more depressive symptoms they reported; for black women, the larger their social network, the more depressive symptoms they experienced, irrespective of their perceived social support. Although removing the constraints that the direct effects were zero reduced the χ^2 associated with the initial model from 24.60 to 13.51, the loss of 12 degrees of freedom made the fit no longer statistically significant ($p = .009$). Moreover, the $\Delta\chi^2$ with 12 degrees of freedom did not indicate a significant statistical improvement in fit by removing the zero constraints on the direct effects.

Discussion

When taken together, differences and similarities observed in the group-sensitive model recommend it for understanding the relationship between perceived adequacy of support and depression, as well as in the ability of social network characteristics to predict satisfaction with support. Moreover, MSEM made it possible to evaluate the adequacy of a theoretically derived model as well as to test the generalizability of parameter estimates across major social groups. Substantively, this multigroup structural equation model suggests that different causal mechanisms may link social support networks with perceived adequacy of support. These data also demonstrate a universal linkage between perceived social support and severity of depressive symptoms in this chronically stressed sample of low-income rural elders who have arthritis.

Palinkas et al. (1990), in summarizing their findings, argued that the structure of support networks

> is influenced by age, physical disability, and mortality of network members, and by culturally-determined rules that define the individuals and institutions available for support. However, these rules appear to differ for men and women. (p. 441)

Data presented here support and extend these conclusions by showing that race interacts with sex to define the availability and benefit associated with informal supportive relationships. For all groups, satisfaction with support was associated with lower depressive symptom severity scores. Beyond this, race differences within gender and gender differences within race were as common as the larger effects of gender or race on both access to support and its utility for promoting or protecting psychological well-being. It may be that some groups must rely more heavily on ties that are stressful as well as supportive. If so, the hypothesized benefits of network size, density, and sex composition would be attenuated for these groups relative to other groups.

These findings must be replicated in other samples before they are used to direct policy decisions. The sampling framework for this study was limited and nonrepresentative. In addition, the snowball technique used to generate the sample was not a random process and may over-sample unusual subgroups. Generalization of these results beyond sex-race comparisons of low-income rural Southern elders who have arthritis is inappropriate, unless the results are first replicated on more representative samples. In addition, the small samples studied, coupled with the use of post-hoc inductive model fitting techniques, and the large number of parameters estimated in these models are known contributors to increased likelihood of Type I errors. To ensure that these results are not serendipitous, they must be replicated on independent samples.

In conclusion, past research anticipated that the subjects in this sample would be particularly vulnerable to psychological distress if their support systems were inadequate. However, because physical health status, functional limitations, income, and age were controlled through sampling, the usual explanation that race or sex differences are artifacts of disadvantages in health or economic status is untenable here. Observed differences in the amount of available support, as well as in the effectiveness of support for protecting or promoting psychological well-being, emphasize the need for a more sophisticated theoretical and methodological appreciation of the impact of sex and race on social worlds. In particular, we need theories integrating social support and social stratification that recognize structural constraints on well-being that sex and race create, and how these operate throughout the life course. Future theories need to address sex and race independently and interdependently as determinants of psychologically protective social environments, so that formal support programs and policies can be developed to meet the needs of chronically stressed elders.

Multigroup structural equation models serve as powerful tools for advancing theory of the roles of sex and race in the psychological effects of social relationships. Rather than accepting a "one-size-fits-all" theory or relying on cumbersome and often uninterpretable complex interaction models, MSEM provides a direct method for simultaneous testing and evaluating of hypotheses about group effects. MSEM also can be used to estimate group-specific measurement error in latent structure equations, including those based on categorical observed variables. The diversity of MSEM estimation techniques available invites more use of these models for theory building and testing in social and behavioral research.

12 Modeling the Relation of Personality Variables to Symptom Complaints

The Unique Role of Negative Affectivity

JAY G. HULL

JUDITH C. TEDLIE

DANIEL A. LEHN

The last decade has witnessed a proliferation of personality constructs theorized to be relevant to health and health behaviors. These include negative affectivity (Watson & Pennebaker, 1989), self-esteem (Antonucci, Peggs, & Marquez, 1989), social anxiety (Snyder, Smith, Augelli, & Ingram, 1985), sense of challenge (Hull, Petterson, Kumar, & McCollum, 1993), optimism (Scheier & Carver, 1985), cynical hostility (Dembroski & Costa, 1987), hardiness (e.g., Hull, Van Treuren, & Virnelli, 1987; Kobasa, 1979), perceived self-efficacy (Bandura, O'Leary, Taylor, Gauthier, & Gossard, 1987), attributional style (Peterson, Seligman, & Vaillant, 1987), and Type A coronary-prone behavior pattern (Booth-Kewley & Friedman, 1987). When confronted with such a list, the question naturally arises: To what extent are all of

AUTHORS' NOTE: Portions of this chapter were presented at the annual meeting of the American Psychological Society, Washington, DC, June, 1991.

these variables related to health because they are tapping into the same general construct? This question involves two separate issues: (a) is there a general construct that underlies many health relevant personality traits and (b) is it the general trait rather than unique aspects of the individual traits that is related to health outcomes?

General Personality Factors and
Their Relation to Health

Recently, considerable progress has been made in specifying a general model of the structure of personality traits. According to this model, personality traits share a five-factor structure (e.g., John, 1990). Typical labels for these factors are neuroticism, extraversion, conscientiousness, agreeableness, and culture. If personality traits have a general structure, then which dimensions of that structure are most strongly related to health behaviors and outcomes? The answer most likely depends on the health outcome of interest. For the present investigation, the domain of principal interest is symptom complaints. Many have suggested that symptom complaints are related to the general factor of neuroticism. This argument has been made both in general reviews of the literature (e.g., Costa & McCrae, 1987; Watson & Pennebaker, 1989) and in research on alternative explanations for the relation of specific personality characteristics to symptom complaints (e.g., as an alternative to hardiness, Funk & Houston, 1987; as an alternative to optimism, Smith, Pope, Rhodewalt, & Poulton, 1989). Others have argued that illnesses are related to variables that are easily recognized as components of neuroticism (e.g., anxiety and depression).

General Factors or Unique Traits?

If one adopts the view that there is a general factor underlying the personality characteristics related to symptom complaints, then one needs to test whether or not a general factor does underlie such traits and whether it is this general factor rather than the unique traits that is responsible for the association of the individual traits with health complaints.

TESTING FOR THE PRESENCE
OF A GENERAL FACTOR

Using a confirmatory factor-analytic approach, it is possible to compare different models of personality traits in order to address the question of whether a single factor is adequate to capture the interrelations of a collection of personality characteristics. The models of greatest interest are (a) a first-order one-factor model, (b) a higher-order factor model with one second-order factor, and (c) a group factor model.

According to a *first-order one-factor model*, all of the items from all of the various trait scales are measuring the same thing. More formally, the reason that items from a particular scale are highly correlated with each other (interitem reliability) and the various scales are highly correlated with each other is that all of these measures assess the same construct (e.g., neuroticism).

In contrast to the first-order one-factor model, according to a *higher-order factor model* the individual scales are associated with discriminable dimensions of a higher-order construct. More formally, the reason that items from a particular scale are highly correlated with each other is that they all measure the same, somewhat specific construct. The reason that these specific constructs correlate with each other is that they are all related to a single, general construct. Despite sharing a significant amount of variance with this general construct, the specific constructs retain a significant amount of variance that is unique (unshared with the general construct).

Finally, according to a *group factor model*, individual scales are associated with discriminable dimensions that are linked in complicated, although theoretically sensible, ways. As a consequence of this complexity, considerable variation exists in the degree to which the specific constructs are related. A single, general construct is inadequate to account for this variation.

Each of these models can be subjected to an explicit statistical test using structural equation modeling techniques (e.g., Bollen, 1989b). Such models are typically evaluated in three ways: (a) using overall fit statistics to judge the general adequacy of a particular model, (b) using component fit statistics to judge the adequacy of individual aspects of a particular model, and (c) using overall fit statistics and rules of parsimony to compare alternative models to each other (see Chapters 2 and 5). An acceptable model should show statistically significant components and good overall fit according to a variety of statistics. Direct comparison should reveal the best model among those hypothesized. Among models that fit equally well, preference is given to the most parsimonious (see Chapter 7). In structural equation modeling, parsimony is judged according to the number of parameters that must be estimated (e.g., Anderson & Gerbing, 1988). In general, first-order factor models are more parsimonious than higher-order factor models, which are in turn more parsimonious than group factor models. If, in fact, a general factor underlies a variety of personality characteristics, then a first-order or higher-order factor model should fit the data as well as a group factor model and should be preferred on the basis of parsimony. Even in cases in which a group factor model fits better than a first-order or higher-order factor model, the latter models might be preferred when a small improvement in fit is gained at the cost of a considerable loss in parsimony.

TESTING FOR THE EFFECTS OF GENERAL FACTORS AND UNIQUE TRAITS

Given evidence that a general factor underlies a variety of health-relevant personality characteristics, it is necessary to test whether the general factor or the unique aspects of individual traits is responsible for an association with health outcomes. Let us take the Watson and Pennebaker (1989) proposition that a variety of personality traits exist that are all related to symptom complaints because they are indicators of neuroticism. This hypothesis is represented in Figure 12.1 as Model 1. In Model 1, each trait (t) is responsible for variation in responses to a number of questionnaire items (i). Variance in the items that is not due to the trait is considered to be a consequence of measurement error (e). At the same time, each trait is associated with the other traits in the model because of their common association with the general latent variable of neuroticism (N). Although each trait is related to N, each also retains some unique variance (u). This unique variance can be thought of as variance in the trait that is unrelated to N but is not simply measurement error. In Model 1, it is the general factor N (rather than the unique aspects of the individual traits) that is responsible for variation in symptom complaints (SC).

Although Model 1 represents our initial theory, let us imagine that we are wrong: Trait t_x is related to symptom complaints because of something unique about it. This can be represented by Model 2 (individual items and errors are not represented in subsequent models for

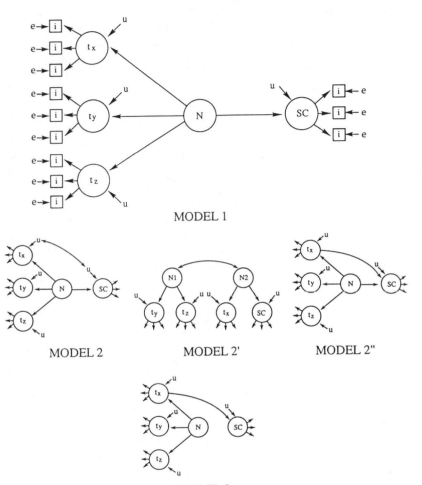

MODEL 1

MODEL 2 MODEL 2' MODEL 2"

MODEL 3

Figure 12.1. Five Models of the Relations Among Personality Traits, General Neuroticism, and Symptom Complaints

the sake of simplicity). In this case, the uniqueness (u) of trait t_x is related to the uniqueness (u) in symptom complaints (i.e., variance in symptom complaints that is not explained by N). Two additional models are statistical (although not conceptual) equivalents to Model 2 and deserve consideration. Model 2' holds that trait t_x and symptom complaints are both indicators of their own factor (N2) that is correlated with neuroticism (N1). Model 2″ holds that N and trait t_x are independently responsible for variance in symptom complaints.

Finally, let us consider the case in which it is trait t_x and not the general factor N that is responsible for symptom complaints. This possibility is represented in Model 3. Model 3 is a slightly simplified version of Model 2″ in which the direct path between N and symptom complaints has been dropped. According to this model, trait t_x can be thought of as mediating the association between neuroticism and symptom complaints. Thus t_x is either *the* aspect of neuroticism responsible for symptom complaints or it is a separate construct that is affected by neuroticism and in turn affects symptom complaints.

Our own preliminary research suggested that, consistent with the reasoning of Watson and Clark (1984) and Watson and Pennebaker (1989), many traits are related to symptom complaints because of their association with a general factor that we labeled neuroticism. However, one particular trait appeared to play a unique role in predicting symptom complaints. Thus negative affectivity, or a general tendency to report negative emotions, was more highly related to symptom complaints than its association with general neuroticism would suggest. We therefore conducted the three studies reported in this chapter to explore the generality of this effect. In each of these studies, we tested the five models illustrated in Figure 12.1. To foreshadow our findings: In Model 1 the general factor N was always related to symptom complaints despite the fact that the particular personality traits used as indicators of N varied widely across the three studies. Furthermore, Model 2 with negative affectivity playing the role of trait t_x always fit better than Model 1. Although Models 2, 2′, and 2″ provided equivalent fits, Model 2′ showed evidence of misspecification and in Model 2″ the general factor N was never associated with symptom complaints when a direct relation was postulated between negative affectivity and symptom complaints. Given the latter finding, we were always led to Model 3 as a more parsimonious account of the data.

Studies 1-3

Although our data were collected as parts of three separate studies, each study differing from the other in terms of measurement instruments, we report them simultaneously for the sake of brevity and clarity. Studies 1-3 differed in terms of the particular personality traits that were measured. In each case, traits were selected that other researchers have argued (a) are associated with neuroticism and (b) predict psychological and physical health. In our view, Watson and Clark (1984) have made the strongest argument that a variety of apparently diverse personality scales are in fact measures of the same stable and pervasive trait of neuroticism (e.g., "a number of personality measures . . . , despite dissimilar names, nevertheless intercorrelate so highly that they must be considered measures of the same construct," p. 465). In Study 1, four constructs that Watson and Clark (1984) identified as components of this trait were investigated: negative affectivity, self-esteem, sense of challenge/threat, and social anxiety. In Study 2, social anxiety and self-esteem were replaced as indicators of neuroticism with another variable discussed by Watson and Clark (1984): optimism-pessimism. Study 3 included all five measures of neuroticism included in Studies 1 and 2, plus the six neuroticism subfacets from the NEO Personality Inventory (Costa & McCrae, 1985).

Watson and Pennebaker (1989) argued that the latent variable underlying neuroticism traits is strongly associated with symptom complaints. As evidence, they cite numerous studies that have found an association between symptom complaints and measures they identify as indicators of neuroticism. These arguments were the basis of Model 1 in the present studies. According to this model, all of the individual traits that we have chosen for the present studies are related to symptom complaints only because of their association with a single higher-order factor.

Method

SUBJECTS

Subjects in Study 1 were 177 undergraduates. Subjects in Study 2 were 187 undergraduates. Subjects in Study 3 were 168 undergraduates. All subjects participated in one and only one of the three studies. In each case, subjects participated in return for extra credit in an introductory psychology course. All subjects completed a multiple questionnaire booklet that included the instruments used in these studies. In each study, some subjects failed to complete all of the items from all of the scales and were excluded from further analysis (11 subjects in Study 1, 16 in Study 2, and 22 in Study 3).

INSTRUMENTS

Study 1. Subjects completed the trait version of the Positive and Negative Affect Schedule (PANAS; Watson, Clark, & Tellegen, 1988) as a measure of dispositional negative affect (Study 1 negative affect subscale α = .82), the Rosenberg Self-Esteem scale (RSE; Rosenberg, 1979) as a measure of global self-esteem (Study 1 α = .88), the Self-Consciousness Scale (SCS; Fenigstein, Scheier, & Buss, 1975) as a measure of dispositional social anxiety (Study 1 α = .72), and the Life Situations Scale (LSS; Hull et al., 1993) as a measure of dispositional challenge (Study 1 α = .86). Finally, subjects completed the Cohen-Hoberman Inventory of Physical Symptoms (CHIPS; Cohen & Hoberman, 1983) as a measure of symptom complaints (Study 1 α = .88).

Study 2. Subjects completed the Life Orientation Test (LOT; Scheier & Carver, 1985) as a measure of dispositional optimism (Study 2 α = .82). As in Study 1, negative affectivity was assessed using the negative emotion traits from the PANAS (Watson et al., 1988; Study 2 α = .83), challenge was assessed using the LSS (Hull et al., 1993; Study 2 α = .84), and symptoms were assessed using the CHIPS (Cohen & Hoberman, 1983; Study 2 α = .81).

Study 3. Subjects completed the NEO-PI (Costa & McCrae, 1985) as a measure of the five major factors of personality. The neuroticism factor is itself divided into six subfacets: self-consciousness, impulsivity, anxiety, depression, hostility, and vulnerability. In the present study, these subfacets were each treated as indicators of neuroticism and were associated with acceptable reliability coefficients (self-consciousness, α = .74; impulsivity, α = .71; anxiety, α = .87; depression, α = .83; hostility, α = .77; vulnerability, α = .79). As in Studies 1 and 2, negative affectivity was assessed using the PANAS (Watson et al., 1988) as a measure of dispositional negative affect, challenge was assessed using the LSS (Hull et al., 1993), and symptoms were assessed using the CHIPS (Cohen & Hoberman, 1983). As in Study 1, social anxiety was assessed using the SCS (Fenigstein et al., 1975) and self-esteem was assessed using the RSE (Rosenberg, 1979). As in Study 2, optimism was assessed using the LOT (Scheier & Carver, 1985). Reliabilities of all scales were similar to those observed in the previous studies.

Results

The first step in analyzing the results involved parcelling each personality trait scale by assigning one third of the items to each of three indicators. Parcelling has multiple advantages over using individual items as indicators (e.g., Rindskopf & Rose, 1988). Of key concern for the present investigation, parcelling allows for the tripartite separation of scale variance into (a) measurement error, (b) variance resulting from the higher-order latent variable of neuroticism, and (c) uniqueness, or variance associated with the individual scale that is not attributed to measurement error or to the higher-order latent variable. Without parcelling, estimates of (b) are attenuated by error, and (a) cannot be distinguished from (c). Finally, specifying three indicators per latent variable is widely recommended as a means of avoiding problems with identification, negative variance estimates, and nonconvergence (e.g., Bollen, 1989b).

PERSONALITY FACTOR MODELS

Before examining the relation of the selected personality traits to symptom complaints, we tested a variety of measurement models of the personality traits themselves. As outlined in the introduction, we specifically compared (a) a one-factor model in which the parcels for all of the individual traits all loaded on a single factor, (b) a higher-order factor model in which parcels for the individual traits loaded on specific trait factors and the latter all loaded on a single higher-order factor, and (c) a group factor model in which parcels for the individual traits loaded on specific trait factors, but the latter correlated in complex ways that were not adequately captured by a single higher-order factor structure. Overall fit was evaluated using χ^2, the Tucker and Lewis (1973) index (TLI), and Bentler's (1990) comparative fit index (CFI). The significance of individual model components was estimated using critical ratios.

One-Factor Model. In Study 1, the one-factor model was associated with 54 degrees of freedom (78 observed variances and covariances, 24 estimated parameters); in Study 2, the one-factor model was associated with 27 degrees of freedom (45 observed variances and covariances, 18 estimated parameters); in Study 3, the one-factor model was associated with 495 degrees of freedom (561 observed variances and covariances,

66 estimated parameters). According to overall fit criteria, the one-factor model resulted in a poor fit to the data in all three studies: Study 1, $\chi^2(54, N = 166) = 341.89$, $p < .001$, TLI = .64, CFI = .71; Study 2, $\chi^2(27, N = 171) = 254.91$, $p < .001$, TLI = .63, CFI = .72; Study 3, $\chi^2(495, N = 146) = 1418.40$, $p < .001$, TLI = .62, CFI = .64 . In each case the model resulted in statistically significant ill fit and accounted for an unacceptably low percentage of the observed covariation.

Second-Order Factor Model. According to overall fit criteria, the second-order factor model resulted in a reasonable fit of the data in Study 1, $\chi^2(50, N = 166) = 99.56$, $p < .01$, TLI = .93, CFI = .95, and Study 2, $\chi^2(24, N = 171) = 33.00$, $p = .10$, TLI = .98, CFI = .99. The data provided a more modest fit of the substantially larger model in Study 3, $\chi^2(484, N = 146) = 835.49$, $p < .001$, TLI = .85, CFI = .87. The factor loadings of the individual parcels on the first-order factors were all sizable and statistically significant. The factor loadings of the first-order latent variables on the second-order latent variable were also all sizable and statistically significant. Furthermore, despite their association with this second-order factor, each of the first-order factors also retained a significant amount of variance that was unique.

Group Factor Model. According to overall fit criteria, the group factor model resulted in a reasonable fit of the data in all three studies: Study 1, $\chi^2(48, N = 166) = 98.56$, $p < .01$, TLI = .93, CFI = .95; Study 2, $\chi^2(24, N = 171) = 33.00$, $p = .10$, TLI = .98, CFI = .99; Study 3, $\chi^2(440, N = 146) = 637.36$, $p < .001$, TLI = .91, CFI = .92. Given the nesting hierarchy, the group factor model can fit no worse than the second-order factor model, although it can fit significantly better than the latter (Rindskopf & Rose, 1988). The individual first-order factor loadings were all statistically significant and their standardized values were all very similar to those that appeared in the second-order factor model. In addition, all of the first-order latent variables were significantly inter-correlated in Studies 1 and 2 and 47 out of 55 of these correlations were significant in Study 3.

Model Comparison. Given that these models are nested versions of each other, they can be directly compared. According to these tests, the one-factor model fits significantly worse than the second-order factor model in all three studies: Study 1, $\Delta\chi^2(4, N = 166) = 242.33$, $p < .001$; Study 2, $\Delta\chi^2(3, N = 171) = 221.91$, $p < .001$; Study 3, $\Delta\chi^2(11, N = 146)$

= 582.91, $p < .001$. Given the number of variables used in Study 2, the second-order and group factor models cannot be directly compared in that sample. In Study 1, however, the second-order factor model is not significantly different from the group factor model, difference $\chi^2(2, N = 166) = 1.00$, n.s. Therefore, given the logic of parsimony the second-order factor model constitutes the preferred solution in Study 1.

In Study 3, the group factor model fit significantly better than the second-order factor model, difference $\chi^2(44, N = 146) = 198.13$, $p < .001$. Modification statistics indicated that this was in large part due to the strong relation between particular personality traits assessed by individual scales and particular subfacets of the NEO-PI. In nearly all cases, these relations were consistent with the logic of convergent validity. Thus, by relating all scales and NEO-subfacets to a single general factor, the original model underestimated relations between particular scales and those NEO-subfacets with which they were closely related conceptually (e.g., self-consciousness and social anxiety, optimism-pessimism and depression, challenge and anxiety). At the same time, the majority of these scales and NEO-subfacets were strongly related to the higher-order factor postulated in the second-order factor model (8 of 11 loaded in excess of .75). Because of the a priori status of the second-order factor model, its degree of parsimony and preferred status in Study 1, and its sizable factor loadings, it was retained for the purpose of testing relations among personality traits and symptom complaints.

On the basis of these results, it makes sense to think in terms of discriminable personality traits that share a simple underlying structure while retaining their own unique characteristics. The question then becomes, is this general factor responsible for variation in symptom complaints that is observed to be associated with these personality traits or is this variation due to unique characteristics of particular traits?

PREDICTING SYMPTOM COMPLAINTS

The relation of these personality characteristics to symptom complaints was modeled within the framework provided by Model 1 illustrated in Figure 12.1. The measure of symptom complaints was parcelled by assigning one third of the items to each of three indicators. An initial model was then specified in which the latent variable of symptom complaints was only related to the second-order factor of neuroticism. In Study 1, Model 1 was associated with 85 degrees of freedom (120 observed variances and covariances, 35 estimated parameters); in Study 2, Model 1 was associated with 50 degrees of freedom (78 observed variances and covariances, 28 estimated parameters); in Study 3, Model 1 was associated with 582 degrees of freedom (666 observed variances and covariances, 84 estimated parameters).

According to overall fit criteria, Model 1 resulted in a reasonable fit to the data in Study 1, $\chi^2(85, N = 166) = 149.88$, $p < .001$, TLI = .94, CFI = .95, and Study 2, $\chi^2(50, N = 171) = 75.03$, $p = .01$, TLI = .97, CFI = .97. Study 3 involved a considerably larger model and resulted in a slightly poorer fit for Model 1, $\chi^2(582, N = 146) = 967.12$, $p < .001$, TLI = .85, CFI = .86.

As expected, in all three studies, component fit criteria indicated that the second-order variable of neuroticism was significantly related to symptom complaints, standardized path Study 1 = .35, $p < .001$; Study 2 = .39, $p < .001$; Study 3 = .43, $p < .001$. In addition, in each study, modification statistics suggested that this Model 1 could be improved by allowing the residual variance in the latent variable of negative affectivity to correlate with residual variance in symptom complaints. Multivariate modification statistics indicated that in all three studies this was the only personality trait residual related to the symptom complaint residual. As noted earlier, this indicates that the second-order factor model is inadequate to account fully for the variance shared by negative affectivity and symptom complaints. At the same time, it is important to note that the second-order factor model was adequate to account fully for the variance shared by symptom complaints and all of the other personality traits in all three studies.

Model 2 was identical to Model 1 except that it allowed residual variance in negative affectivity to correlate with residual variance in symptom complaints (see Figure 12.1). In each study, the result was a significant improvement in fit, Study 1, $\Delta\chi^2(1, N = 166) = 8.03$, $p < .01$; Study 2, $\Delta\chi^2(1, N = 171) = 7.46$, $p < .01$; Study 3, $\Delta\chi^2(1, N = 146) = 4.33$, $p < .05$. The interpretation of the altered model is as follows: Although it is useful to think of many traits as redundant for the sake of predicting symptom complaints (and these traits vary widely across Studies 1-3), this is not true of negative affectivity. Although negative affectivity is related to the general variable of neuroticism, it is more strongly related to symptom complaints than would be expected given its association with neuroticism.

We considered two additional ways to model the unique relation of negative affectivity and symptom complaints within the framework of the higher-order factor model of neuroticism. These two models are identical in overall fit to Model 2 and are simply alternative ways of conceiving the observed relations (see Breckler, 1990; Chapter 2, this volume). Model 2′ allowed the personality traits other than negative affectivity to load on one second-order factor (neuroticism 1) and negative affectivity and symptom complaints to load on their own separate second-order factor (neuroticism 2). The two second-order factors were then allowed to correlate. Although this model resulted in the same χ^2 as Model 2, it also yielded a negative residual variance estimate for negative affectivity in both Study 1 and Study 2. Such results may indicate that the model is misspecified (e.g., Bollen, 1989b).

Model 2″ allowed all personality traits to load on the second-order factor of neuroticism; however, both neuroticism and negative affectivity were used as independent predictors of symptom complaints. Again, this model yields a χ^2 identical to that observed for Models 2 and 2′. However, when modeled in this way, the independent association of neuroticism and symptom complaints is nonsignificant in all three studies (standardized path Study 1 = −.20, n.s.; Study 2 = −.29, n.s.; Study 3 = .15, n.s.), whereas the path associating negative affectivity and symptom complaints is significant in all three studies (standardized path Study 1 = .58, $p < .01$; Study 2 = .64, $p < .01$; Study 3 = .35, $p < .05$). Dropping the nonsignificant neuroticism-symptom complaints path results in Model 3. In this model, negative affectivity was significantly related to symptom complaints in all three studies (standardized path Study 1 = .40, $p < .001$; Study 2 = .40, $p < .001$; Study 3 = .48, $p < .001$). Because Model 3 is a nested version of Model 2″, it can be directly compared to it. The resulting χ^2 is not significant in any of the three studies, Study 1, $\Delta\chi^2(1, N = 166) = .94$, n.s.; Study 2, $\Delta\chi^2(1, N = 171) = 1.44$, n.s.; Study 3, $\Delta\chi^2(1, N = 146) = .84$, n.s. Because Model 3 estimates one less parameter, it may be preferred on the basis of parsimony. Model 3 for Study 3 is shown in Figure 12.2.

Discussion

On the basis of these studies, it would appear that (a) a variety of personality traits that have been argued to relate to physical and psychological health might usefully be considered to share a common association with an underlying general factor of neuroticism; (b) despite their association with neuroticism, each of these traits retains a

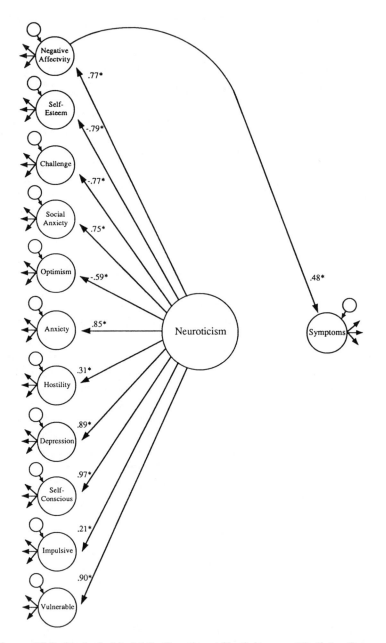

Figure 12.2. Study 3, Model 3: Negative Affectivity as a Mediator Between General Neuroticism and Symptom Complaints

substantial amount of unique variance; and (c) in most cases these personality traits are related to symptom complaints because of their association with general neuroticism rather than because of their unique characteristics; however, (d) negative affectivity is more strongly related to symptom complaints than can be explained by its association with the general factor of neuroticism.

Given that negative affectivity would appear to be ill-conceived as simply an indicator of general neuroticism, we considered a variety of ways to model its association with symptom complaints and the remaining personality characteristics. Model 3 was offered as providing the most parsimonious account. This model has a rather straightforward interpretation: A variety of different personality traits are to some extent overlapping constructs that share a common source of variance with a general factor of neuroticism. These variables are related to each other and to negative affectivity because of their shared association with neuroticism rather than because of anything unique about them as personality traits. Negative affectivity in turn serves to mediate the influence of general neuroticism on symptom complaints.

THE UNIQUE QUALITIES OF NEGATIVE AFFECTIVITY

The results of these studies naturally lead one to ask: What is unique about negative affectivity? Obviously, the answer to this question goes beyond the data at hand. Nevertheless, in comparing personality trait measures used in the present studies, it became apparent to us that they vary in their assessment of subjects' dispositional tendencies to think, feel, and/or act in particular ways. Specifically, some scales are dominated by questions regarding thoughts (e.g., the Rosenberg Self-Esteem Scale, the Life Orientation Test of optimism-pessimism) and others are dominated by questions regarding acts (e.g., the NEO impulsivity subfacet), but most contain a mix of questions regarding thoughts and feelings (e.g., the NEO depression subfacet, the NEO anxiety subfacet, the Life Situation Scale of challenge). In contrast to the other scales, the negative affectivity subscale of the PANAS exclusively asks about subjects' feelings or emotions. Thus one way to view the present results is that general neuroticism is composed of a variety of thoughts, feelings, and behaviors; however, the feeling component (best assessed by the PANAS measure of negative affectivity) is responsible for symptom complaints. From this perspective, thoughts and behaviors give rise to symptom complaints only to the extent that they are associated with negative emotionality.

Why should negative emotions be especially likely to yield symptom complaints? Salovey (1991) has offered several distinct reasons for such an effect. Negative emotions may (a) focus attention inward, leading to increased awareness of all internal states including physical symptoms (see also Watson & Pennebaker, 1989), (b) bias memory and hence reporting of physical complaints, (c) lead to behaviors that damage health (e.g., smoking, alcohol consumption) and hence increased illness, (d) damage the immune system leading to increased susceptibility to illness, or (e) motivate a desire for attention from others and hence increased likelihood to express symptom complaints to elicit sympathy. To this list we would add that physiological changes associated with chronic negative emotions may be confused with symptoms of physical illness.

Regardless of the specific interpretation of the unique association of negative affectivity and symptom complaints, it is apparent that negative affectivity does not operate like other indicators of neuroticism. As a consequence, we recommend that measures be developed that clearly separate affective from nonaffective components of personality so that the effects of these components can be independently observed. Development of such measures is particularly important to the extent that personality variables have effects that are not affectively mediated and trait affectivity has sources that are not personality based (e.g., life circumstances). In addition, separation of affective from nonaffective aspects of personality will yield models whose affective components can be subjected to more rigorous tests of causality through independent manipulation. For example, in research relevant to the current studies, Salovey and Birnbaum (1989) demonstrated that manipulations of negative affect do in fact increase symptom complaints.

METHOD AND KNOWLEDGE:
THE UTILITY OF STRUCTURAL EQUATION MODELING

General and Specific Effects. Elsewhere we have detailed the advantages of structural equation modeling approaches to evaluating multidimensional personality constructs (Hull, Lehn, & Tedlie, 1991; Hull & Mendolia, 1991). The principal advantage in the present research has been to identify the existence and predictive utility of the unique variance in different health relevant personality constructs. In all of the models, this was accomplished by dividing the variance in the observed measures into (a) variance resulting from the general, second-order construct, (b) variance resulting from the unique aspects of the specific construct, and (c) variance resulting from measurement error. Traditional approaches obscure these sources and as a consequence make it difficult to assess the unique versus redundant aspects of personality measures.

In this context, it is worth noting that although the unique aspects of the personality traits other than negative affectivity were not useful in predicting symptom complaints, the estimated size of these variances is large and statistically significant. It is quite reasonable to expect that the unique aspects of these variables will prove useful in predicting variables other than symptom complaints.

Modeling Strategy. In addition to adopting a measurement approach that allows more detailed examination of the source of observed effects, we also used data-analytic strategies that we recommend to anyone using structural equation modeling. First, we adopted a measurement model (the second-order factor model) that tried to balance the twin criteria of quality of fit and parsimony. Second, we examined a variety of a priori structural models (Models 1-3) including some that were statistically identical in fit (Models 2, 2', and 2''). Third, we attempted to document the robust character of the observed effects by conducting replications in multiple samples while varying the specific indicators of the latent variable of interest.

LIMITATIONS OF THE PRESENT RESEARCH

Although our approach has definite advantages over alternative approaches, the methods used in the present studies also have distinct limitations. These limitations include (a) a select range of neuroticism indicators, (b) the potential for misunderstanding the status of models as evidence, and (c) reliance on symptom complaints as a measure of health behavior.

Neuroticism Indicators. As in any research, we have been forced to rely on a limited number of measured variables to make a more general case. In doing so, we have tried to sample broadly from the variety of measures available. Most of the measures included in our models have been identified as key components of neuroticism in general reviews of the literature. For example, Watson and Clark (1984) explicitly identified self-esteem, negative emotions, pessimism, and a tendency to perceive the environment as threatening (i.e., low challenge) as aspects of general negative affectivity. Similarly, Costa and McCrae (1987) identified self-esteem, negative affectivity, social anxiety, and a perceived inability to cope (i.e., low challenge) as aspects of neuroticism. In addition to including a wide variety of measures, we have also varied these measures across studies in an attempt to demonstrate that our results are not dependent on a particular combination of items. As a consequence, we are reasonably confident as to the generalizability of our results. Nevertheless, the variety of health relevant personality constructs is large enough that not all constructs may be subsumed under this general model. In particular, constructs that are unrelated to neuroticism need to be identified and validated.

Interpreting the Results of Structural Equation Modeling. Despite its distinct advantages, structural equation modeling does not provide evidence of causality, and it does not "prove" the superiority of one model over all possible alternative models (e.g., Breckler, 1990; Cliff, 1983; Chapters 1 and 2, this volume). With respect to the latter issue, although we have shown that certain models are superior to specific alternatives, we have not eliminated the universe of alternative models.

Measures of Health and Health Behaviors. We have no illusions that by predicting symptom complaints we have demonstrated a link between personality and disease. Many researchers have provided extensive evidence calling into question the use of symptom reports as valid measures of physical illness (e.g., Costa & McCrae, 1987; Watson & Pennebaker, 1989). Most of these researchers see symptom complaints as health relevant behaviors that are to some extent a function of personality neuroticism. It is from this perspective that we view symptom complaints as providing an appropriate context for testing the unique predictive utility of the various subcomponents of neuroticism.

Conclusion

Based on the present research, it is our view that some researchers have moved too quickly toward the view that a variety of health relevant personality constructs are simply surrogates for neuroticism. With respect to the alternative models described in the introduction, the one-factor model is clearly wrong. Furthermore, the single higher-order factor model, although adequate in some respects, clearly fails to account fully for the association of negative affectivity and symptom complaints. Finally, the group factor model appears to be unnecessarily complex. The model that was ultimately derived and replicated combines a higher-order factor model with a group factor model. According to this approach, some health relevant personality constructs have their influence on symptom complaints via the general factor of neuroticism, whereas others (i.e., negative affectivity) actually serve to mediate the influence of general neuroticism on symptom complaints. Future research should be directed toward determining the aspect of negative affectivity that distinguishes it from other traits related to neuroticism in such a way that it is a uniquely strong predictor of symptom complaints.

13 Predictors of Change in Antisocial Behavior During Elementary School for Boys

MIKE STOOLMILLER

TERRY E. DUNCAN

GERALD R. PATTERSON

Lykken (1993) recently came to some rather startling and discomforting conclusions about the level of antisocial and aggressive behavior in the United States:

> The United States has the highest per capita incidence of interpersonal violence of any nation not actively engaged in civil war. In a comparison of homicide rates (per 100,000 inhabitants) of 20 industrialized countries, the United States not only ranks first but has a rate more than four times greater than the nearest competitor. (p. 17)

The above quotation underscores the importance of understanding the emergence, escalation, and eventual maintenance of serious antisocial behavior.

This chapter utilizes structural equation modeling (SEM) techniques to test a social learning perspective on the development of antisocial

AUTHORS' NOTE: Preparation of this chapter was supported in part by grant MH 46690 from the Prevention Research Branch, NIH; grant MH 37940 from the Center for Studies of Antisocial and Violent Behavior, NIH; grant MH 38318 from the Mood, Anxiety, and Personality Disorders Research Branch, NIH; and grants DA 07031 and DA 03706 from the National Institute on Drug Abuse.

behavior in grade-school boys that has emerged from years of research by Patterson and his colleagues on coercive family interaction (see Patterson, Reid, & Dishion, 1992, for details). Coercion theory emphasizes simple, well-founded principles of positive and negative reinforcement from learning theory to explain the emergence, escalation, and eventual maintenance of serious antisocial behavior in children. Specifically, coercion theory holds that over many thousands of trials during family interaction, the problem child learns via negative reinforcement to shut off irritable, aversive intrusions from parents and siblings with his or her own aversive counterattacks. With parents, these attack-counterattack sequences typically occur during discipline encounters and undermine the parents' abilities to socialize and supervise the child properly. Although it does not emphasize biological or temperamental variables, coercion theory is still consistent with the view of Lykken (1993) that some children may be more susceptible to the detrimental effects of coercive family interaction than others. As the result of an abrasive, aggressive interpersonal style and low parental supervision, the child is rejected by normal peers, fails to learn at school, and eventually winds up in a delinquent peer group as an adolescent (Dishion, Patterson, Stoolmiller, & Skinner, 1991).

It is increasingly clear that antisocial behavioral patterns begin early and are highly stable across development (Loeber, 1982; Loeber & Dishion, 1983). Robins (1978) concluded that nearly all adults with antisocial personality disorder had demonstrated troublesome and oppositional behavior beginning between 8 and 10 years of age. More recent studies strongly suggest that the pattern begins before first grade (Campbell, Ewing, Breaux, & Szumowski, 1986; Loeber & Dishion, 1983). West and Farrington (1977) concluded that about 7% of the adolescent population who were chronically antisocial accounted for between 50% and 70% of all the reported juvenile criminal acts. Thus, on the basis of the continuity and intensity of the problem, identifying potentially malleable predictors of childhood antisocial behavior such as parenting practices could have important implications for efforts to prevent or reduce such behavior.

The focus of this chapter is on expanding the test of key coercion theory variables such as parental discipline skill and monitoring practices. This is accomplished by including other potentially competing explanatory variables in a model of changes in antisocial behavior in the school setting from Grade 4 to Grade 5.

Focusing on changes in antisocial behavior in the school setting as an outcome has several advantages. First, it minimizes any potential biases or distortions that might arise when all information comes from one informant in one setting (e.g., the mother reporting about child behavior at home). Second, it demonstrates that aggressive and antisocial behavior learned at home will generalize or spill over to school settings. Third, it focuses attention on antisocial behavior that would tend to undermine success in school, which in turn carries negative long-term implications for successful adult adjustment.

Emphasizing dynamic change in antisocial behavior from Grade 4 to Grade 5 as opposed to just status at Grade 5 also strengthens the test of coercion theory. It avoids the implicit, untested, and unreasonable assumption that predictors of Grade 5 antisocial status are equivalent to predictors of change. This assumption will hold only when antisocial behavior essentially emerges de novo in the school setting at Grade 5 or change is completely determined by Grade 4 status. Neither of these conditions seems plausible. A focus on models of change enables an examination of how key coercion theory variables exert an influence on an ongoing process.

Studying competing predictors also strengthens the test of coercion theory. Meehl (1990) has argued persuasively that, in general, rejecting the statistical null hypothesis of no effect is a very weak test of a substantive theory in psychology. Thus a large number of other plausible explanatory variables will be examined for their independent contribution to the prediction of changes in antisocial behavior. Grade 4 characteristics of the child such as self-esteem, depressed moods, and peer relations; parent characteristics such as depression, antisocial tendency, irritability, and marital adjustment; and family characteristics such as parental socioeconomic status, family income, and family problem solving skill will all be included. In addition, the key coercion theory variables of parent discipline skill, parent monitoring practices, and child coerciveness will be included.

The hypothesis to be examined for this study is that key coercion theory variables will exert significant, direct effects on two measures of change in antisocial behavior at school, even when controlling for the effects of the competing variables. The statistical model that will be utilized will be a measured variable path model that is essentially a simultaneous multiple regression model with two correlated outcome measures.

Method

The sample used for these analyses comes from two successive Grade 4 cohorts of the Oregon Youth Study (OYS) being conducted by Patterson and his associates. Schools in the metropolitan Eugene-Springfield area of Oregon were ranked from highest to lowest by police statistics for rates of delinquency. For Cohort I, six schools were randomly selected from the top 10 and all families with a boy in Grade 4 were invited to participate. For Cohort II, recruited one year later, seven schools were randomly selected from the top 10. This scheme generated a sample of 206 families (102 for Cohort I and 104 for Cohort II), for an overall participation rate of 74.4%. The sample is primarily European-American (86%), and a majority of the boys come from two-parent families (70%). For these analyses, 10 single-father families were excluded because of the small sample size, which brought the total sample size to 196. At least 50% of the families in both cohorts were of either low socioeconomic status or working class. The families were paid up to $300 for participating in the annual assessments.

INSTRUMENT DESCRIPTION

The OYS annual assessment battery includes structured interviews and telephone interviews with the study boy and his parents; question-naires administered to the boy, his parents, and the boys' teachers; three home observation sessions lasting one hour each; and a structured family problem solving task completed in the lab. Data for these analyses were taken from the initial assessment at Grade 4 and again one year later at Grade 5.

To complete the telephone interview, each family is called six times over approximately three weeks. Items for the telephone interview consist of the occurrence of behaviors of interest either in the last 24 hours or in the last three days. In all cases, the average score from the six calls is used as the basic item in scales.

Each family was observed three times over approximately three weeks for one hour each time in order to complete the home observations. In addition, home observers filled out observer impressions inventories immediately after each observation session. Observations were conducted in the late afternoon near the dinner hour. Behavior was recorded during home observations using the Family Process Coding (FPC) system, which was described in detail by Dishion et al. (1983).

In general, scales were created separately for each unique combination of respondent and assessment method. A priori item pools were created on the basis of strong face validity. Items were standardized prior to item analyses to ensure that arbitrary scaling differences across respondents and instruments did not influence the total variance of the construct score. Item analysis was conducted on the a priori item pools; items with nonsignificant, corrected item-to-total correlations were dropped from the scales. Scales had to produce a coefficient of internal consistency above .60 or they were dropped. Scales were computed if at least 60% of the items were present; otherwise, the score was coded as missing. All scales for a given respondent were averaged to form a respondent-specific indicator of the construct. Finally, construct scores were computed by averaging over all the respondents, given that at least 60% of the respondent-specific indicators were present. Computing constructs by aggregating across methods and respondents minimizes any bias unique to a method or respondent that would tend to limit the generalizability of the findings.

CHILD CONSTRUCTS

School antisocial behavior at Grade 4 was obtained from teacher ratings using the CBC-L (Achenbach & Edelbrock, 1986) and peer nominations for aggressive and troublesome behavior. Peer nominations were standardized within classrooms. At Grade 5, two school antisocial construct scores were derived. The first was based solely on teacher ratings on the CBC-L and was available for all 196 subjects. The second was a much richer measure that included direct observation of behavior in the classroom (amount of time on task) and on the playground (negative social interaction), discipline contacts, attendance, and a teacher rating of positive school adjustment from the Walker-McConnell scale of social competence and school adjustment (Walker & McConnell, 1988). Unfortunately, the additional school antisocial measures were obtained for only a subsample ($n = 79$) of the OYS. Therefore, SEM techniques for missing data (described in greater detail in the modeling section) were utilized in order to include both antisocial outcome measures in a single model.

The *playground negative social interaction* measure was derived from the Target/Peer Interaction Code (TPIC; O'Neil, Ramsey, Shinn,

Todis, & Spira, 1985), which recorded the free play and social behavior of the target subjects and their peers in playground settings. The playground measure is a combination of the total negative behaviors by the target subject and the total negative behaviors by peers directed at the target subject. *Academic engaged time* was assessed within each subject's classroom using a definition and duration recording procedure developed by Walker, Severson, Haring, and Williams (1986). A student was defined as academically engaged if he was attending to the assigned material and the academic tasks involved, was making appropriate motor responses (e.g., writing or computing), or was appropriately asking for assistance in an acceptable manner. Direct observation of engaged time was conducted during two 15-minute sessions in which reading or math was being taught and the students were expected to do independent seat work. *Attendance and discipline contacts* with the school principal were obtained at the end of the school year from official school records. Change in school antisocial behavior for these analyses refers to residual change; that is, the part of Grade 5 school antisocial behavior that is not accounted for by Grade 4 school antisocial behavior.

Tantrums and disobedience was derived from parents' ratings on the CBC-L (Achenbach & Edelbrock, 1983), the parent interview, and parent telephone interview. Scores were first derived for tantrums and disobedience separately and then combined so that each would contribute more or less equally. Separate ratings of *depressed mood* and *good peer relations* were obtained from parents' and teachers' ratings on the CBC-L. *Self-esteem* was based on self-report using Rosenberg's (1965) Self-Esteem Scale.

PARENT CONSTRUCTS

Depression was derived from the CES-D (Radloff, 1977). *Irritability* was based on observers' impressions of observed irritability during the home observations. *Antisocial* was computed from arrest records obtained from the Oregon Department of Motor Vehicles and from FBI records. *Marital adjustment* was based on the proportion of behavior by one partner directed toward their spouse that was coded as aversive using a priori aversive categories of the FPC. *Good discipline* includes both observed rates of behavior and observer impressions items pertaining to discipline practices and lack of discipline control of the boy. The observed rates included nattering, the proportion of the parents' behavior directed at the child that was coded as low intensity aversive (i.e., not physically aggressive), and abusing (i.e., physically aggressive) using a priori aversive categories of the FPC. *Inept monitoring* was based on separate interviewers' impressions for the mother, father, and child concerning the adequacy of parental monitoring and supervision of the study boy. *Problem solving* was based on a structured problem-solving task that was conducted in the lab and includes the total number of positive solutions suggested by family members, a binomial z-score reflecting the tendency of the parents to encourage the child's participation, and observers' impressions concerning the quality of the problem-solving process and proposed solutions. *SES* was scored using the method of Hollingshead (1975) and includes educational attainment and occupational prestige. *Poverty* is computed by dividing the total family income by the number of family members, standardizing over the sample, and reversing the scaling. *Family type* is a nominal code indicating at Grade 4 whether the family is a two-parent family ($n = 54$ with complete data, $n = 86$ with missing Grade 5 data) or a single-mother family ($n = 25$ with complete data, $n = 31$ with missing Grade 5 data).

MODELING DESCRIPTION

Some additional description of modeling techniques is warranted because of the additional complexity involved in handling missing data on the Grade 5 school antisocial measure. A subsample of 79 boys was selected from the larger sample of 196 for more intensive study in the school setting. Selection was based on a global measure of antisocial behavior obtained at Grade 4 that included parent, peer, and teacher ratings and direct observation in the home and lab. The 40 most antisocial boys on the global index were included along with a random sample of 39 from the remaining 166 boys. Clearly, the subsample of 79 cannot be considered a completely random sample from the larger sample of 196. However, the use of SEM techniques for missing data can proceed under the much milder assumption that the missing data at Grade 5 are missing at random (MAR) once the sampling mechanism is accounted for (Little & Rubin, 1990; Muthén, Kaplan, & Hollis, 1987). In other words, the school antisocial data that are missing at Grade 5 are not systematically related to the (unobserved) level of school antisocial at Grade 5 once the Grade 4 selection criteria are considered. In the terminology of Little and Rubin (1990), the missing data mechanism is said to be ignorable and the techniques suggested by Allison and Hauser (1991), Bentler (1989), and Muthén et al. (1987) can be used. Interested readers should refer to the above references for more details and sample programs.

Briefly, the strategy for handling missing data consists of expanding the usual SEM model to include means and intercepts, and partitioning the sample into subgroups with distinct patterns of missing data. Equality constraints across the missing data groups are used in a multisample analysis to obtain unbiased, consistent estimates. It should be emphasized that these equality constraints across the missing data subsamples are not substantively interesting; they function solely to ensure correct estimation of model parameters. For these data, preliminary regression analyses indicated that there were also significant differences in the models across family-type groups (two-parent vs. single-mother). Thus the sample was split into four separate groups defined by family type (single-mother vs. two-parent) and missing data (complete vs. missing data on additional Grade 5 school antisocial measures). Equality constraints across the missing data groups within family-type groups were employed to obtain correct parameter estimates.

Results

Regression imputation was used separately in the two-parent and single-mother subsamples to replace a small number of missing values that were scattered over the data (eight subjects missing one value each). Missing values on the predictor variables were estimated from regressions using the other predictors with complete data. One missing value on the Grade 5 teacher CBC-L ratings of school antisocial behavior was estimated using the Grade 4 school antisocial behavior measure.

The teacher ratings of school antisocial behavior showed a significant mean level increase from Grade 4 to Grade 5. Boys in stepparent families increased the most relative to boys in intact or single-mother families, although the difference was only marginally significant at the .07 level.

Separate, preliminary regression analyses for each Grade 5 outcome were conducted using the entire sample ($N = 196$) for the Grade 5 teacher ratings of school antisocial behavior and the subsample ($n = 79$) for the general school antisocial behavior measure. The purpose of these analyses was to reduce the number of potential predictors and to examine the data for outliers and highly influential observations. The following variables were dropped from the models because they had no impact on either Grade 5 outcome measure when controlling for other predictors: depressed mood (both parent and teacher ratings), self-esteem, good peer relations (parent ratings), irritability, marital adjustment, SES, and problem solving. Variables retained for further consideration either had significant effects in the preliminary analyses or were considered key theoretical variables.

Because the model includes an interaction term, Figure 13.1 shows estimated, unstandardized regression weights for the two outcome variables and means and variances for the predictor variables for single-mother versus two-parent families with no constraints across family-type groups. The overall model χ^2 is 194.63 with 130 degrees of freedom (df) and a p-value less than .001. The large χ^2 value and df result from the constraints across missing data groups. If there were no missing data, the model shown in Figure 13.1 would be completely saturated, using up all available df and fitting the data perfectly. The missing data constraints represent a test of the hypothesis that the data are missing completely at random. As mentioned earlier, this is not substantively interesting because the sampling mechanism is known and is definitely not a simple random sampling scheme. The obtained χ^2 value is useful, however, as a baseline for testing more substantively interesting hypotheses about the equality of regression weights across family-type groups. The df for each family-type group can be obtained by noting that the group with missing data will contribute 65 df (45 covariances, 10 variances, and 10 means), and the group with no missing data will contribute 77 df (55 covariances, 11 variances, and 11 means) for a total of 142 df. The model being fit has 77 estimated parameters: 54 covariances, variances, and means for the 9 predictors; 1 residual variance and 1 intercept for the outcome with no missing data; 18 regression weights linking the predictors to the outcomes—all of which are constrained to be equal across missing data groups—and, finally, 1 residual variance, 1 intercept, and 1 residual covariance for the outcome that has missing data. Subtracting the 77 df for the 77 estimated parameters from the total available 142 df leaves 65 df per family-type group. For the model with no constraints across the two family-type groups, there are 284 total available df (142 df per family-type group × two family-type groups) and 154 estimated parameters, leaving the model df equal to 130.

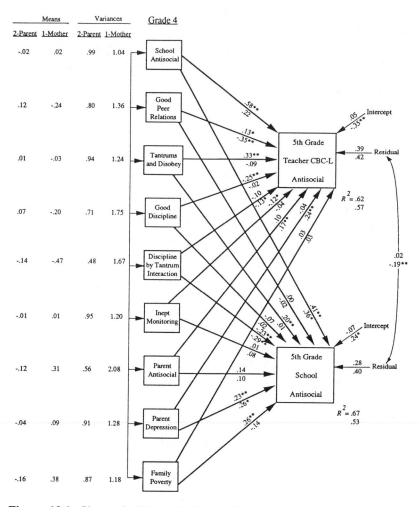

Figure 13.1. Change in School Antisocial Behavior, No Constraints Across Family Type

NOTE: Estimates are unstandardized. Two-parent family values shown on top, single-mother values on bottom.
*p < .05, **p < .01.

For the model with complete constraints across family-type groups, the total available df is still 284 but now only 77 parameters are estimated, leaving the model df equal to 207 with a χ^2 of 421.79 and a

p-value less than .001. The difference in χ^2s between the full constraints model and the no constraints model can be used as a statistical test of the hypothesis that the models are the same in two-parent and single-mother families. This $\Delta\chi^2$ is equal to 227.16 with 77 df and a p-value less than .001. The test indicates that some aspect(s) of the model differ significantly across the two family-type groups. The comparative fit index (CFI) for comparing the completely constrained versus the unconstrained models is a substantial .699.

In order to explore differences in the model across family types, modification indices were used to identify 16 constraints across family-type groups that seemed untenable. Once these 16 constraints were relaxed, the model generated a χ^2 of 263.80 with 191 df for a p-value less than .001. The test of the significance of the 16 relaxed constraints was obtained by subtracting this χ^2 from the full constraints model χ^2 to obtain a $\Delta\chi^2$ of 157.99 with 16 df and a p-value less than .001. The CFI corresponding to this comparison is .661. Clearly, relaxing the 16 constraints results in a large and significant improvement in fit of the model. A test of the tenability of the remaining constraints is obtained by subtracting the no constraints model χ^2 from the partially constrained model χ^2 to obtain a $\Delta\chi^2$ of 69.17 with 61 df and p-value greater than .05. The CFI for this comparison is only .112. Thus the rest of the constraints can be considered reasonable. Most of the model parameters (61 out of 77) can be considered the same across the two family-type groups. Note that results concerning differences in specific parameter values across family types should be considered exploratory, and significance tests should not be taken too seriously.

Unstandardized regression weights for both outcomes and means and variances for the predictors for the partially constrained model are shown in Figure 13.2. Different values in Figure 13.2 across family groups indicate significant differences in parameter estimates across family groups. Single-mother families were significantly higher on both poverty and depression. Single-mother families also had significantly larger variances on good discipline, the interaction term of tantrums and disobedience with good discipline, antisocial, and poverty.

The effects of the predictors were much more variable across family groups for teacher ratings than for general school antisocial behavior. Seven of the eleven estimated parameters for the teacher ratings were different across family groups as compared to only one of the eleven for general school antisocial behavior. In fact, for the teacher ratings of school antisocial behavior, teacher ratings of good peer relations had

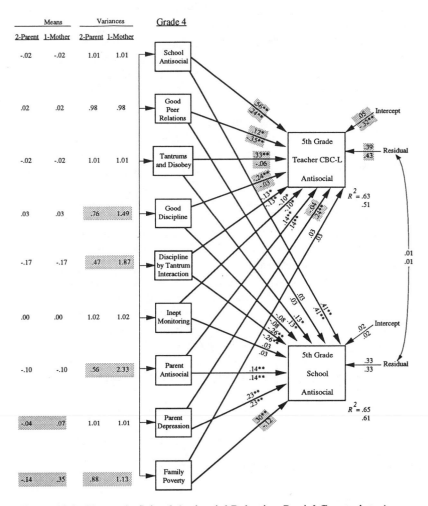

Figure 13.2. Change in School Antisocial Behavior, Partial Constraints Across Family Type

NOTE: Estimates are unstandardized. Two-parent family values shown on top, single-mother values on bottom. Pairs of parameters allowed to be different across family types are indicated by shaded boxes. Two additional pairs of parameters not shown in the diagram, covariances, were allowed to be different across family types.
*$p < .05$, **$p < .01$.

opposite effects in the two family-type groups. The effect was negative and strongly significant in the single-mother families but positive and marginally significant in the two-parent families. In contrast, the effect was essentially zero in both family types for the general school antisocial behavior measure. Poverty was the only variable that had significantly different effects across family groups for general school antisocial behavior. Poverty was positive and significant for two-parent families and nonsignificant for single-mother families.

Main effects of key coercion theory variables were variable, but the interaction of tantrums and disobedience with good discipline was significant for both outcomes across both family types. The interaction indicates that the effect of good discipline depends on the level of tantrums and disobedience, and vice versa. The main effects represent the effect of good discipline when tantrums and disobedience is zero, and vice versa. More specifically, because the means of good discipline and tantrums and disobedience are essentially zero in both family-type groups, the main effects represent the effect of good discipline at the mean level of tantrums and disobedience, and vice versa. Following Aiken and West (1991), the basic regression equation can be algebraically manipulated to clarify the dependence of the good discipline effect on the level of tantrums and disobedience. Omitting the other predictors for clarity, the equation becomes

$$(B_{Disc} + B_{Disc\ by\ Tantrums}Tantrums)Discipline = School\ Antisocial.$$

$$(13.1)$$

The terms in parentheses represent the simple slope or the effect of discipline at some specified level of tantrums and disobedience. For example, for a tantrums and disobedience score of zero (i.e., the mean level), the simple slope is just the estimated main effect of good discipline, B_{Disc}.

Figure 13.2 shows that the main effects of good discipline and tantrums and disobedience are significant only for two-parent families on teacher ratings of school antisocial behavior. In other words, good discipline is an important predictor of change in teacher ratings of school antisocial behavior at average levels of tantrums and disobedience only for two-parent families. For the other three models, good discipline is important only for above-average levels of tantrums and disobedience. The bulk of the findings in these analyses indicate that changes in school antisocial behavior are primarily related to the cooccurrence of both a highly coercive child and a lack of good discipline practices. The other key coercion variable, inept monitoring, had small and variable effects across outcomes.

In addition to the key coercion theory variables, both depression and antisocial had significant effects on changes in school antisocial behavior. The effect of parent depression was more variable than was the effect of parent antisocial, being significant for single mothers but nonsignificant for two-parent families on teacher ratings of school antisocial behavior.

In summary, changes in both measures of school antisocial behavior from Grade 4 to Grade 5 are significantly predicted by the interaction of tantrums and disobedience with good discipline for both single-mother families and two-parent families. The cooccurrence of both the lack of skilled parental discipline and a coercive child is at the heart of coercion theory. In addition, measures of parent depression and antisocial had significant effects.

Discussion

Structural equation modeling techniques were used to test a theoretical model for residual change in boys' antisocial behavior at school from Grade 4 to Grade 5. The theoretical model stipulated that family management practices such as skilled parental discipline should be the most proximal predictors of changes in antisocial behavior, whereas parent characteristics such as antisocial tendencies and depression would not contribute once family management practices were included in the model. In addition, other characteristics of the child such as depressed mood, peer relations, and self-esteem, and other family characteristics such as income and socioeconomic status, were tested in preliminary models. Teacher ratings of problematic behavior were collected for the entire sample, and direct observation of classroom and playground behavior, discipline contacts, and additional teacher ratings, combined into an additional antisocial outcome measure, were obtained for a subset of the complete sample. A multisample regression model was estimated across both single-mother families and two-parent families for both Grade 5 school antisocial outcome measures, simultaneously controlling for Grade 4 school antisocial using SEM techniques for missing data.

COERCION THEORY AND
CHANGE IN ANTISOCIAL BEHAVIOR

Following previous work by Patterson and his colleagues (i.e., Patterson & Bank, 1989; Patterson, Bank, & Stoolmiller, 1990), it was hypothesized that one of the significant contributors to the preadolescent's antisocial behavior would be the contribution made by the preadolescent himself or herself to the disruption of appropriate parenting practices. Findings from the present study appear to support the contention that coercive behavior of the child, in conjunction with unskilled and coercive parental discipline practices, adequately describe a process that may, in fact, be one of the most significant contributors to the developmental change of the child's antisocial behavior. That is, boys who exhibited higher levels of coercive behavior at home and whose parents demonstrated a lack of appropriate discipline practices were more at risk for experiencing an increase in their antisocial behavior in the school setting.

Parental monitoring practices, however, appeared to be unrelated to changes in antisocial behavior at school from Grade 4 to Grade 5. In other work on the OYS sample, lax supervision has been found to be both an important outcome and predictor of antisocial behavior for boys during middle adolescence (Forgatch & Stoolmiller, 1994; Patterson et al., 1990). Thus it may be that parental discipline practices are more important in childhood whereas supervision practices become more important in adolescence.

Another facet of the present investigation was concerned with examining competing predictors that have been implicated in the formation of adolescent antisocial behavior. Results indicated that parental depression and antisocial behavior were those contextual variables contributing most to the child's development of antisocial behavior between the 4th and 5th grades, effects that were evident for both family types and for both outcome measures. In addition, although restricted to the teacher report of school-based antisocial behavior, findings also support previous work that has demonstrated inadequate peer relations to be a factor in the at-risk adolescent's subsequent submersion into the coercion process. However, results from the present study appear consistent with our position that even when specific contextual and personal variables are accounted for, key coercion theory predictions are still tenable.

It is increasingly clear that antisocial behavior begins early in childhood and is highly stable across development (Loeber & Dishion,

1983). The linchpin of our theoretical model is that the antisocial child's constant conflict with others at both individual and institutional levels is at the core of the youngster's development or continuation of antisocial behavior in each new setting and with each new relationship. Children who have developed an early coercive pattern of interacting with parents will quickly involve themselves in coercive cycles in new settings that will sustain and exacerbate their development toward antisocial behaviors. This demonstrable developmental continuity makes antisocial children acutely at risk for a panoply of other problems such as substance abuse, chronic unemployment, divorce, a range of physical and psychiatric disorders, and dependence on welfare services (Caspi, Elder, & Bem, 1987; Robins & Ratcliff, 1979).

Not only is antisocial behavior highly stable, costly to society, and disruptive to the long-term adjustment of the child, it also is extremely difficult to change. In reviewing the intervention research with antisocial behaviors, Kazdin (1987) concluded that the most promising strategies included a focus on family-management practices, broad based interventions that targeted the child's adjustment in the school, and community interventions that emphasized changing contextual influences on the determinants of antisocial behaviors. Nonetheless, research clearly indicates that as the age-at-referral of the child increases, the probability of successfully intervening and preventing the continued development of antisocial behavior decreases (Dishion, 1984).

ANALYZING INCOMPLETE LONGITUDINAL DATA

Despite the best efforts of researchers, few studies interested in the etiology of antisocial behaviors are completed without the loss of subjects over time or the collection of incomplete data. Data gathered from such studies are most often analyzed using traditional methods such as listwise deletion of missing cases; however, loss of data through attrition, unforeseen budget problems, or other missing data mechanisms can sometimes cause the sample of subjects with complete data to differ substantially from the original sample (Brown, 1990).

Research has shown that traditional estimation methods are inferior to likelihood estimators that use all available information in terms of large sample bias and efficiency (Muthén et al., 1987). The present study involved a situation in which the data could not be considered missing completely at random. However, utilizing SEM techniques, correct maximum-likelihood estimation for the model parameters was obtained.

Such analytical techniques are not, however, without limitations. One problem with the computational approach utilized in the present study is that in many situations there may be a number of missing data patterns so that the number of observations in each group frequently falls below the number of variables. When this occurs it may be necessary to delete some parts of the data, much like the approach of listwise deletion, so that a reasonable number of groups with large sample sizes remain (Muthén et al., 1987). Unless this loss of data introduces strong selective missingness not predictable by observed variables for which there is no missingness, little bias is likely to result. Regardless of the mechanism for the pattern of missingness, utilizing information from a few substantial missing data pattern groups will likely yield more appropriate results than the use of data from only the complete-data group. However, the usual caution concerning generalizability is necessary in that results may be limited not only by the regression model and the pattern of missingness studied but also by the particular specification of the missing data mechanism.

The method described here should make collecting and analyzing longitudinal data in which missing data are likely to occur more attractive to researchers. By combining data from a complete-case subsample and nonresponse subsample, efficient estimates of the coefficients and consistent estimates of their standard errors for a linear model are possible. The method does so introducing only mild assumptions concerning the missing data mechanism beyond those generally made for structural equation modeling.

Summary and Conclusions

In summary, these preliminary analyses of the effect of the key coercion theory variables on the ongoing process of antisocial behavior acknowledge the necessity for differentiating between those developmentally threatening events (e.g., the disruption of family management skills) and those pathogenic processes that are proximal to the development of behavioral problems in the child. Although studies conducted over the past 20 years have demonstrated the ability to predict the likelihood of subsequent delinquency with relative accuracy (e.g., Loeber & Dishion, 1983, 1987), our understanding of the processes by which some children start early and persist into adolescence lags far behind. Of interest, therefore, is whether the present findings add sufficiently to our understanding of this process to facilitate the development of intervention strategies designed to interrupt the progression of antisocial behaviors.

There is an obvious need for additional research that integrates our basic knowledge of how key coercion variables exert their influence on the ongoing development of serious antisocial behavior, with the assumption that different combinations of these factors are set into motion for different subpopulations of children exposed to major risk factors (Reid, 1991). This assumption becomes increasingly important to efforts aimed at interrupting the coercion process, because it is likely that an increased understanding of the role these mediators play in the etiology of antisocial behavior will ultimately lead to the development of distinct interventions tailored to the needs of the individual.

References

Achenbach, T. M., & Edelbrock, C. S. (1983). *Manual for the Child Behavior Checklist and the Revised Child Behavior Profile*. Burlington, VT: University of Vermont.

Achenbach, T. M., & Edelbrock, C. S. (1986). *Manual for the Teacher's Report Form and Teacher Version of the Child Behavior Profile*. Burlington, VT: University of Vermont.

Aiken, L. S., & West, S. G. (1991). *Multiple regression: Testing and interpreting interactions*. Newbury Park, CA: Sage.

Aitchison, J. (1962). Large-sample restricted parametric tests. *Journal of the Royal Statistical Society, Series B, 24*, 234-250.

Akaike, H. (1974). A new look at the statistical model identification. *IEEE Transactions on Automatic Control, AC-19*, 716-723.

Akaike, H. (1987). Factor analysis and AIC. *Psychometrika, 52*, 317-332.

Allison, P. D. (1987). Estimation of linear models with incomplete data. In C. C. Clogg (Ed.), *Sociological methodology 1987* (Vol. 17, pp. 68-119). San Francisco: Jossey-Bass.

Allison, P. D., & Hauser, R. M. (1991). Reducing bias in estimates of linear models by remeasurement of a random subsample. *Sociological Methods and Research, 19*, 466-492.

Amemiya, Y., & Anderson, T. W. (1990). Asymptotic chi-square tests for a large class of factor analysis models. *The Annals of Statistics, 18*, 1453-1463.

American Psychological Association. (1994). *Publication manual of the American Psychological Association* (4th ed.). Washington, DC: Author.

Anderson, J. C., & Gerbing, D. W. (1984). The effects of sampling error on convergence, improper solutions, and goodness-of-fit indices for maximum likelihood confirmatory factor analysis. *Psychometrika, 49*, 155-173.

254

References   255

Anderson, J. C., & Gerbing, D. W. (1988). Structural equation modeling in practice: A review and recommended two-step approach. *Psychological Bulletin, 103*, 411-423.

Anderson, T. W. (1959). On some scaling models and estimation procedures in the latent class model. In O. Grenander (Ed.), *Probability and statistics, The Harold Cramer Volume* (pp. 9-38). New York: Wiley.

Anderson, T. W., & Amemiya, Y. (1988). The asymptotic normal distribution of estimators in factor analysis under general conditions. *The Annals of Statistics, 16*, 759-771.

Antonucci, T. C., Peggs, J. F., & Marquez, J. T. (1989). The relationship between self-esteem and physical health in a family practice population. *Family Practice Research Journal, 9*, 65-72.

Arminger G., & Schoenberg, R. (1989). Pseudo maximum likelihood estimation and a test for misspecification in mean and covariance structure models. *Psychometrika, 54*, 409-425.

Babakus, E., Ferguson, C. E., & Jöreskog, K. G. (1987). The sensitivity of confirmatory maximum likelihood factor analysis to violations of measurement scale and distributional assumptions. *Journal of Marketing Research, 37*, 72-141.

Bacon, F. (1858). Novum organum. In J. Devey (Ed.), *The physical and metaphysical works of Lord Bacon* (pp. 380-567). London: Bohn. (Original work published 1620)

Bagozzi, R. P. (Ed.). (1982). Causal modeling [Special issue]. *Journal of Marketing Research, 19*(4).

Bagozzi, R. P. (1991). Structural equation modeling in marketing research. In W. D. Neal (Ed.), *First annual advanced research techniques forum* (pp. 335-379). Chicago: American Marketing Association.

Bagozzi, R. P., & Yi, Y. (1990). Assessing method variance in multitrait-multimethod matrices: The case of self-reported affect and perceptions at work. *Journal of Applied Psychology, 75*, 547-560.

Bagozzi, R. P., & Yi, Y. (1992). Testing hypotheses about methods, traits, and communalities in the direct-product model. *Applied Psychological Measurement, 16*, 373-380.

Bandura, A., O'Leary, A., Taylor, C. B., Gauthier, J., & Gossard, D. (1987). Perceived self-efficacy and pain control: Opiod and nonopiod mechanisms. *Journal of Personality and Social Psychology, 53*, 563-571.

Baron, R. M., & Kenny, D. A. (1986). The moderator-mediator variable distinction in social psychological research: Conceptual, strategic, and statistical considerations. *Journal of Personality and Social Psychology, 51*, 1173-1182.

Bearden, W. D., Sharma, S., & Teel, J. E. (1982). Sample size effects on chi-square and other statistics used in evaluating causal models. *Journal of Marketing Research, 19*, 425-430.

Bechtel, W. (1988). *Philosophy of science*. Hillsdale, NJ: Erlbaum.

Beck, A. T., Steer, R. A., & Garbin, M. G. (1988). Psychometric properties of the Beck Depression Inventory: Twenty-five years of evaluation. *Clinical Psychology Review, 8*, 77-100.

Beck, A. T., Ward, C. H., Mendelson, M., Mock, J., & Erbaugh, J. (1961). An inventory for measuring depression. *Archives of General Psychiatry, 4*, 561-571.

Bentler, P. M. (1980). Multivariate analysis with latent variables: Causal modeling. *Annual Review of Psychology, 31*, 419-456.

Bentler, P. M. (1983). Some contributions to efficient statistics for structural models: Specification and estimation of moment structures. *Psychometrika, 48*, 493-571.

Bentler, P. M. (1986). *Lagrange Multiplier and Wald tests for EQS and EQS/PC.* Los Angeles: BMDP Statistical Software.

Bentler, P. M. (1989). *EQS structural equations program manual.* Los Angeles: BMDP Statistical Software.

Bentler, P. M. (1990). Comparative fit indices in structural models. *Psychological Bulletin, 107*, 238-246.

Bentler, P. M. (1992a). *EQS structural equations program manual.* Los Angeles: BMDP Statistical Software.

Bentler, P. M. (1992b). On the fit of models to covariances and methodology to the *Bulletin. Psychological Bulletin, 112*, 400-404.

Bentler, P. M., & Bonett, D. G. (1980). Significance tests and goodness-of-fit in the analysis of covariance structures. *Psychological Bulletin, 88*, 588-606.

Bentler, P. M., & Chou, C.-P. (1987). Practical issues in structural modeling. *Sociological Methods and Research, 16*, 78-117.

Bentler, P. M., & Chou, C.-P. (1988). Practical issues in structural modeling. In J. S. Long (Ed.), *Common problems/proper solutions: Avoiding error in quantitative research* (pp. 161-192). Newbury Park, CA: Sage.

Bentler, P. M., & Dijkstra, T. (1985). Efficient estimation via linearization in structural models. In P. R. Krishnaiah (Ed.), *Multivariate analysis* (Vol. VI, pp. 9-42). Amsterdam: North-Holland.

Bentler, P. M., & Stein, J. A. (1992). Structural equation modeling in medical research. *Statistical Methods in Medical Research, 1*, 159-181.

Bentler, P. M., & Weeks, D. G. (1980). Linear structural equations with latent variables. *Psychometrika, 45*, 289-307.

Bentler, P. M., & Wu, E. J. C. (1993). *EQS/Windows user's guide.* Los Angeles: BMDP Statistical Software.

Biddle, B. J., & Marlin, M. M. (1987). Causality, confirmation, credulity, and structural equation modeling. *Child Development, 58*, 4-17.

Bielby, W. T., & Hauser, R. M. (1977). Structural equation models. *Annual Review of Sociology, 3*, 137-161.

Blazer, D. G. (1982). *Depression in late life.* St. Louis: Mosby.

Bollen, K. A. (1986). Sample size and Bentler and Bonett's nonnormed fit index. *Psychometrika, 51*, 375-377.

Bollen, K. A. (1989a). A new incremental fit index for general structural equation models. *Sociological Methods and Research, 17*, 303-316.

Bollen, K. A. (1989b). *Structural equations with latent variables.* New York: Wiley.

Bollen, K. A. (1990). Overall fit in covariance structure models: Two types of sample size effects. *Psychological Bulletin, 107*, 256-259.

Bollen, K. A., & Arminger, G. (1991). Observational residuals in factor analysis and structural equation models. In P. V. Marsden (Ed.), *Sociological methodology 1991* (Vol. 21, pp. 235-262). Oxford: Blackwell.

Bollen, K. A., & Barb, K. H. (1981). Pearson's r and coarsely categorized measures. *American Sociological Review, 46*, 232-239.

Bollen, K. A., & Lennox, R. (1991). Conventional wisdom on measurement: A structural equation perspective. *Psychological Bulletin, 110*, 305-314.

Bollen, K. A., & Liang, J. (1988). Some properties of Hoelter's CN. *Sociological Research and Methods, 16*, 492-503.

Bollen, K. A., & Long, J. S. (Eds.). (1993). *Testing structural equation models.* Newbury Park, CA: Sage.

Bollen, K. A., & Stine, R. A. (1992). Bootstrapping goodness-of-fit measures in structural equation models. *Sociological Methods and Research, 21*, 205-229.

Boomsma, A. (1983). *On the robustness of LISREL (maximum likelihood estimation) against small sample size and non-normality.* Unpublished doctoral dissertation, University of Gröningen, Gröningen.

Booth-Kewley, S., & Friedman, H. S. (1987). Psychological predictors of heart disease: A quantitative review. *Psychological Bulletin, 101*, 343-362.

Box, G. E. P., & Cox, D. R. (1964). An analysis of transformations. *Journal of the Royal Statistical Society, Series B, 26*, 211-252.

Bozdogan, H. (1987). Model selection and Akaike's information criteria (AIC): The general theory and its analytical extensions. *Psychometrika, 52*, 345-370.

Breckler, S. J. (1990). Application of covariance structure modeling in psychology: Cause for concern? *Psychological Bulletin, 107*, 260-273.

Brown, C. H. (1990). Protection against nonrandomly missing data in longitudinal studies. *Biometrics, 46*, 143-155.

Browne, M. W. (1974). Generalized least squares estimators in the analysis of covariance structures. *South African Statistical Journal, 8*, 1-24.

Browne, M. W. (1982). Covariance structures. In D. M. Hawkins (Ed.), *Topics in multivariate analysis* (pp. 72-141). Cambridge, England: Cambridge University.

Browne, M. W. (1984a). Asymptotically distribution-free methods for the analysis of covariance structures. *British Journal of Mathematics and Statistical Psychology, 37*, 62-83.

Browne, M. W. (1984b). The decomposition of multitrait-multimethod matrices. *British Journal of Mathematical and Statistical Psychology, 37*, 1-21.

Browne, M. W. (1989). Relationships between an additive model and multiplicative model for multitrait-multimethod matrices. In R. Coppi & S. Bolasco (Eds.), *Multiway data analysis* (pp. 507-520). Amsterdam: North-Holland.

Browne, M. W. (1990). *MUTMUM PC users's guide* [Computer program and manual]. Pretoria, South Africa: University of South Africa.

Browne, M. W., & Cudeck, R. (1989). Single sample cross-validation indices for covariance structures. *Multivariate Behavioral Research, 24*, 445-455.

Browne, M. W., & Cudeck, R. (1993). Alternative ways of assessing model fit. In K. A. Bollen & J. S. Long (Eds.), *Testing structural equation models* (pp. 136-162). Newbury Park, CA: Sage.

Browne, M. W., & Mels, G. (1992). *RAMONA PC user's guide.* Columbus: Ohio State University, Department of Psychology.

Browne, M. W., & Shapiro, A. (1988). Robustness of normal theory methods in the analysis of linear latent variate models. *British Journal of Mathematical and Statistical Psychology, 41*, 193-208.

Buse, A. (1982). The likelihood ratio, Wald, and Lagrange multiplier tests: An expository note. *The American Statistican, 36*, 153-157.

Byrne, B. M. (1989). *A primer of LISREL: Basic applications and programming for confirmatory factor analytic models.* New York: Springer-Verlag.

Byrne, B. M. (1994). *Structural equation modeling with EQS and EQS/Windows: Basic concepts, applications, and programming.* Newbury Park, CA: Sage.

Byrne, B. M., & Baron, P. (1993). The Beck Depression Inventory: Testing and cross-validating an hierarchical factor structure for nonclinical adolescents. *Measurement and Evaluation in Counseling and Development, 26,* 164-178.

Byrne, B. M., & Baron, P. (1994). Measuring adolescent depression: Tests of equivalent factorial structure for English and French versions of the Beck Depression Inventory. *Applied Psychology: An International Review, 43,* 33-47.

Byrne, B. M., Baron, P., & Campbell, T. L. (1993). Measuring adolescent depression: Factorial validity and invariance of the Beck Depression Inventory across gender. *Journal of Research on Adolescence, 3,* 127-143.

Byrne, B. M., Baron, P., & Campbell, T. L. (1994). The Beck Depression Inventory (French version): Testing for gender-invariant factorial structure for nonclinical adolescents. *Journal of Adolescent Research, 9,* 166-179.

Byrne, B. M., Baron, P., Larsson, B., & Melin, L. (1993a). *The Beck Depression Inventory: Testing and cross-validating a second-order structure for Swedish nonclinical adolescents.* Manuscript submitted for publication.

Byrne, B. M., Baron, P., Larsson, B., & Melin, L. (1993b). *Measuring depression for Swedish nonclinical adolescents: Factorial validity and equivalence of the Beck Depression Inventory across gender.* Manuscript submitted for publication.

Byrne, B. M., Shavelson, R. J., & Muthén, B. (1989). Testing for the equivalence of factor covariance and mean structures: The issue of partial measurement invariance. *Psychological Bulletin, 105,* 456-466.

Campbell, D. T., & Fiske, D. W. (1959). Convergent and discriminant validation by multitrait-multimethod matrix. *Psychological Bulletin, 56,* 81-105.

Campbell, D. T., & O'Connell, E. J. (1967). Method factors in multitrait-multimethod matrices: Multiplicative rather than additive? *Multivariate Behavioral Research, 2,* 409-426.

Campbell, S. B., Ewing, L. J., Breaux, A. M., & Szumowski, E. K. (1986). Parent-referred problem three-year-olds: Follow up at school entry. *Journal of Child Psychology and Psychiatry, 27,* 473-488.

Carlson, M., & Mulaik, S. (1993). Trait ratings from descriptions of behavior as mediated by components of meaning. *Multivariate Behavioral Research, 28,* 111-159.

Caspi, A., Elder, G. H., & Bem, D. J. (1987). Moving against the world: Life course patterns of explosive children. *Developmental Psychology, 23,* 308-313.

Cattell, R. B., & Burdsal, C. A., Jr. (1975). The radial parcel double factoring design: A solution to the item-vs-parcel controversy. *Multivariate Behavioral Research, 10,* 165-179.

Chaplin, W. F. (1994, June). *Methodological issues in reporting findings in personality.* Paper presented at the Seventh Annual Nags Head International Conference on Personality and Social Behavior, Highland Beach, FL.

Chatterjee, S., & Yilmaz, M. (1992). A review of regression diagnostics for behavioral research. *Applied Psychological Measurement, 16,* 209-227.

Chatters, L. M., Taylor, R. J., & Jackson, J. S. (1985). Size and composition of informal helper networks of elderly Blacks. *Journal of Gerontology, 40,* 605-614.

Chou, C.-P., & Bentler, P. M. (1990). Model modification in covariance structure modeling: A comparison among likelihood ratio, Lagrange multiplier, and Wald tests. *Multivariate Behavioral Research, 25,* 115-136.

Chou, C.-P., Bentler, P. M., & Satorra, A. (1991). Scaled test statistics and robust standard errors for non-normal data in covariance structure analysis: A Monte Carlo study. *British Journal of Mathematical and Statistical Psychology, 44*, 347-357.

Cliff, N. (1983). Some cautions concerning the application of causal modeling methods. *Multivariate Behavioral Research, 18*, 115-126.

Cohen, P., Cohen, J., Teresi, J., Marchi, M., & Velez, C. N. (1990). Problems in the measurement of latent variables in structural equations causal models. *Applied Psychological Measurement, 14*, 183-196.

Cohen, S., & Hoberman, H. M. (1983). Positive events and social support as buffers of life change stress. *Journal of Applied Social Psychology, 13*, 99-125.

Connell, J. P., & Tanaka, J. S. (Eds.). (1987). Structural equation models in developmental psychology [Special section]. *Child Development, 58*, 1-175.

Cook, H. L., De Vellis, R. F., Gillings, D. B., Price, L. J., Sauter, S. V. H., & Whitehead, T. L. (1986). *Refinement of arthritis psychosocial research measures.* Unpublished manuscript.

Costa, P. T., & McCrae, R. R. (1985). *The NEO Personality Inventory Manual.* Odessa, FL: Psychological Assessment Resources.

Costa, P. T., & McCrae, R. R. (1987). Neuroticism, somatic complaints, and disease: Is the bark worse than the bite? *Journal of Personality, 55*, 299-316.

Crystal, S. & Shea, D. (1990). Cumulative advantage, cumulative disadvantage, and inequality among elderly people. *The Gerontologist, 30*, 437-443.

Cudeck, R. (1988). Multiplicative models and MTMM matrices. *Journal of Educational Statistics, 13*, 131-147.

Cudeck, R. (1989). Analysis of correlation matrices using covariance structure models. *Psychological Bulletin, 105*, 317-327.

Cudeck, R., & Browne, M. W. (1983). Cross-validation of covariance structures. *Multivariate Behavioral Research, 18*, 147-167.

Cudeck, R., & Henly, S. J. (1991). Model selection in covariance structures analysis and the "problem" of sample size: A clarification. *Psychological Bulletin, 109*, 512-519.

Cunningham, L. S., & Kelsey, J. L. (1984). Epidemiology of musculoskeletal impairments and associated disability. *American Journal of Public Health, 74*, 574-579.

Curran, P. J., West, S. G., & Finch, J. F. (1994). *The robustness of test statistics and goodness-of-fit indices in confirmatory factor analysis.* Manuscript submitted for publication.

D'Agostino, R. B. (1986). Tests for the normal distribution. In R. B. D'Agostino & M. A. Stephens (Eds.), *Goodness-of-fit techniques* (pp. 367-390). New York: Dekker.

Dancy, J. (1985). *An introduction to contemporary epistemology.* Oxford: Blackwell.

Daniel, C., & Wood, F. S. (1980). *Fitting equations to data.* New York: Wiley.

Dean, A., Kolody, B., & Wood, P. (1990). Effects of social support from various sources on depression in elderly persons. *Journal of Health and Social Behavior, 31*, 148-161.

de Leeuw, J., Keller, W. J., & Wansbeek, T. (Eds.). (1983). Interfaces between econometrics and psychometrics [Special issue]. *Journal of Econometrics, 22*(1/2).

Dembroski, T. M., & Costa, P. T., Jr. (1987). Coronary-prone behavior: Components of the Type A pattern and hostility. *Journal of Personality, 55*, 211-235.

Descartes, R. (1901). Discourse on the method of rightly conducting the reason and seeking truth in the sciences. In *The method, meditations, and philosophy of Descartes* (J. Veitch, Trans.). Washington: Dunne. (Original work published 1637) de Veaux, R. D. (1990). Finding transformations for regression using the ACE algorithm. In J. Fox & J. S. Long (Eds.), *Modern methods of data analysis* (pp. 177-208). Newbury Park, CA: Sage.

Dillon, W. R., Kumar, A., & Mulani, N. (1987). Offending estimates in covariance structure analysis: Comments on the causes of and solutions to Heywood cases. *Psychological Bulletin, 102,* 126-135.

Dishion, T. J. (1984). *Changing child social aggression within the context of the family: Factors predicting improvement in parent training.* Unpublished manuscript. (Available from the Oregon Social Learning Center, 207 E. 5th Ave., Suite 202, Eugene, OR 97401)

Dishion, T. J., Gardner, K., Patterson, G. R., Reid, J. B., Spyrou, S., & Thibodeaux, S. (1983). *The family process code: A multidimensional system for observing family interaction.* (Tech. Rep.). Eugene, OR: Oregon Social Learning Center.

Dishion, T. J., Patterson, G. R., Stoolmiller, M., & Skinner, M. L. (1991). Family, school, and behavioral antecedents to early adolescent involvement with antisocial peers. *Developmental Psychology, 2,* 172-180.

Dwyer, J. H. (1983). *Statistical models for the social and behavioral sciences.* New York: Oxford University.

Efron, B., & Tibshirani, R. (1986). Bootstrap methods for standard errors, confidence intervals and other measures of statistical accuracy. *Statistical Science, 1,* 54-74.

Emerson, J. D., & Stoto, M. A. (1983). Transforming data. In D. C. Hoaglin, F. Mosteller, & J. W. Tukey (Eds.), *Understanding robust and exploratory data analysis* (pp. 97-127). New York: Wiley.

Engle, R. F. (1984). Wald, likelihood ratio, and Lagrange multiplier tests in econometrics. In Z. Griliches & M. Intriligator (Eds.), *Handbook of econometrics* (pp. 776-826). Amsterdam: North-Holland.

Ensel, W. M., & Woelfel, M. (1986). Measuring instrumental and expressive functions of social support. In N. Lin, A. Dean, & W. M. Ensel (Eds.), *Social support, life events, and depression* (pp. 129-152). Orlando: Academic.

Fenigstein, A., Scheier, M. F., & Buss, A. H. (1975). Public and private self-consciousness: Assessment and theory. *Journal of Consulting and Clinical Psychology, 43,* 522-527.

Finch, J. F., Curran, P. J., & West, S. G. (1994). *The effects of model and data characteristics on the accuracy of parameter estimates and standard errors in confirmatory factor analysis.* Unpublished manuscript.

Forgatch, M. S., & Stoolmiller, M. S. (1994). Emotions as contexts for adolescent delinquency. *Journal of Research on Adolescence, 4,* 601-614.

Freedman, D. A. (1987). As others see us: A case study in path analysis. *Journal of Educational Statistics, 12,* 101-128.

Funk, S. C., & Houston, B. K. (1987). A critical analysis of the Hardiness Scale's validity and utility. *Journal of Personality and Social Psychology, 53,* 572-578.

Garrison, J. W. (1986). Some principles of post-positivistic philosophy of science. *Educational Researcher, 15,* 12-18.

George, L. K. (1989). Stress, social support and depression over the life-course. In K. S. Markides & C. L. Cooper (Eds.), *Aging, stress, and health* (pp. 241-267). Chichester, England: Wiley.

Gerbing, D. W., & Anderson, J. C. (1993). Monte Carlo evaluations of goodness-of-fit indices for structural equation models. In K. A. Bollen & J. S. Long (Eds.), *Testing structural equation models* (pp. 40-65). Newbury Park, CA: Sage.

Goffin, R. D. (1993). A comparison of two new indices for the assessment of fit of structural equation models. *Multivariate Behavioral Research, 28,* 205-214.

Goffin, R. D., & Jackson, D. N. (1992). Analysis of multitrait-multirater performance appraisal data: Composite direct product method versus confirmatory factor analysis. *Multivariate Behavioral Research, 27,* 363-385.

Gratch, H. (Ed.). (1973). *25 years of social research in Israel.* Jerusalem: Jerusalem Academic.

Haines, V. A., & Hurlbert, J. S. (1992). Network range and health. *The Journal of Health and Social Behavior, 33,* 254-266.

Hanson, N. R. (1958). *Patterns of discovery.* Cambridge, England: Cambridge University.

Harlow, L. L. (1985). *Behavior of some elliptical theory estimators with non-normal data in a covariance structures framework: A Monte Carlo study.* Unpublished doctoral dissertation, University of California, Los Angeles.

Hayduk, L. A. (1987). *Structural equation modeling with LISREL: Essentials and advances.* Baltimore: Johns Hopkins.

Heise, D. R. (1975). *Causal analysis.* New York: Wiley.

Hempel, C. G. (1965). Aspects of scientific explanation. In C. G. Hempel (Ed.), *Aspects of scientific explanation and other essays in the philosophy of science* (pp. 331-496). New York: Macmillan.

Hoelter, J. W. (1983). The analysis of covariance structures: Goodness-of-fit indices. *Sociological Methods and Research, 11,* 325-344.

Holland, P. W. (1986). Statistics and causal inference. *Journal of the American Statistical Association, 81,* 945-970.

Hollingshead, A. B. (1975). *Four factor index of social status.* Unpublished manuscript. (Available from A. B. Hollingshead, Department of Sociology, Yale University, New Haven, CT)

Hoyle, R. H. (1994a). Introduction to the special section: Structural equation modeling in clinical research. *Journal of Consulting and Clinical Psychology, 62,* 427-428.

Hoyle, R. H. (Ed.). (1994b). Structural equation modeling in clinical research [Special section]. *Journal of Consulting and Clinical Psychology, 62,* 427-521.

Hoyle, R. H., & Smith, G. T. (1994). Formulating clinical research hypotheses as structural equation models: A conceptual overview. *Journal of Consulting and Clinical Psychology, 62,* 429-440.

Hu, L.-T., & Bentler, P. M. (1993). *Fit indexes in covariance structural equation modeling.* Unpublished manuscript.

Hu, L.-T., Bentler, P. M., & Kano, Y. (1992). Can test statistics in covariance structure analysis be trusted? *Psychological Bulletin, 112,* 351-362.

Huba, G. J., & Harlow, L. L. (1987). Robust structural equation models: Implications for developmental psychology. *Child Development, 58,* 147-166.

Hull, J. G., Lehn, D. A., & Tedlie, J. C. (1991). A general approach to testing multifaceted personality constructs. *Journal of Personality and Social Psychology, 61,* 932-945.

Hull, J. G., & Mendolia, M. (1991). Modeling the relations of attributional style, expectancies, and depression. *Journal of Personality and Social Psychology, 61,* 85-97.

Hull, J. G., Petterson, K. E., Kumar, N., & McCollum, C. (1993). *The personality construct of challenge.* Unpublished manuscript.

Hull, J. G., Van Treuren, R. R., & Virnelli, S. (1987). Hardiness and health: A critique and alternative approach. *Journal of Personality and Social Psychology, 53,* 518-530.

Hume, D. (1968). *A treatise of human nature*. Oxford: Clarendon. (Original work published 1739)

Husaini, B. A., Castor, R. S., Linn, J. G., Moore, S. T., Warren, H. A., & Whitten-Stovall, R. (1990). Social support and depression among the Black and White elderly. *Journal of Community Psychology, 18*, 12-18.

Husaini, B. A., Moore, S. T., Castor, R. S., Neser, W., Whitten-Stovall, R., Linn, J. G., & Griffin, D. (1991). Social density, stressors, and depression: Gender differences among the Black elderly. *Journal of Gerontology, 46*, 236-242.

James, L. R., Mulaik, S. A., & Brett, J. M. (1982). *Causal analysis: Assumptions, models, and data*. Beverly Hills, CA: Sage.

Jason, G. (1989). *The logic of discovery*. New York: Lang.

Jastrow, J. (1900). *Fact and fable in psychology*. Boston: Houghton-Mifflin.

John, O. P. (1990). The "big five" factor taxonomy: Dimensions of personality in the natural language and questionnaires. In L. A. Pervin (Ed.), *Handbook of personality: Theory and research* (pp. 66-100). New York: Guilford.

Johnston, J. (1984). *Econometric methods* (3rd ed.). New York: Wiley.

Jöreskog, K. G. (1969). A general approach to confirmatory maximum likelihood factor analysis. *Psychometrika, 34*, 183-202.

Jöreskog, K. G. (1971). Statistical analyses of sets of congeneric tests. *Psychometrika, 36*, 109-134.

Jöreskog, K. G. (1973). A general method for estimating a linear structural equation system. In A. S. Goldberger & O. D. Duncan (Eds.), *Structural equation models in the social sciences* (pp. 85-112). New York: Academic.

Jöreskog, K. G. (1974). Analyzing psychological data by structural analysis of covariance matrices. In R. C. Atkinson, D. H. Krantz, R. D. Luce, & P. Suppes (Eds.), *Contemporary developments in mathematical psychology: Measurement, psychophysics, and neural information processing* (Vol. 2, pp. 1-56). San Francisco: Freeman.

Jöreskog, K. G. (1993). Testing structural equation models. In K. A. Bollen & J. S. Long (Eds.), *Testing structural equation models* (pp. 294-316). Newbury Park, CA: Sage.

Jöreskog, K. G., & Goldberger, A. S. (1972). Factor analysis by generalized least squares. *Psychometrika, 37*, 243-260.

Jöreskog, K. G., & Sörbom, D. (1979). *Advances in factor analysis and structural equation models*. Cambridge, MA: Abt.

Jöreskog, K. G., & Sörbom, D. (1981). *LISREL V: Analysis of linear structural relationships by the method of maximum likelihood*. Chicago: National Educational Resources.

Jöreskog, K. G., & Sörbom, D. (1984). *LISREL VI user's guide* (3rd ed.). Mooresville, IN: Scientific Software.

Jöreskog, K. G., & Sörbom, D. (1988). *LISREL 7: A guide to the program and applications*. Chicago: SPSS.

Jöreskog, K. G., & Sörbom, D. (1989). *LISREL 7: A guide to the program and applications* (2nd ed.). Chicago: SPSS.

Jöreskog, K. G., & Sörbom, D. (1992). *LISREL VIII: A guide to the program and applications*. Mooresville, IN: Scientific Software.

Jöreskog, K. G., & Sörbom, D. (1993a). *LISREL 8: Structural equation modeling with the SIMPLIS command language*. Hillsdale, NJ: Erlbaum.

Jöreskog, K. G., & Sörbom, D. (1993b). *LISREL 8: User's reference guide*. Chicago: Scientific Software.

Jöreskog, K. G., & Sörbom, D. (1993c). *PRELIS 2: User's reference guide*. Chicago: Scientific Software.

Judd, C. M., Jessor, R., & Donovan, J. E. (1986). Structural equation models and personality research. *Journal of Personality, 54,* 149-198.

Kano, Y., Berkane, M., & Bentler, P. M. (1990). Covariance structure analysis with heterogenous kurtosis parameters. *Biometrika, 77,* 575-585.

Kant, I. (1965). *The critique of pure reason* (N. K. Smith, Trans.). New York: St. Martin's. (Original work published 1781)

Kaplan, D. (1988). The impact of specification error on the estimation, testing, and improvement of structural equation models. *Multivariate Behavioral Research, 23,* 69-86.

Kaplan, D. (1989a). Model modification in covariance structure analysis: Application of the expected parameter change statistic. *Multivariate Behavioral Research, 24,* 285-305.

Kaplan, D. (1989b). The problem of error rate inflation in covariance structure models. *Educational and Psychological Measurement, 49,* 333-337.

Kaplan, D. (1989c). A study of the sampling variability and z-values of parameter estimates from misspecified structural equation models. *Multivariate Behavioral Research, 24,* 41-57.

Kaplan, D. (1990). Evaluating and modifying covariance structure models: A review and recommendation. *Multivariate Behavioral Research, 25,* 137-155.

Kaplan, D., & George, R. (in press). A study of the power associated with testing factor mean differences under violations of factorial invariance. *Structural Equation Modeling: A Multidisciplinary Journal.*

Kaplan, D., & Wenger, R. N. (1993). Asymptotic independence and separability in covariance structure models: Implications for specification error, power, and model modification. *Multivariate Behavioral Research, 28,* 483-498.

Kazdin, A. E. (1987). Treatment of antisocial behavior in children: Current status and future directions. *Psychological Bulletin, 102,* 187-203.

Keesling, J. W. (1972). *Maximum likelihood approaches to causal analysis*. Unpublished doctoral dissertation, University of Chicago.

Kenny, D. A. (1976). An empirical application of confirmatory factor analysis to the multitrait-multimethod matrix. *Journal of Experimental Social Psychology, 12,* 247-252.

Kenny, D. A., & Kashy, D. A. (1992). The analysis of the multitrait-multimethod matrix by confirmatory factor analysis. *Psychological Bulletin, 112,* 165-172.

Kobasa, S. C. (1979). Stressful life events, personality, and health: An inquiry into hardiness. *Journal of Personality and Social Psychology, 37,* 1-11.

Krause, N. (1989). Issues of measurement and analysis in studies of social support, aging and health. In K. S. Markides & C. L. Cooper (Eds.), *Aging, stress, and health* (pp. 43-66). Chichester, England: Wiley.

Kuhn, D. (1991). *The skills of argument*. Cambridge, England: Cambridge University.

Kumar, A., & Dillon, W. R. (1992). An integrative look at the use of additive and multiplicative covariance models in the analysis of MTMM data. *Journal of Marketing Research, 29,* 51-64.

La Du, T. J., & Tanaka, J. S. (1989). The influence of sample size, estimation method, and model specification on goodness-of-fit assessments in structural equation models. *Journal of Applied Psychology, 74*, 625-636.

Lazarsfeld, P. F. (1958). Latent structure analysis. In S. Koch (Ed.), *Psychology: A study of a science* (Vol. 3, pp. 476-543). New York: McGraw-Hill.

Lee, S., & Hershberger, S. (1990). A simple rule for generating equivalent models in covariance structure modeling. *Multivariate Behavioral Research, 25*, 313-334.

Lee, S.-Y. (1985). On testing functional constraints in structural equation models. *Biometrika, 57*, 239-251.

Leffler, A., Krannick, R. S., & Gillespie, D. L. (1986). Contact, support, and friction: Three faces of networks in community life. *Sociological Perspectives, 29*, 337-355.

Levy, S., & Guttman, L. (1981). Structure and level of values for rewards and allocation criteria in several areas of life. In I. Borg (Ed.), *Multidimensional data representations: When and why* (pp. 153-192). Ann Arbor: Mathesis.

Lin, N. (1986). Epilogue: In retrospect and prospect. In N. Lin, A. Dean, & W. M. Ensel (Eds.), *Social support, life events, and depression* (pp. 333-342). Orlando, FL: Academic.

Lin, N. (1989). Measuring depressive symptomology in China. *Journal of Nervous and Mental Disease, 177*, 212-231.

Linn, J. G., Husaini, B. A., Whitten-Stovall, R., & Broomes, L. R. (1989). Community satisfaction, life stress, social support, and mental health in rural and urban southern Black communities. *Journal of Community Psychology, 17*, 78-88.

Little, R. J., & Rubin, D. B. (1990). The analysis of social science data with missing values. *Sociological Methods and Research, 18*, 292-326.

Loeber, R. (1982). The stability of antisocial child behavior: A review. *Child Development, 53*, 1431-1446.

Loeber, R., & Dishion, T. J. (1983). Early predictors of male delinquency: A review. *Psychological Bulletin, 94*, 68-99.

Loeber, R., & Dishion, T. J. (1987). Antisocial and delinquent youths: Methods for their early identification. In J. D. Burchard & S. N. Burchard (Eds.), *Prevention of delinquent behavior* (Vol. 10, pp. 75-89). Newbury Park, CA: Sage.

Loehlin, J. C. (1987). *Latent variable models.* Hillsdale, NJ: Erlbaum.

Lord, F. M., & Novick, M. R. (1968). *Statistical theories of mental test scores.* Reading, MA: Addison-Wesley.

Losee, J. (1980). *A historical introduction to the philosophy of science* (2nd ed.). Oxford: Oxford University.

Lykken, D. T. (1993). Predicting violence in the violent society. *Applied and Preventive Psychology, 2*, 13-20.

MacCallum, R. C. (1986). Specification searches in covariance structure modeling. *Psychological Bulletin, 100*, 107-120.

MacCallum, R. C., & Browne, M. W. (1993). The use of causal indicators in covariance structure models: Some practical issues. *Psychological Bulletin, 114*, 533-541.

MacCallum, R. C., Roznowski, M., & Necowitz, L. B. (1992). Model modifications in covariance structure analysis: The problem of capitalization on chance. *Psychological Bulletin, 111*, 490-504.

MacCallum, R. C., Wegener, D. T., Uchino, B. N., & Fabrigar, L. R. (1993). The problem of equivalent models in applications of covariance structure analysis. *Psychological Bulletin, 114*, 185-199.

Maiti, S. S., & Mukherjee, B. N. (1991). Two new goodness-of-fit indices for covariance matrices with linear structures. *British Journal of Mathematical and Statistical Psychology, 28,* 205-214.

Mardia, K. V. (1970). Measures of multivariate skewness and kurtosis with applications. *Biometrika, 57,* 519-530.

Marsden, P. V. (1987). Core discussion networks of Americans. *American Sociological Review, 52,* 122-131.

Marsh, H. W. (1988). Multitrait-multimethod analyses. In J. P. Keeves (Ed.), *Educational research methodology, measurement, and evaluation: An international handbook* (pp. 570-578). Oxford: Pergamon.

Marsh, H. W. (1989). Confirmatory factor analyses of multitrait-multimethod data: Many problems and a few solutions. *Applied Psychological Measurement, 13,* 335-361.

Marsh, H. W. (1993). Multitrait-multimethod analyses: Inferring each trait/method combination with multiple indicators. *Journal of Applied Educational Measurement, 6,* 49-81.

Marsh, H. W., Antill, J. K., & Cunningham, J. D. (1989). Masculinity, femininity, and androgyny: Bipolar and independent constructs. *Journal of Personality, 57,* 625-663.

Marsh, H. W., & Bailey, M. (1991). Confirmatory factor analysis of multitrait-multimethod data: A comparison of alternative models. *Applied Psychological Measurement, 15,* 47-70.

Marsh, H. W., Balla, J. R., & McDonald, R. P. (1988). Goodness-of-fit indexes in confirmatory factor analysis: The effect of sample size. *Psychological Bulletin, 103,* 391-411.

Marsh, H. W., Byrne, B. M., & Craven, R. (1993). Overcoming problems in confirmatory factor analyses of MTMM data: The correlated uniqueness model and factorial invariance. *Multivariate Behavioral Research, 27,* 489-507.

Marsh, H. W., & Grayson, D. (in press). Multitrait-multimethod analyses. In T. Husen & T. N. Postlewaite (Eds.), *International encyclopedia of education* (2nd ed.). Oxford: Pergamon.

Marsh, H. W., & Hocevar, D. (1988). A new, more powerful approach to multitrait-multimethod analyses: Application of second-order confirmatory factor analysis. *Journal of Applied Psychology, 73,* 107-117.

Martin, J. A. (1987). Structural equation modeling: A guide for the perplexed. *Child Development, 58,* 33-37.

Matsueda, R. L., & Bielby, W. T. (1986). Statistical power in covariance structure models. In N. B. Tuma (Ed.), *Sociological methodology 1986* (pp. 120-158). San Francisco: Jossey-Bass.

McArdle, J., & McDonald, R. P. (1984). Some algebraic properties of the reticular action model for moment structures. *British Journal of Mathematical and Statistical Psychology, 37,* 234-254.

McDonald, R. P. (1978). A simple comprehension model for the analysis of covariance structures. *British Journal of Mathematical and Statistical Psychology, 31,* 59-72.

McDonald, R. P. (1989). An index of goodness-of-fit based on noncentrality. *Journal of Classification, 6,* 97-103.

McDonald, R. P., & Marsh, H. W. (1990). Choosing a multivariate model: Noncentrality and goodness-of-fit. *Psychological Bulletin, 107,* 247-255.

Meehl, P. E. (1990). Appraising and amending theories: The strategy of Lakatosian defense and two principles that warrant it. *Psychological Inquiry, 2,* 108-141.

Mercier, J. M., & Powers, E. A. (1984). The family and friends of the rural aged as a natural support system. *Journal of Community Psychology, 12*, 334-346.

Micceri, T. (1989). The unicorn, the normal curve, and other improbable creatures. *Psychological Bulletin, 105*, 156-166.

Mill, J. S. (1874). *A system of logic* (8th ed.). New York: Harper.

Mooney, C. Z., & Duval, R. D. (1993). *Bootstrapping: A nonparametric approach to statistical inference.* Newbury Park, CA: Sage.

Mulaik, S. A. (1986). Toward a synthesis of deterministic and probabilistic formulations of causal relations by the functional relation concept. *Philosophy of Science, 52,* 410-430.

Mulaik, S. A. (1987). Toward a conception of causality applicable to experimentation and causal modeling. *Child Development, 58*, 18-32.

Mulaik, S. A. (1990, June). *An analysis of the conditions under which the estimation of parameters inflates goodness-of-fit indices as measures of model validity.* Paper presented at the annual meeting of the Psychometric Society, Princeton, NJ.

Mulaik, S. A. (1991). Factor analysis, information-transforming instruments, and objectivity: A reply and discussion. *British Journal for the Philosophy of Science, 42,* 87-100.

Mulaik, S. A. (1993a). *The metaphoric origins of subjectivity and objectivity in the breakdown of consciousness.* Manuscript submitted for publication.

Mulaik, S. A. (1993b). Objectivity and multivariate statistics. *Multivariate Behavioral Research, 28*, 171-203.

Mulaik, S. A. (1994). Kant, Wittgenstein, objectivity, and structural equation modeling. In C. R. Reynolds (Ed.), *Cognitive assessment: A multidisciplinary perspective* (pp. 209-236). New York: Plenum.

Mulaik, S. A. (in press). Metaphoric origins of objectivity, subjectivity, and consciousness in the direct perception of reality. *Philosophy of Science.*

Mulaik, S. A., James, L. R., Van Alstine, J., Bennett, N., Lind, S., & Stillwell, C. D. (1989). An evaluation of goodness-of-fit indices for structural equation models. *Psychological Bulletin, 105*, 430-445.

Muthén, B. (1984). A general structural equation model with dichotomous, ordered categorical, and continuous latent variable indicators. *Psychometrika, 49,* 115-132.

Muthén, B. (1988). *LISCOMP: Analysis of linear structural equations with a comprehensive measurement model.* Chicago: Scientific Software.

Muthén, B. (1989). Latent variable modeling in heterogeneous populations. *Psychometrika, 54,* 557-585.

Muthén, B. (1991). Tobit factor analysis. *British Journal of Mathematical and Statistical Psychology, 42,* 241-250.

Muthén, B. (1993). Goodness of fit with categorical and nonnormal variables. In K. A. Bollen & J. S. Long (Eds.), *Testing structural equation models* (pp. 205-234). Newbury Park, CA: Sage.

Muthén, B., & Christofferson, A. (1981). Simultaneous factor analysis of dichotomous variables in several groups. *Psychometrika, 46*, 485-500.

Muthén, B., & Kaplan, D. (1985). A comparison of methodologies for the factor analysis of non-normal Likert variables. *British Journal of Mathematical and Statistical Psychology, 38*, 171-189.

Muthén, B., & Kaplan, D. (1992). A comparison of some methodologies for the factor analysis of non-normal Likert variables: A note on the size of the model. *British Journal of Mathematical and Statistical Psychology, 45,* 19-30.

Muthén, B., Kaplan, D., & Hollis, M. (1987). On structural equation modeling for data that are not missing completely at random. *Psychometrika, 52,* 431-462.

O'Neil, R. E., Ramsey, E., Shinn, M., Todis, B., & Spira, D. (1985). *Observer training manual for the target/peer interaction code (TPIC).* Eugene: Center on Human Development, University of Oregon.

Palinkas, L. A., Wingard, D. L., & Barrett-Connor, E. (1990). The biocultural context of social networks and depression among the elderly. *Social Science and Medicine, 30,* 441-447.

Patterson, G. R., & Bank, L. (1989). Some amplifying mechanisms for pathologic processes in families. In M. R. Gunnar & E. Thelan (Eds.), *Systems and development: Minnesota symposium on child psychology* (Vol. 22, pp. 167-210). Hillsdale, NJ: Erlbaum.

Patterson, G. R., Bank, L., & Stoolmiller, M. (1990). The preadolescent's contributions to disrupted family process. In R. Montemayor, G. R. Adams, & T. P. Gullotta (Eds.), *From childhood to adolescence: A transitional period?* (pp. 107-133). Newbury Park, CA: Sage.

Patterson, G. R., Reid, J. B., & Dishion, T. J. (1992). *A social learning approach: IV. Antisocial boys.* Eugene, OR: Castalia.

Peterson, C., Seligman, M. E. P., & Vaillant, G. E. (1987). Pessimistic explanatory style is a risk factor for physical illness: A thirty-five year longitudinal study. *Journal of Personality and Social Psychology, 55,* 23-27.

Pollock, J. L. (1986). *Contemporary theories of knowledge.* Totowa, NJ: Rowman & Littlefield.

Popper, K. (1959). *The logic of discovery.* London: Hutchinson. (Original work published 1935)

Quevillon, R. P., & Trennery, M. R. (1983). Research in rural depression: Implications of social networks for theory and treatment. *International Journal of Mental Health, 12,* 45-61.

Radloff, L. S. (1977). The CES-D scale: A self report depression scale for research in the general population. *Applied Psychological Measurement, 1,* 385-401.

Rasch, G. (1960). *Probabilistic models for some intelligence and attainment tests.* Chicago: University of Chicago.

Raykov, R., Tomer, A., & Nesselroade, J. R. (1991). Reporting structural equation modeling results in *Psychology and Aging*: Some proposed guidelines. *Psychology and Aging, 6,* 499-503.

Reid, J. B. (1991). Mediational screening as a model for prevention research. *American Journal of Community Psychology, 19,* 867-872.

Reis, H. T., & Stiller, J. (1992). Publication trends in *JPSP*: A three-decade review. *Personality and Social Psychology Bulletin, 18,* 465-472.

Rindskopf, D., & Rose, T. (1988). Some theory and applications of confirmatory second-order factor analysis. *Multivariate Behavioral Research, 23,* 51-67.

Robins, L. N. (1978). Sturdy childhood predictors of adult antisocial behavior: Replication from longitudinal studies. *Psychological Medicine, 8,* 611-622.

Robins, L. N., & Ratcliff, K. S. (1979). Risk factors in the continuation of childhood anti-social behaviors into adulthood. *International Journal of Mental Health, 7,* 96-116.

Rosenberg, M. (1965). *Society and the adolescent self-image.* Princeton, NJ: Princeton University.

Rosenberg, M. (1979). *Conceiving the self.* New York: Basic.

Salovey, P. (1991, October). *Affective influences on health related judgments*. Paper presented at the annual meeting of Society for Experimental Social Psychology, Columbus, OH.

Salovey, P., & Birnbaum, D. (1989). Influence of mood on health-relevant cognitions. *Journal of Personality and Social Psychology, 57*, 539-551.

Saris, W. E., den Ronden, J., & Satorra, A. (1987). Testing structural equation models. In P. Cuttance & R. Ecob (Eds.), *Structural modeling by example* (pp. 202-221). Cambridge, England: Cambridge University.

Saris, W. E., & Satorra, A. (1987). Characteristics of structural equation models which affect the power of the likelihood ratio test. In W. E. Saris & I. N. Gallhofer (Eds.), *Sociometric research* (Vol. 2). London: Macmillan.

Saris, W. E., & Satorra, A. (1993). Power evaluations in structural equation models. In K. Bollen and J. S. Long (Eds.), *Testing structural equation models* (pp. 181-204). Newbury Park, CA: Sage.

Saris, W. E., Satorra, A., & Sörbom, D. (1987). The detection and correction of specification errors in structural equation models. In C. C. Clogg (Ed.), *Sociological methodology 1987* (pp. 105-129). San Francisco: Jossey-Bass.

Saris, W. E., & Stronkhorst, H. (1984). *Causal modeling in nonexperimental research*. Amsterdam: Sociometric Research Foundation.

SAS Institute, Inc. (1991). *The CALIS procedure: Analysis of covariance structures*. Cary, NC: Author.

Satorra, A. (1989). Alternative test criteria in covariance structure analysis: A unified approach. *Psychometrika, 54*, 131-151.

Satorra, A. (1990). Robustness issues in structural equation modeling: A review of recent developments. *Quality & Quantity, 24*, 367-386.

Satorra, A., & Bentler, P. M. (1988a). Scaling corrections for chi-square statistics in covariance structure analysis. *Proceedings of the Business and Economics Sections* (pp. 308-313). Alexandria, VA: American Statistical Association.

Satorra, A., & Bentler, P. M. (1988b). *Scaling corrections for statistics in covariance structure analysis* (UCLA Statistics Series 2). Los Angeles: University of California, Department of Psychology.

Satorra, A., & Bentler, P. M. (1990). Model conditions for asymptotic robustness in the analysis of linear relations. *Computational Statistics and Data Analysis, 10*, 235-249.

Satorra, A., & Bentler, P. M. (1991). Goodness-of-fit test under IV estimation: Asymptotic robustness of a NT test statistic. In R. Gutierrez & M. J. Valderrama (Eds.), *Applied stochastic models and data analysis* (pp. 555-567). Singapore: World Scientific.

Satorra, A., & Bentler, P. M. (1994). Corrections to test statistic and standard errors in covariance structure analysis. In A. Von Eye & C. C. Clogg (Eds.), *Analysis of latent variables in developmental research* (pp. 399-419). Newbury Park, CA: Sage.

Satorra, A., & Saris, W. E. (1985). Power of the likelihood ratio test in covariance structure analysis. *Psychometrika, 50*, 83-90.

Scheier, M. F., & Carver, C. S. (1985). Optimism, coping, and health: Assessment and implications of generalized outcome expectancies. *Health Psychology, 4*, 219-247.

Schlick, M. (1959). Causality in everyday life and in recent science. In E. Sprague & P. W. Taylor (Eds.), *Knowledge and value* (pp. 193-210). New York: Harcourt, Brace.

Schmitt, N., & Stults, D. M. (1986). Methodological review: Analysis of multitrait-multimethod matrices. *Applied Psychological Measurement, 10,* 1-22.

Schoenberg, R. J., & Arminger, G. (1989). Latent variable models of dichotomous data: The state of the method. *Sociological Methods and Research, 18,* 164-182.

Schulte, J. (1992). *Wittgenstein.* (W. H. Brenner & J. F. Holley, Trans.). Albany: State University of New York.

Scott, J. P., & Roberto, K. A. (1985). Use of informal and formal support networks by rural elderly poor. *The Gerontologist, 25,* 624-630.

Sewell, W. H., Haller, A. O., & Ohlendorf, G. W. (1970). The educational and early occupational status attainment process: Replication and revision. *American Sociological Review, 34,* 82-92.

Shye, S. (1978). On the search for laws in the behavioral sciences. In S. Shye (Ed.), *Theory construction and data analysis in the behavioral sciences* (pp. 2-24). San Francisco: Jossey-Bass.

Silvia, E. S. M., & MacCallum, R. C. (1988). Some factors affecting the success of specification searches in covariance structure modeling. *Multivariate Behavioral Research, 23,* 297-326.

Simon, H. A. (1977). *Models of discovery.* Dordrecht, Holland: Reidel.

Smith, T. W., Pope, M. K., Rhodewalt, F., & Poulton, J. L. (1989). Optimism, neuroticism, coping, and symptom reports: An alternative interpretation of the Life Orientation Test. *Journal of Personality and Social Psychology, 56,* 640-648.

Snyder, C. R., Smith, T. W., Augelli, R. W., & Ingram, R. E. (1985). On the self-serving function of social anxiety: Shyness as a self-handicapping strategy. *Journal of Personality and Social Psychology, 48,* 970-980.

Sobel, M. E., & Bohrnstedt, G. W. (1985). Use of null models in evaluating the fit of covariance structure models. In N. B. Tuma (Ed.), *Sociological methodology 1985* (pp. 152-178). San Francisco: Jossey-Bass.

Sörbom, D. (1974). A general method for studying differences in factor means and factor structure between groups. *British Journal of Mathematical and Statistical Psychology, 27,* 229-239.

Sörbom, D. (1982). Structural equation models with structured means. In K. G. Jöreskog & H. Wold (Eds.), *Systems under indirect observation* (pp. 183-195). Amsterdam: North-Holland.

Sörbom, D. (1989). Model modification. *Psychometrika, 54,* 371-384.

Spirtes, P., Glymour, C., & Scheines, R. (1993). *Causation, prediction, and search.* New York: Springer-Verlag.

Steiger, J. H. (1989). *EZPATH: A supplementary module for SYSTAT and SYGRAPH.* Evanston, IL: SYSTAT.

Steiger, J. H., & Lind, J. C. (1980, May). *Statistically-based tests for the number of common factors.* Paper presented at the Annual Meeting of the Psychometric Society, Iowa City, IO.

Stelzl, I. (1986). Changing causal relationships without changing the fit: Some rules for generating equivalent LISREL-models. *Multivariate Behavioral Research, 21,* 309-331.

Stelzl, I. (1991). Rival hypotheses in linear structure modeling: Factor rotation in confirmatory factor analysis and latent path analysis. *Multivariate Behavioral Research, 26,* 199-225.

Strogatz, D. S., & James, S. A. (1986). Social support and hypertension among Blacks and Whites in a rural, southern community. *American Journal of Epidemiology*, *124*, 949-956.

Swain, A. J. (1975). *Analysis of parametric structures for variance matrices.* Unpublished doctoral dissertation, University of Adelaide.

Tanaka, J. S. (1984). *Some results on the estimation of covariance structure models.* Unpublished doctoral dissertation, University of California, Los Angeles.

Tanaka, J. S. (1987). How big is big enough?: Sample size and goodness-of-fit in structural equation models with latent variables. *Child Development*, *58*, 134-146.

Tanaka, J. S. (1993). Multifaceted conceptions of fit in structural equation models. In K. A. Bollen & J. S. Long (Eds.), *Testing structural equation models* (pp. 10-39). Newbury Park, CA: Sage.

Tanaka, J. S., & Huba, G. J. (1985). A fit index for covariance structural models under arbitrary GLS estimation. *British Journal of Mathematical and Statistical Psychology*, *42*, 233-239.

Tanaka, J. S., & Huba, G. J. (1989). A general coefficient of determination for covariance structure models under arbitrary GLS estimation. *British Journal of Mathematical and Statistical Psychology*, *42*, 233-239.

Tanaka, J. S., Panter, A. T., Winborne, W. C., & Huba, G. J. (1990). Theory testing in personality and social psychology with structural equation models: A primer in 20 questions. In C. Hendrick & M. S. Clark (Eds.), *Review of personality and social psychology* (Vol. 11, pp. 217-242). Newbury Park, CA: Sage.

Tiles, M. (1984). *Bachelard: Science and objectivity.* Cambridge: Cambridge University.

Tucker, L. R., & Lewis, C. (1973). A reliability coefficient for maximum likelihood factor analysis. *Psychometrika*, *38*, 1-10.

Turner, R. J., & Wood, D. W. (1985). Depression and disability: The stress process in a chronically strained population. *Research in Community and Mental Health*, *5*, 77-109.

Vale, C. D., & Maurelli, V. A. (1983). Simulating multivariate non-normal distributions. *Psychometrika*, *48*, 465-471.

Vaux, A. (1985). Variations in social support associated with gender, ethnicity, and age. *Journal of Social Issues*, *41*, 89-110.

Wald, A. (1943). Tests of statistical hypotheses concerning several parameters when the number of observations is large. *Transactions of the American Mathematical Society*, *54*, 426-482.

Walker, H. M., & McConnell, S. R. (1988). *Walker-McConnell scale of social competence and school adjustment.* Austin, TX: Pro-Ed.

Walker, H. M., Severson, H., Haring, N., & Williams, G. (1986). Standardized screening and identification of behavior disordered pupils in the elementary age range: A multiple gating approach. *Direct Instruction News*, *5*, 7-9.

Watson, D., & Clark, L. A. (1984). Negative affectivity: The disposition to experience aversive emotional states. *Psychological Bulletin*, *96*, 465-490.

Watson, D., Clark, L. A., & Tellegen, A. (1988). Development and validation of brief measures of positive and negative affect: The PANAS scales. *Journal of Personality and Social Psychology*, *54*, 1063-1070.

Watson, D., & Pennebaker, J. W. (1989). Health complaints, stress, and distress: Exploring the central role of negative affectivity. *Psychological Review*, *96*, 233-253.

West, D. J., & Farrington, D. P. (1977). *The delinquent way of life.* London: Heinemann.

Widaman, K. F. (1985). Hierarchically nested covariance structure models for multitrait-multimethod data. *Applied Psychological Measurement, 9*, 1-26.

Wiley, D. E. (1973). The identification problem for structural equation models with unmeasured variables. In A. S. Goldberger & O. D. Duncan (Eds.), *Structural equation models in the social sciences* (pp. 69-83). New York: Academic.

Wittgenstein, L. (1953). *Philosophical investigations* (G. E. M. Anscombe, Trans.). New York: Macmillan.

Wittgenstein, L. (1975). *Philosophical remarks* (R. Rhees, Ed., and R. Hargreaves & R. White, Trans.). Oxford: Blackwell.

Wothke, W. (1993). Nonpositive definite matrices in structural modeling. In K. A. Bollen and J. S. Long (Eds.), *Testing structural equation models* (pp. 256-293). Newbury Park, CA: Sage.

Author Index

Subject Index

Campbell-Fiske guidelines, 178-
180, 196-197
confirmatory factor analysis, 180-
187, 197-198
direct product model, 187-190, 197-
198
Multivariate normality, 47, 59, 60-61,
78, 89
See also Distribution, (non)normal

Nested models, 8, 135-137, 169
See also Model comparison
Noncentrality parameter. *See* Parameter,
noncentrality
Nonconvergence. *See* Convergence
Nonstandard effect. *See* Specific effect
Normality. *See* Distribution, normal
See also Multivariate normality
Notation, 13, 24-26, 43-44, 170
Null (independence) model, 7, 82, 136-
137

Observed variable. *See* Variable, observed (measured)
Omnibus fit. *See* Evaluation of fit,
overall
Ordered categorical data. *See* Scale of
measurement, ordered categorical
Outliers, 61-62
Overall model fit. *See* Evaluation of fit,
overall
Overidentification. *See* Identification,
overidentification

Parameter, 21-24
defined, 3, 18-19, 37
fixed, 3, 22-24
See also Constraints on parameter,
equality; set to zero or constant
free, 3, 24
identification. *See* Identification
noncentrality, 80-81, 84-85
standardized estimate, 9, 194-195,
211
unstandardized estimate, 9, 151, 245,
247

See also Confirmatory factor analysis,
factor loading; Constraints on
parameters
Parcel, 70-71, 225
Parsimony, 17, 97-98, 219-220
Path diagram, 11-12, 24-45, 26, 140-141,
160
example of, 26, 142, 143, 182, 183,
184, 203, 221, 230, 245, 247
Power:
and model evaluation, 107-108, 117,
173-174
and modification, 101, 115
calculation of, 102
individual parameters, 102-104
multiple parameters, 104-105,
116

R^2, 82, 167
Relations between variables, 3, 18
Residual matrix, 5, 7, 98-99
Robust statistics, 46, 52-54

Sample size, 47, 62-63, 74, 87-88, 89-93,
95-96, 107
Scale of measurement, 57
continuous, 70-71
coursely categorized, 59-60, 63-64,
68-70
ordered categorical, 68-70
SEMNET, xix, xxi
Significance test. *See* Evaluation of fit,
overall; component
Simulation (Monte Carlo), 46-54, 79-80,
109
Simultaneous equations, 20, 40
Skewness. *See* Distribution, skewness
Software. *See* Computer program
Specification:
defined, 2
example of, 25-27
Specific effect, 228-229, 230, 232-233
Standard error. *See* Bias, in standard
errors
Standardized estimate. *See* Parameter,
standardized estimate
Start values, 5

About the Contributors

Peter M. Bentler is Professor of Psychology at the University of California, Los Angeles. His research deals with theoretical and statistical problems in psychometrics, especially structural equation models, as well as with personality and applied social psychology, especially drug use and abuse.

Barbara M. Byrne is Professor in the School of Psychology at the University of Ottawa, where she has taught since 1987. Subsequent to obtaining her Ph.D. in 1982, Dr. Byrne worked as Research Associate at the Child Study Centre, University of Ottawa, held a one-year appointment in the Department of Psychology at Carleton University, held a two-year postdoctoral fellowship at the UCLA Graduate School of Education, where she worked with Richard J. Shavelson and consulted with Bengt Muthén, and recently spent a six-month sabbatical as a visiting scholar in the Department of Psychology at UCLA, where she worked with Peter M. Bentler. She is the author of two books: *A Primer of LISREL: Basic Applications and Programming for Confirmatory Factor Analytic Models*, and the more recent, *Structural Equation Modeling With EQS and EQS/Windows: Basic Concepts, Applications, and Programming*. Additionally, Dr. Byrne has published over 40 journal articles and five book chapters, most of which have involved applications of structural equation modeling. Her research interests

283

focus on construct validation issues related to the structure and measurement of self-concept, burnout, and depression.

Chih-Ping Chou is Assistant Professor of Research in the Department of Preventive Medicine at the University of Southern California. His research interests include structural equation modeling, multivariate statistical analysis, and evaluation.

Patrick J. Curran received his Ph.D. in clinical psychology from Arizona State University and currently holds a National Institute on Alcoholism and Alcohol Abuse National Research Service Award for postdoctoral study in quantitative methods with Bengt Muthén at the University of California, Los Angeles. His primary research interests include the application of structural equation modeling and latent growth curve analysis to the study of individual differences in adolescent alcohol and drug use.

Terry E. Duncan is affiliated with the Oregon Research Institute, where his responsibilities include the implementation of statistical analytic methods for several longitudinal studies, including community based intervention programs focused on the reduction of adolescent substance abuse and on the prevention of high-risk sexual behavior. His research interests include statistical methods for the analysis of change, health and exercise psychology, and social support processes. Dr. Duncan's most recent publications include "Modeling Social and Psychological Determinants of Exercise Behaviors via Structural Equation Systems" (with Stoolmiller) in *Research Quarterly for Exercise and Sport* and "The Effect of Family Cohesiveness and Peer Encouragement on the Development of Adolescent Alcohol Use: A Cohort-Sequential Approach to the Analysis of Longitudinal Data" (with S. C. Duncan and Hops), to appear in *Journal of Studies on Alcohol*.

John F. Finch received his Ph.D. from Arizona State University and is currently Assistant Professor of Psychology at Texas A & M University. His primary research interests include the effects of nonnormality on parameter estimation in latent variable and mediational models.

David Grayson has a Ph.D. in (mathematical) psychology, with undergraduate majors in psychology, pure mathematics, and mathematical statistics. He is the author of about thirty journal articles, covering a range of theoretical and substantive areas, including epidemiology, psychometrics, psychiatry, behavior genetics, and medical statistics. His current research interests are in the fields of the history and philosophy of statistics, multitrait-multimethod designs, psychosocial health of Australian veterans of the Vietnam War (of whom he is one), and health in the elderly. He has worked as a full-time researcher in social psychiatry and, currently, in geriatric medicine, and also has lectured in quantitative methods to psychology undergraduate and postgraduate students.

Rick H. Hoyle is Assistant Professor of Psychology at the University of Kentucky. He completed his Ph.D. in psychology (social and quantitative) at the University of North Carolina at Chapel Hill in 1988. After a year in the Department of Psychology at Duke University, he joined the faculty in the social area of the Department of Psychology at Kentucky, where he teaches introductory statistics and social psychology at the undergraduate level and seminars on research methods, structural equation modeling, and the self at the graduate level. Dr. Hoyle's research interests include the self-concept, interpersonal attraction, and psychometrics. Recent publications focusing on applications of structural equation modeling have appeared in *Multivariate Behavioral Research* and *Journal of Consulting and Clinical Psychology*. He is on the editorial boards of *Journal of Personality and Social Psychology*, *Journal of Personality*, and *Journal of Consulting and Clinical Psychology*.

Li-tze Hu is Assistant Professor of Psychology at the University of California, Santa Cruz. Her research areas include both applied and theoretical social psychology, mental health, and statistical methodology, especially structural equation modeling.

Jay G. Hull is Professor of Psychology at Dartmouth College. His research interests include the structure of self-knowledge and its utility in processes related to self-regulation.

Lawrence R. James holds the Pilot Oil Chair of Excellence in Management and Industrial-Organizational Psychology at the University of Tennessee. He is the author of numerous articles and papers and co-author of books on causal analysis and organizational climate. He is a leading researcher in organizational psychology. His statistical contributions have been designed to make possible tests of new models in areas such as organizational climate, leadership, and personnel selection. He is a member of the editorial boards of *Journal of Applied Psychology, Organizational Behavior and Human Decision Processes, Human Performance, Human Resources Management, Journal of Management,* and *Research Methods and Analysis.*

David Kaplan is Associate Professor in the Department of Educational Studies at the University of Delaware. Professor Kaplan specializes in educational statistics and psychometrics with applications to educational policy. He has published extensively on the problem of nonnormality, specification error, and power in covariance structure models. His papers have appeared in *British Journal of Mathematical and Statistical Psychology, Educational and Psychological Measurement, Journal of Educational Statistics, Multivariate Behavioral Research,* and *Sociological Methods and Research.* Professor Kaplan's current program of research focuses on the development of multilevel simultaneous equation systems with applications to policy simulation modeling.

Daniel A. Lehn is Assistant Professor of Psychology at Coe College. His current research interests include statistical models of the structure of personality trait knowledge.

Richard D. Lennox completed his Ph.D. in social psychology at Texas Tech University. After three years at the University of North Carolina's Institute for Research in Social Science, he moved to the UNC Medical School's Multipurpose Arthritis Center. In his current position as Senior Research Scientist at the Pacific Institute for Research and Evaluation at Chapel Hill, NC, Dr. Lennox studies health service utilization among patients treated for drug or alcohol problems.

Robert C. MacCallum is currently Professor of Psychology at Ohio State University. He received his Ph.D. in quantitative psychology from the University of Illinois in 1974, after which he joined the faculty in the quantitative psychology program at Ohio State. There he has taught primarily graduate level courses in quantitative methods, especially regression, factor analysis, and structural equation modeling. His research interests in recent years focus on methodological issues in latent variable models. In the area of structural equation modeling, he has published papers on topics such as model modification, the problem of equivalent models, and the use of causal indicators. Another recent paper delineates sources of error in factor analysis. He is also extensively involved in a large-scale research program studying effects of stress on psychological and physiological functioning. This program involves multiple projects investigating people undergoing stress in different environments (e.g., Alzheimer's Disease caregivers, cancer patients, and married couples in conflict). Under study are relationships among stress, psychosocial constructs, and the functioning of the immune and endocrine systems and the autonomic and sympathetic nervous systems.

Herbert W. Marsh is the Research Professor of Education at the University of Western Sydney-Macarthur in Australia. He completed his B.A. in psychology at Indiana University and his M.A. and Ph.D. in psychology at University of California, Los Angeles. His research spans a broad array of methodological (research design, statistical analysis, psychological measurement, multitrait-multimethod analyses, covariance structural modeling) and substantive (students' evaluations of teaching effectiveness, self-concept, school effectiveness, gender differences, sports psychology) concerns and he has published widely in these areas. He is the most widely cited Australian educational researcher as well as being among the most widely cited researchers in several fields of research. He reviews regularly for a wide variety of Australian and international journals and is on the editorial boards of *Journal of Personality and Social Psychology*, *Journal of Educational Psychology*, *Child Development*, *Structural Equation Modeling*, and *Journal of Experimental Education*. In 1992 he received the W. J. McKeachie Career Achievement Award from the American Educational Research Association in recognition of 20 years of student evaluation research. He is the author of several psychological instruments including the set of self-concept instruments, the Self Description Questionnaires (SDQ) I, II and III, the Physical Self Description Questionnaire (PSDQ), and the Academic Self Description Questionnaire (ASDQ), as well as the student evaluation instrument, Students' Evaluations of Educational Quality (SEEQ).

Stanley A. Mulaik is Professor of Psychology at the Georgia Institute of Technology. He is the author of *The Foundations of Factor Analysis* and the second author with L. R. James and J. M. Brett of *Causal Analysis: Assumptions, Models, and Data*. He is the author of numerous book chapters and technical papers on topics related to factor analysis, confirmatory factor analysis, and structural equation modeling. His most recent publications are on the topics of causality and objectivity in the philosophy and history of science and statistics. He is currently the editor of *Multivariate Behavioral Research*.

Abigail T. Panter is Assistant Professor in the L. L. Thurstone Psychometric Laboratory in the Department of Psychology at the University of North Carolina at Chapel Hill. Her research interests include links between structural equation models and latent variables and item response models, especially as these models apply to personality assessment. As part of the Quantitative graduate program, she teaches courses in advanced statistical methods, structural equation modeling, exploratory factor analysis, and test theory. In her applied work she conducts scaling and methodological research with at-risk populations across the lifespan on issues such as chronic illness, drug use, and homelessness.

Gerald R. Patterson is affiliated with the Oregon Social Learning Center. He has been conducting research on coercive family interaction for over 20 years and has published numerous books and journal articles on the development of antisocial behavior. His recent research interests have included predicting the onset of early- and late-starting official offending and studying developmental changes in the form of antisocial behavior. Recent publications include "Predicting Risk for Early Police Arrest" (with Crosby and Vuchinich) in *Journal of Quantitative Criminology* and "Orderly Change in a Stable World: The Antisocial Trait as a Chimera" in *Journal of Consulting and Clinical Psychology*.

Jane A. Scott-Lennox obtained her Ph.D. in Sociology at the University of North Carolina at Chapel Hill. After completing postgraduate work at Duke's Center for the Study of Aging and Human Development, she joined the Applied Healthcare Research Division of Glaxo Research Institute. As a manager of pharmacoeconomic research studies, she evaluates quality-of-life impacts and cost efficacy of new drug therapies.

Mike Stoolmiller is affiliated with the Oregon Social Learning Center. He serves as a methodologist for several current longitudinal grants. His research interests include developmental models for antisocial and delinquent behavior, observational techniques for studying parent-child interaction, and the prevention of antisocial and delinquent behavior. Recent publications include "Some Problems and Solutions in the Study of Change: Significant Patterns in Client Resistance" (with Duncan, Bank, and Patterson) in *Journal of Consulting and Clinical Psychology* and "Using Latent Growth Curve Models to Study Developmental Processes," a chapter to appear in the edited volume, *The Analysis of Change*.

Judith C. Tedlie is a Post-Doctoral Fellow at the University of California, San Francisco Center for AIDS Prevention Studies. Her current research interests include coping styles and adaptation to illness.

Stephen G. West is currently Professor of Psychology and coprincipal investigator of the National Institute of Mental Health funded Prevention Intervention Research Center at Arizona State University. He is the past editor of *Journal of Personality*. He is the coauthor of *Multiple Regression: Testing and Interpreting Interactions* (1991) and *Applied Multiple Regression/Correlation Analysis for the Behavioral Sciences* (forthcoming). His primary research interests are in the design and statistical analysis of field research and the development and evaluation of theory-based preventive interventions.